The
Education
of Catholic
Americans

norc

NATIONAL OPINION RESEARCH CENTER
MONOGRAPHS IN SOCIAL RESEARCH

The Education of Catholic Americans

By

ANDREW M. GREELEY

and

PETER H. ROSSI

ALDINE PUBLISHING COMPANY
Chicago

*The study reported in this volume was supported
by a grant from the Carnegie Corporation of New York,
whose generosity and interest is hereby gratefully
acknowledged. The Corporation is not responsible,
however, for any of the statements made in this volume.*

*The research reported herein was completed under
Office of Education Cooperative Research Project No.
3964, Contract No. OE-5-10-019, U. S. Department
of Health, Education and Welfare.*

*First published 1966 by
ALDINE Publishing Company
320 West Adams Street
Chicago, Illinois 60606*

*Library of Congress Catalog Card Number 66-10867
Designed by Greer Allen
Printed in the United States of America*

Preface

"Education, beyond all other devices of human origin, is the great equalizer of conditions of men—a balance wheel of the social machinery." Thus wrote Horace Mann in a plea for the establishment of universal free public education in the United States. Belief in universal education as the means to prevent the development of sharp divisions among social classes has long been an important element in American society. From the beginning of the public school movement in the early nineteenth century, supporters of the public schools have stressed the importance of education to the individual's occupational achievement and to the economic prosperity of the country as a whole. Investment in human capital, as exemplified in the public school system, probably plays the most important role in creating and maintaining an egalitarian society.

An educational system, however, does not exist entirely because of the economic benefits that the individual and society derive from it. Education is also an important instrument in developing the moral, social, and political values that underlie the American political system and help maintain the "American way of life." For many Americans the development of these values is inextricably interwoven with the teaching of religious values, and for them the question of religious instruction in the schools is a vital one.

Religious instruction was excluded from the curriculum early in the history of public schools. While elements of religious symbolism and practices survive in varying degrees in many public schools, most frequently with nondenominational Christian overtones, the schools teach a social and political "morality" which has only a vague connection with religion. This exclusion has been a source of great concern for many organized religious bodies and has led several denominations to establish separate religious schools. By far the largest of these, of course, is the school system established and maintained by the Catholic Church in the United States. While it is by no means the only "parochial" school system in the country, it is by a wide margin the biggest, the costliest, and the most controversial.

In view of the general emphasis on education in American society and the size and importance of the Catholic school system, it is surprising that systematic studies of the Catholic school have never before been undertaken. Perhaps this relative lack of interest was due to a belief that the existence of Catholic schools was a phenomenon associated with the large waves of immigration of the late nineteenth and early twentieth centuries which were predominantly from Catholic countries and that the schools would begin to disappear as these Catholic immigrant groups were absorbed into the mainstream of American society. But the fact that the Catholic school system increased after World War II suggests that the opposite is happening and that Catholic schools are showing a continued vigor.

Because of our belief in the importance of a comprehensive study of the education of Catholic Americans in the Catholic school system, the National Opinion Research Center approached the Carnegie Corporation with a view to financing a national survey. The Carnegie Corporation, which has long been interested in the excellence of education in America, shared our belief in the importance of such a study and generously agreed to underwrite its costs. This book is the report of that research project.

In designing their research project, Professors Greeley and Rossi have focused their attention on those issues which appear to be the concerns of both the defenders and the critics of Catholic schools. These concerns are centered on four general issues which run throughout much of the discussion of the relative merit of public versus Catholic schools.

The first of these concerns is the major manifest reason for the establishment and maintenance of the Catholic school system— the preservation of religious faith. Since the *raison d'être* of religious schools is that they assist in the teaching of religion, it is crucial that any research project on Catholic schools address itself to the question: "Are the people who attend Catholic schools better Catholics?" The problem of measuring the "goodness" of a Catholic is an exceedingly difficult one which taxes the ingenuity of the researcher. The authors have considered many possible indicators of religious "goodness" and have attempted to show the consequences of Catholic education for each of these possible indicators. How adequately they have succeeded in this endeavor the reader will have to decide for himself.

A second issue of major concern in discussions of Catholic education has been the question of the potentially divisive nature of a separate, value-oriented educational system. Does the Catholic school system set its students apart from other Americans and create barriers to their cooperation with Protestants and Jews? To complicate the problem, many Catholic schools have been identified with particular ethnic groups that formed significant blocs of immigrants. Many critics believe that a separate school system tends to preserve these ethnic solidarities and prevent these groups from being absorbed into American life. Since it is generally held that the educational system is one of the important elements in welding the social and political value-structure that underlies an effective democratic system, much of the most heated debate over the Catholic schools has been focused on this issue. Because people generally associate with those of similar values and beliefs, it is a particularly difficult problem to assess the Catholic educational system's contribution to the creation or maintenance of particular subgroups in the population that are based on ethnic or religious ties. The authors address themselves specifically to this problem and show considerable skill in untangling these complicated interrelationships.

A third issue which underlies the research project is the evaluation of the part which Catholic education plays in preparing individuals for economic success. The significant question here concerns the competency of Catholic schooling to prepare one for life in a secular world, where occupational success not only contributes to his general level of economic well-being but also has a significant impact on his general social status. Since education plays such a crucial role in the social mobility which, for better or worse, is highly valued in our culture, it is important to know whether those attending Catholic schools are in any sense disadvantaged, compared with the Catholics educated in public schools, or whether they receive an education which gives them an advantage over public school Catholics in the competition for worldly success.

Finally, the authors explore a range of issues which center on the problem of internal criticism of the Catholic school system. Not all—perhaps not even the larger part—of the criticism directed against the Catholic schools comes from non-Catholics. Much comes from within the Catholic Church itself, both from some of the younger members of the clergy and from intellectual laymen. For any social institution that depends on voluntary contributions to sustain itself, the problem of maintaining the support of its members is vital. Because of the ever rising cost of maintaining an educational system, the Catholic school system has been subjected to strong pressures to raise more money. With greater amounts of federal funds available for public school education, the comparative advantage of public schools makes it more difficult to sustain the Catholic school system at the level a progressively better-educated Catholic population demands. Whether Catholic parents will continue to increase their support is an issue to which the authors have given attention and have attempted to provide some speculative answers.

That Andrew M. Greeley is a Catholic priest may indicate to some readers that he cannot be truly objective in his evaluations, although no one who knows him personally or who is acquainted with his other sociological writings would doubt his scientific detachment. That Peter H. Rossi is not a Catholic may indicate to others that he will be antipathetic to those who feel religious instruction is an integral part of education. But anyone familiar with his other writings on the sociology of education will have no doubt that he brings a sympathetic understanding as well as his social scientific skills to the examination of the problem. The authors, I believe, have examined the data with as much objectivity as is humanly possible, and it is my hope that the reader, whichever side of the fence he may be on, will bring the same standards to his own reading of the report.

Both advocates and critics of Catholic schools will find much here to support their respective views; consequently, neither side will be entirely happy with the results. As with most controversial issues, the reality is much more complex than the rhetoric of the disputants would have us believe. Many will regret that the authors do not come down firmly either for or against the Catholic school system but content themselves with pointing out, as clearly as the data will permit, the strengths and weaknesses of the system as it has worked over the past fifty years. The practical implications of the analysis must be left to the policy-makers and the polemicists.

The study, financed by a grant from the Carnegie Corporation, was aided by supplementary funds from the Office of Education of the United States Department of Health, Education, and Welfare. The national advisory committee that helped in the design of the questionnaire was composed of Anthony Downs, Joseph Fichter, Charles Glock, Bernard Lazerwitz, Gerhard Lenski, John Hotchkin, William McManus, Robert McNamara, Lloyd Morrisett, James O'Gara, Michael Schiltz, George Shuster, and Marshal Sklare. Leonard Pinto and C. Edward Noll acted as associate study directors during the course of the project—the former during the design, data-collection, and preliminary-analysis stages, the latter during the final-analysis stage. Thaddeus O'Brien analyzed the material comparing the effects of grammar school with the effects of high school. Sampling was directed by Seymour Sudman, fieldwork by Galen Gockel, coding by Carol Bowman, and data processing by Harold Levy, Patrick Page, and William Van Cleve. Richard Jaffe, assistant director of NORC, supervised the budgeting of the survey and Fansayde Calloway acted as office manager. Among our colleagues at NORC who provided special assistance were Jacob J. Feldman, James A. Davis, Seymour Warkov, John W. C. Johnstone, and Joe L. Spaeth. Research assistance at various times was provided by James Squyres, James Vanecko, John Denvir, Daniel Farrell, Harold Abramson, William McCready, and Thomas Philpot. The final manuscript was typed by Lillian Rochon and Nella Siefert. Mary A. Spaeth prepared the index.

NORMAN M. BRADBURN
Acting Director
National Opinion Research Center

Contents

List of Tables

1
The Nature of the Problem

History and affluence have combined to give America a system of primary and secondary education which has many outstanding features. The size of the system, the amount of resources and personnel allocated to it, the decentralized pattern of control, and its extensive coverage of the population are all characteristics which mark American education as different in degree and kind from the educational systems of other modern industrialized societies. Yet these are characteristics which, when taken singly, can be found in other societies. Extensive coverage of the population exists in the Soviet Union and Japan. There are many countries which allocate larger proportions of their gross national product to education, although none can match the United States expenditures in terms of absolute sums. Even certain degrees of local control occur in Great Britain and Canada, whose autonomy comes close to that of our local school system.

Often overlooked by observers of our educational system is one truly unique characteristic: of all modernized countries, the United States is the only one which maintains an extensive denominational school system financed by nongovernmental sources. To be sure, there are denominational school systems with extensive coverage in other countries, but none is financed almost entirely through tuition and private contributions as is the large and complex system of schools administered by the American Roman Catholic Church. With more than 300 institutions of higher learning, 2,500 secondary schools, and 10,000 elementary schools, the Catholic educational "system" enrolls approximately 14 per cent of the children and youths in school. Its 200,000 teachers (two-thirds of them priests, nuns, and brothers; one-third of them laity) instruct more than six million students.[1]

The Roman Catholic schools show no sign of disappearing from the American scene. On the contrary, they have grown at a very rapid rate. In 1900 (sixteen years after the American hierarchy decreed the establishment of a Catholic school in each parish) some 5 per cent of the elementary and secondary school students in the country were in Catholic schools. By 1940 the proportion had risen to 7 per cent, but in the last twenty-five years the percentage has doubled so that approximately one-seventh of the grammar- and high-school students in the nation are in Catholic schools. Since 1940 Catholic primary and secondary school enrollment has increased from 2.4 to 5.8 million, and there is no evidence of a decline in this expansion.

The historical roots of the Catholic school lead back mainly to the nineteenth century, when the commitment of the American population to mass public schooling began to be formed. The "common schools" of the eighteenth century were spotty in their coverage: the northeastern colonies were much more likely to provide schools than were the southern colonies, which did not begin to provide education on any extensive scale until after the Revolution. The common schools of the eighteenth century were, furthermore, community schools in the sense that they took on the doctrinal coloration of the communities which supported them. In this earlier period, where Catholics existed in large numbers either the publicly supported schools had a Roman doctrinal coloration, or else individual churches attempted to provide some sort of religiously oriented education to some portion of their parishioners.

In the early nineteenth century two trends developed to produce a different kind of "common school." First, as schisms developed within the major Protestant denominations, and Roman Catholic immigrants began to arrive in fairly large numbers, local communities lost their religious homogeneity. Second, state and local governments began to adopt the principle of providing education to all children at public expense. Universal compulsory education

[1] These figures are taken from the annual *National Catholic Directory*, as are all the statistics in this paragraph.

began to be written into state constitutions, especially in the new states that were admitted into the Union from the western territories.

The public schools that emerged in the nineteenth century were nondenominational but Protestant in flavor. Local communities tended to be overwhelmingly Protestant in composition but heterogeneous as far as specific Protestant denominations were concerned. The schools sought out and incorporated into their atmosphere those elements which Protestant denominations had in common. These common elements—readings from the King James version of the Old Testament, the singing of Protestant hymns, etc.—were, however, precisely ones which accentuated the doctrinal differences between Protestants and Roman Catholics. To the American Catholic hierarchy of the nineteenth century, the public schools appeared to be increasingly neutral *against* Roman Catholicism.

American Roman Catholics, partly in reaction to the schools and partly out of post-Reformation retreatism, came to the conclusion that the public schools were endangering the faith of the children of the rapidly growing Catholic population. The American Catholics could only survive by preserving their faith in the security of their own schools. There can be no question that Archbishop Hughes began Catholic schools in New York in the 1840's only after concluding that he could not arrange a satisfactory working agreement with the public school system. Nor can there be much doubt that "protection of the faith" has been part of the ideology of many of the defenders of Catholic schools.[2] Some Catholics have always been skeptical of this argument, and a large proportion of American Catholics have been educated in public secular schools (cf. Cross, 1958, pp. 130–38).

The Catholic immigrants of the nineteenth century were only partly of Anglo-Saxon stock. Preservation of their ethnic identities was another source of educational separatism (cf. Cross, 1965). Thus the strongest defenders of the Catholic schools during the "school controversy" at the end of the century were the German Catholics; in later years Polish Catholics became staunch sup-

[2] For an account of the founding of the Catholic schools in New York, see Glazer and Moynihan (1963, pp. 233–38).

porters of Catholic schools as a means of preserving their own cultural tradition. On the other hand, in cities where the Irish influence was dominant, Catholic education was not nearly so extensive.

These historical roots account for the existence of a Catholic school system, but as time goes on they become less and less adequate as reasons for its present vigor—especially the remarkable growth since the end of World War II, when ethnic identities were presumably less strong, when the public school had long since ceased to be Protestant (at least in areas where most Catholics live), and when American Catholics were well on their way to becoming fully accepted in the larger society.

To be sure there is organizational inertia, a force that preserves institutions long after their reasons for being brought into existence have disappeared. But organizational inertia accounts merely for persistence, not for growth and vigor. The Catholic schools exist and grow today because they serve important functions both for the Roman Catholic Church and for the Roman Catholic population.

It seems to us that Catholic education persists and grows because of a number of reasons. First, as we shall document in later chapters, American Catholics are a very religious group, existing in a cultural milieu in which almost everyone is at least nominally religious. Agnosticism and atheism have hardly taken root in this country, in large part because the major denominations are liberal and have modernized their theology and religious practices continuously. Religion is valued, and "to be religious" is a personal characteristic which is highly regarded and rarely viewed negatively. Religious education is by extension also valued.

Second, the Roman Catholic schools have neither developed into a very expensive type of private education nor provided second-class education for their students. By and large, Catholic schools and colleges appear to be about as good as the public schools, although there have been no schools of eminence supported by the Catholic Church. Inexpensive religious education of good quality—a tribute largely to the devotion of the religious working as educator at a nominal salary and the layman who has contributed more than tuition alone—has enabled Catholics to have their religious education at "below cost." Indeed the recent spurt of growth in Catholic education indicates the rising socio-economic status of the Catholic segment of the American population.

For historical and doctrinal reasons, Catholic schools as a means of religious education were not merged into the "common school." Having survived as separate entities for reasons that were largely defensive, they expanded and grew for reasons that were not primarily defensive at all but rather reflected the typical American concern for religious education. We would therefore expect survival and growth among other sectarian educational systems which, for one reason or another, were not amalgamated into the common school. More detailed study would be required, however, before we could apply this theory to the Missouri Synod Lutheran, Seventh-Day Adventist, and Jewish parochial school systems. Surely the size of the Catholic population (25 per cent of the national population), the relatively efficient organizational structure of Roman Catholicism, and the strong Catholic concern with overt religious behavior have also contributed their share to the expansion of Catholic education. Coupled with these factors have been, first, the amazing ability of the Church to absorb the educational costs to parents of school children who would otherwise be unable to send them to Catholic schools and, second, enough affluence in the Catholic group to afford the individual and collective costs involved.

Although a matter of considerable interest in its own right, we are not concerned in this volume with either the historical roots of the Catholic school or its present function. Rather, we are concerned with it as an institution designed to produce effects upon the individuals who go through it as students. There are two main reasons for this concern. First, as sociologists, we are concerned with the process of socialization. Second, much of the current discussion of the Catholic schools both within the Catholic community and in the larger society has been concerned with the effects of Catholic schooling on individuals. Hence, we are presented with one of those rare occasions on which both theoretical and applied interests in a particular social phenomenon coincide.

From the point of view of the sociologist, both interests focus on the socialization process. The continuity of cultural traditions is an inescapable fact, but the mechanisms by which they are maintained are still not fully understood. Surely formal schooling plays a part in this cultural transmission, but it is not at all clear to sociologists that the part of the school is as important in the socialization experience as most Americans think. Many who are critical of separate school systems assume that a common experience in public education is essential to the development of a cultural consensus within the United States. According to this view, the United States was (and to a considerable extent still is) a nation composed of groups whose interests and ideologies are potentially divisive. The manners of socialization of its various groups are thought to be considerably different from each other and from those of a presumed central core of American tradition. Therefore a universal school system must be expected to provide a socialization experience common to all groups—one that will inculcate the types and values of the "core culture." If this common socialization experience in a universal school system were absent, diversities among the various American cultural groups might lead to a chaotic, at best a divided, social system.

The proponents of religious education similarly take a position of high regard for the efficacy of formal education. Education in the context of religious schools is needed because secular schools inculcate, at best, no values at all, and at worst, the wrong ones. Parents can do part of the job, but religious schooling is needed to provide that special expertise in theological matters that resides in the religious. Therefore religion must be taught in school, preferably a school which will train its graduates in the usual academic subjects and prepare them for entry into American society and, in addition, develop in these graduates the proper value orientations and a strong sense of attachment to the Church.

Investigating the *factual* bases for these assumptions is the purpose of this volume. We hope to discern in what significant ways adults who have gone through the schools maintained by the Roman Catholic Church differ from others. Obviously, the kind of person one is as an adult is a product of many experiences.

Hence, in order to sharpen our discernment, we need to compare persons who are as closely identical as possible in all respects except attendance at Catholic schools as a child and youth. These kinds of comparisons can be made only imperfectly, as we shall relate below.

As social scientists, we maintain a skeptical view concerning the efficacy of formal schooling for the teaching of values. To the social scientist a view of formal education as an omnipotent socializing agent shows an exaggerated regard for education. The social scientist is not convinced that institutions of formal education are capable of accomplishing all the mammoth tasks that some apparently expect of them. The classroom may well be a place where formal skills are learned; it may also contribute to the transition from the family to the larger society. Finally, it may contribute somewhat to the maintenance of a core culture or the creation of a cultural synthesis. But whether formal education really has much influence on either cultural values or social behavior is not evident. Most sociological inquiries suggest that the more intimate settings of household, neighborhood, friendship, and workplace provide more effective modes of socialization than formal indoctrination. Social scientists are ready to concede that a considerable amount of socialization occurs in the school milieu, but they suggest that it takes place, not as a result of formal instruction in the classroom, but rather in the informal groups which grow up among the students. Most of the research literature available indicates that the changes in value orientations which do occur in the schools are limited and are conditioned by the previous experiences of the student in his family milieu.

Furthermore, whatever socialization does take place in the school environment may be substantially modified in adult life by the influence of postschool experiences. Marriage, parenthood, work, neighborhood, and aging may all weaken the impact on life values of formal instruction in childhood and youth.

Thus, while the average American has great faith in the efficacy of the school as a developer of values, whether religious or secular, the social scientist finds himself holding guarded views. He is extremely skeptical of the ability of the schools to develop value orientations and will only grudgingly accept proof for the proposition that schools indeed develop values.

The research reported here cannot fail to be influenced by the social scientist's skeptical posture. But it is also the work of two Americans deeply concerned with the problems of our society. The authors—one a Catholic and the other a non-Catholic—will cheerfully concede that the study is not concerned merely with the theoretical questions whether religious values can be taught in a separate school system and whether such a separate school system isolates members of a religion from other people in their society. Furthermore, we are hardly likely to be blind to the considerable controversy raging over Catholic schools in American society, between Catholic and non-Catholic, but perhaps even more between Catholic and Catholic. In the midst of controversy, the desire of the social scientist to find answers to the heated questions being discussed is a strong one. Hence, while we are interested in the theoretical issues at stake, we are also quite interested in the practical consequences.

The skeptical viewpoint expressed above is reinforced by the scanty research that has already been conducted on the effects of Catholic education. Although the results of such researches are inconclusive because their coverage of the Catholic population and the possible effects of Catholic education is limited, they do point strongly to the conclusion that the effects of formal religious schooling are considerably attenuated in Catholic adults. For example, Rossi and Rossi (1961), in summarizing the results of four studies, concluded that the differences between Catholic schooling and non-Catholic schooling are shown most dramatically in areas in which the Church has traditionally taken a strong stand, for example, the performance of ritual duties or attitudes toward the support of religious schools. In other areas of life—participation in the community, values concerning occupational achievement, or the political goals of American society—the differences between Catholic school and public school Catholics are nonexistent. Fichter (1958), in his study of a Catholic school in South Bend, Indiana, found few value differences between the students in the Catholic school and those in a nearby public school. Greeley (1963), in studying the effects of denominational education in high school and college, found little difference in occupational values and career plans, moderate differences in church attendance, and moderate differences in expectations of life happiness between Catholics from the denominational colleges and Catholics from other schools.

It was not possible in any of these studies to take into account the religiousness of the families from which those studied came. Yet such a control is of crucial importance, since children of devout Catholic families would be the most likely to go to Catholic schools, and thus there is a strong possibility that Catholic school attendance merely reflects having been born to religious parents. However, there is some indication that Catholic schooling has an independent effect on behavior. Westoff *et al.* (1963), who did contrast Catholics from families of varying religiousness, discovered that Catholic schools did produce a considerable effect on both values and behavior in the area of family planning and fertility and that this effect did not disappear under a control for the religiousness of the family of origin.

THE KEY RESEARCH ISSUES

Our research cannot help being affected in its conception and enduring concerns by both the theoretical and practical issues concerning religious education. These are reflected below in the eight key issues on which we hoped to shed some light. Of course, we cannot claim that these are the only issues involved in an empirical investigation of Catholic schools. For example, we have little if anything to say about the quality of Catholic education as judged by current educational standards. We are concerned mainly with those effects which still manifest themselves in adulthood rather than with those which are evident among students or recent graduates.

Furthermore, nothing is more tentative than the results of scientific investigation. Although we believe that a national survey can shed some light on each of these issues, these are results conditioned both by the historical context of our investigation and the instruments of observation which we employed.

1. If the principle goal of Catholic schools is to provide religious education, the first question we must ask is whether they

have succeeded in doing so. Are the Catholics who went to Catholic schools "better" Catholics than those who did not, especially when the comparison is between Catholics from highly religious family backgrounds? Do they go to church more often and receive the sacraments more frequently? Are they more orthodox in their doctrinal and ethical attitudes? Do they have a better grasp of doctrinal propositions? Are they more inclined to accept the authority of the Church as a teacher?

Catholic schools would not exist if there were not a fairly strong belief within the Church that the schools did in fact have some success in achieving such results. However, Catholic opinion has never been unanimous on the subject; the recent "modernization" within the Church has led to a renewed skepticism on the part of some Catholic writers whether the Catholic school Catholic was indeed a "better" Catholic.[3] Some have even argued that Catholic school training was an actual hindrance to "ecumenical dialogue" and had little relevance in the era of the Second Vatican Council. Such writers contend that whatever differences might exist between Catholic school Catholics and other Catholics result from family training, not from schooling, and that the Church would be much wiser to "phase out" its schools and entrust religious education to the family and to "released time" classes.

2. The second question is whether the Catholic school Catholic is more likely to be involved in the organizational activity of his church. On the one hand, it might be argued that frequent contact with the Church as an organization and with the religious functionaries of the Church during his childhood and adolescence would establish patterns of behavior that would continue into his later life. Thus he would be more likely to belong to Catholic organizations, to be friendly with the clergy, to contribute money to the upkeep of his church and to engage in the quasi-religious activities which are expected of the "active" Catholic. On the other hand, there is some research evidence in the work of Brothers (1964) that, in England at least, there is no relationship be-

---

[3] See the turn-of-the-century controversy documented by Cross (1958, Chap. 8). Many of the quotations cited by Cross could be part of the present controversy. Apparently, as far as Catholic schools go, there is nothing too much new under the sun.

tween Catholic secondary education and associational activity in later life, and the Rossi and Rossi (1961) study of a New England town could not find any association between Catholic schooling and membership in Church organizations.

3. Catholic education in a literal sense is segregated education. For at least eight years Catholic children attending their Catholic schools are, for all practical purposes, in contact only with other Catholics as teachers and as fellow students. The issue that stems from this segregated pattern is whether such schools have "divisive" effects that are manifest among Catholic adults. While it seems reasonable to assume that attending Catholic schools will affect the friendship patterns of school children, it is still very much an open question what effects this pattern may have upon the engagement of the Catholic adult population in the larger community (e.g., participation in political, community, and other voluntary associations) and the extent to which Catholics as a group are, through their separate school system, more likely to exist as a self-conscious political and social collectivity acting in unison on questions of nonreligious import in American society.

The question of divisiveness is raised both within the Church and outside it. Arguing against private schools in general and Catholic schools in particular, Conant charges that religiously segregated schools must necessarily weaken the consensus of American society. Similarly, Catholic critics argue that Catholic schools develop and maintain a "ghetto" mentality in Catholics.

This is an issue which has generated perhaps a greater proportion of heat to light than any of the others we will consider in this volume. Part of the problem resides in the question of the meaning we are to give to the term "divisiveness." For example, is a pattern of differential marriage divisive when partners to the marriage tend to be members of the same religion? Should the referent of divisiveness be restricted primarily to the political sphere, or should it cover the gamut of human interaction? Obviously the answer to the question whether Catholic schools are divisive depends on the meaning of divisiveness one adopts. For example, Rossi and Rossi (1961) found that Catholic school Catholics were quite like their public school counterparts with respect to membership in community organizations and political party preferences, but they were more likely to say they would accept the leadership of the clergy in forming an opinion on a local political issue.

4. Closely related to the question of divisiveness is the issue whether Catholic schools develop a sense of social distance between their graduates and other non-Catholic members of our society. Are Catholics who went to Catholic schools more intolerant than those who did not? If their Catholic school experience isolated them from members of other groups, it might well be that they would be more inclined to have stereotyped attitudes and therefore tend to be higher on measures of anti-Semitism, anti-Protestantism, and anti-Negro prejudice. Furthermore, the "authoritarian" nature of Catholic education would perhaps produce adults who would be less tolerant of religious differences and less concerned about the civil liberties of people who were not members of their own religious group. On the other hand, the supporters of Catholic education could argue that the emphasis on morals and values in Catholic schools might produce a graduate who was more tolerant, more open, and more concerned with the rights of others, especially if the teachings of some of the social encyclicals of recent popes were stressed.

5. Catholic schools are also schools in the ordinary sense, and one of the issues to which a study of this sort must address itself is whether attendance at a Catholic school is a help or a hindrance in coming to grips with the world outside the Church. There is no doubt that historically the rise of modern industry and commerce was associated with Protestant countries and, within a country, with the Protestant portion of the country. How much of that association still remains? Is the Catholic Church so otherworldly in its orientation that the graduates of its schools are handicapped in making their way through the modern American economic system and are less inclined to achieve economic and social success?

6. Whether a separate religious educational system can be expected to survive in the future American society depends in part on how its constituency views the institution. A number of articles have appeared in popular Catholic journals suggesting that the newly well-to-do upper-middle-class Catholic views his school

with extreme skepticism. Indeed, the articles give the impression that educated Catholics are strongly inclined to remove their children from such schools. If a "drift" away from the Catholic schools could be discovered, and if there were evidence that the Catholic elite groups are becoming increasingly dissatisfied with their schools, then there would be serious doubt whether the Catholic educational system had a reliable future. However, we know from previous research that middle-class people in general tend to be more concerned about and more critical of their schools; therefore, the increasing level of criticism of Catholic education among the middle and upper classes reflects more the intense concern of this group than its disaffection.

7. Of considerable theoretical and practical importance is the question whether any level of education is more effective than other levels in the development of religious values. We know very little about how young people develop their religious attitudes and beliefs, and what we do know from research into other aspects of socialization indicates that there are several processes at work. During the infancy and latency years, religion is intimately bound up with the primordial ties between child and parent. During early adolescence a very different kind of religious experience seems to be related to the emergence of an autonomous self. In later adolescence religion may become the focus around which an "ideology" (to use Erik Erikson's term) will develop to give articulate meaning to the life goals of the young adult. These three general stages of development (and there may well be others) are clearly very different, and the word "religion" seems to have rather different meanings at each stage. It is not at all clear which stage has the greatest importance for adult religious behavior. Or to put the matter more precisely, we do not know which stage influences which kinds of adult religious behavior for most people.

On the practical level a religious institution must inquire whether education during a certain period of the developmental process is more important for inducing the preferred adult religious behavior than education at other periods. Within American Catholicism there has been a group which has always emphasized the "forming of youthful minds" in the early years of school, another group which has stressed the necessity of seeing the young person through the "crisis of adolescence," and yet another which has insisted that in the final analysis the Church must be most concerned with the ideological and intellectual commitment of young adulthood. In recent years this debate has become quite intense as the rapid expansion of demand for classroom desks has led to the suggestion that certain levels be eliminated from the Catholic system. (As might be expected, the grades which are recommended for the ax are usually those in which a given speaker is not working; there are always excellent theoretical reasons not to preside over the liquidation of one's own function.)

There is very little evidence at hand to clarify this issue, though one finding in a previous NORC report (Greeley, 1963) might suggest that, with regard to certain values, the Catholic college is much more effective than the Catholic high school. Nor must we overlook the possibility that no level is more effective than any other and that the impact of Catholic education may result rather from a cumulation of years in Catholic schools.

8. Finally, we must inquire about the effect on Catholic education of the profound changes going on within the Church of Rome. The American Church is in the midst of two monumental transitions, as it moves from the immigrant ghetto to the upper-middle-class suburb and from the "garrison" Church of the Counter-Reformation to the "open" Church of the ecumenical age. While both the fact and the degree of these transitions are of considerable interest, our concern with them will be only indirect. As the emphases and concerns of American Catholicism change, we might readily expect a change in the consequences of Catholic education—even though educational systems are traditionally slow in adjusting to changing societies. It may well be that, as some defenders of Catholic schools contend, the younger Catholics who have come out of Catholic schools since the end of World War II will show traces of the mutations which have been going on within the Roman Church for the last quarter of a century. Thus the younger Catholics who went to Catholic schools may reflect the Church's increasing attention to the problems of interracial justice; they may also be more interested in academic excellence and better disposed to interact with Americans not

of their own religious faith; finally, they may be more strongly inclined to share in the broad value consensus of the larger society.

If such a change in the consequences of Catholic education can be discovered, it would indicate that we must take great care in essaying a judgment about the long-run effects on American society and on the American Church of a separate school system. The effects of a generation ago may not be the effects of the present or the effects of the next quarter of a century. Writers who describe Catholic schools as they were in the 1930's would be recording interesting history but would not be contributing directly to the discussion about the present or future impact of the schools.

On the other hand, the normal pace of social change—especially in an age-old religious body—can be expected to be slow, and the reflection of change in an educational system may be even slower. If our twenty-year-old respondents from Catholic schools prove to be different from those who are in their fifties, especially with social class held constant, we will have recorded only the fact of change; we will have said nothing about the pace. The crucial question is not so much whether Catholic schools have changed—it would have been hard for them not to have changed. The important question, rather, is whether we can find in the total picture of Catholic education's impact in the last half-century any evidence that a separate school system can be expected to develop in a direction and at a speed at which its dysfunctions for both the Church and the larger society will become minimal.

AN ASIDE ON METHOD

Whether we can produce empirical evidence appropriate to each of the issues we have raised depends on how wisely and insightfully we have designed this study. There can be no doubt that our study departs from the model that one would employ were there not human considerations (let alone considerations of time) to contend with. In some world where human values as we know them were grotesquely distorted, one could conduct the kind of classical experiment which would generate definitive findings. All one need do is arbitrarily send some Catholics to Catholic schools and others to public schools and wait for the "subjects" to grow old enough to manifest steady readings on the variables of interest.

The best we can do in our human environment is to isolate, from a representative sample of Catholics, those who went to Catholic schools and compare them with those who did not. There are obvious defects in this approach, as any novice in the scientific method can discern: the act of going to a Catholic school may represent a condition of family life or of individual qualities which may markedly affect behavior and values in adult life. We have attempted to meet this objection to our ·procedures as best we can by analyzing our data in a way that tends to eliminate the effects of factors other than attendance at Catholic schools.

The data of this study were obtained mainly through personal interviews with a representative national sample of American Catholics during the winter of 1963–64. From a previously existing national sample of Catholics (drawn in a 1962 study of adult education in the United States), 2,753 Catholic respondents between the ages of twenty-three and fifty-seven were selected for personal interviewing. In addition, 1,000 self-administered questionnaires were left at the homes of remaining Catholic respondents of the 1962 sample who were in the proper age brackets. In households where there were adolescents, another self-administered questionnaire was left to be completed by those currently in high school. Finally, a questionnaire was mailed to a randomly selected sample of 1,000 readers of *Commonweal* so that the analysis could compare the liberal intelligentsia and the total population in their attitudes toward Catholic education.[4]

Although the major focus of attention in the present study is on a comparison of Catholics who went to Catholic schools with Catholics who did not, proper evaluation of the size and direction of differences between public school and Catholic school Catholics required a "control" group of non-Catholics. Therefore, interviews were conducted with a small sample of Protestants

---

[4] Further details about the sample design and the technical aspects of the study will be found in Appendix 1.

who were chosen to match the regional distribution of Catholics. A shortened version of the questionnaire used for the Catholic part of the sample was employed.

The general mode of analysis employed in assessing the effects of denominational schooling is to contrast Catholic adults who have attended Catholic schools with those who have attended public schools. It is obvious that the analyst's ability to make strong statements about the origins of differences is compromised by the extent of self-selection of those who attend one type of school rather than another. Catholics who have attended Catholic schools may be different from those who have attended public schools because they have come from backgrounds and environments which were more religious. Thus a difference between Catholic school and public school Catholics may be merely masking differences in kinds of parental influences, rather than differences generated by different educational experiences.

Since it is the pious, though perhaps naïve, hope of the authors that some readers will be fortunate enough not to be sociologists, it would be discreet at this point to make explicit some of the assumptions on which survey research is based, as well as to describe briefly the tools of analysis which will be used in this report.

First of all, we assume that our sample is a reasonably accurate representation of the Catholic population of the United States. Selected according to the laws of probability (by techniques described in Appendix 1), the sample is such that tests of "significance" can be made which will reveal the dimensions for the corresponding figures for the total Catholic population. This is not the place to engage in a long apologia for sample surveys; the reader who is dubious that some two thousand respondents could truly be "typical" of a much larger population is referred to a standard college statistics text.

Second, we assume that our respondents will tell the truth—unless they have reason not to. The problem, of course, is being certain that there is no reason for deception, and one can never completely exclude the possibility that deception is taking place. The arrangement of the questionnaire, the wording of questions, the manner of the interviewer, the nature of the subject—all can increase or decrease the probability that the responses of those being interviewed are valid. In this particular study, for example, it is possible (though one is not sure how possible) that we were not told the truth about how often our respondents went to church. It might be that Catholics, highly conscious of their obligation to attend Sunday Mass, would not be altogether honest in answering a question on this subject, especially since it surely must have been clear after the first ten or fifteen minutes of the interview that this particular questionnaire was almost inordinately concerned with religion. On the other hand, the proportion saying they went to Mass every Sunday is approximately the same as that reported in other surveys and is not inconsistent with the findings of the various studies of individual Catholic parishes. Furthermore, Sunday Mass attendance in our data correlates with sex, education, and nationality as we expected it might. At least on this particular question we have another check on the accuracy of a respondent's answer, since, in addition to his self-report, we also have a report on the respondent's church attendance from his spouse. Table 1.1 shows a remarkable agreement between the two reports. Only 6 per cent of those who claimed to go to Mass every week are contradicted by their spouses (although the spouse seems to be more generous to the nonattending respondent than the respondent is to himself). While

Table 1.1 Respondent's Description of His Church Attendance Compared with Spouse's Description of That Attendance (Per Cent of Catholic Marriages Only)

Spouse's Description of Respondent's Frequency of Attendance	Male Respondent's Self-description of His Frequency of Attendance		Female Respondent's Self-description of Her Frequency of Attendance	
	Weekly	Less than Weekly	Weekly	Less than Weekly
Weekly or more often	94	17	93	20
Less often than weekly	6	83	7	80
Total	100	100	100	100
N^a	528	227	572	170

[a] Only those respondents whose spouses were also interviewed are represented in this table. In addition to the main sample on which the report is based, the sample of those who filled out the self-administered questionnaire (for details, see Appendix 1) are included here.

there is the possibility that both reporters are lying, the consistency demonstrated would require a nationwide conspiracy if it obscured a pattern of church attendance radically different from that indicated by our statistics. Finally, in the present study some respondents administered the questionnaire to themselves instead of being interviewed, and there was no difference between the answers of these respondents and the answers of those who participated in a personal interview.[5] In addition, it might be noted that the question which is relevant in this study is not whether all respondents might have deceived us but, rather, whether there is any reason for those who went to Catholic schools to be more likely to lie about their religious behavior than those who went to public schools. It could be maintained that their Catholic schooling had made them more conscious of their obligations and hence more likely to attempt to hide their failings; but then this greater consciousness of obligation would be, at a minimum, an effect of Catholic education.

Third, we assume that the use of indices (multiple measures combining responses to several questions) substantially reduces the effect of misunderstanding a question or inadvertently giving a wrong answer. The indices used are composed of clusters of attitudinal or behavioral responses which correlate with each other; they do not of themselves necessarily represent anything more "true" than a response to a single question. However, they do indicate a pattern of consistency in the way a respondent reacts to our questions. Thus a man who gives anti-Semitic responses on several questions can safely be assumed to have a response "set" which indicates anti-Semitism, while one who gives tolerant answers on the same questions displays a more tolerant "set." While the index is a very useful tool, it should be kept in mind that, no matter what impressive label is attached to it, it represents nothing more than a pattern of answers to a given cluster of questions. The wise reader will keep in the back of his mind a notion of what these questions were.

Fourth, we assume that the behavioral and attitudinal questions we use in our interview reflect with some kind of accuracy the values of the respondents. It is quite possible of course that

[5] Full data are given in an article by Sudman, Greeley, and Pinto (1965).

a man may go to church every day and not be religious in any sense of the word; it is also possible that a man may say he would not live next door to a Negro but change his mind when faced with a situation in which a Negro has in fact appeared on the front lawn. However, in the ordinary course of human events, attitudes and behavior represent values for most of the people most of the time. If this were not so, human interaction would be quite impossible.

Having deliberately listed some of the ways in which we could have made mistakes, we might well be asked whether the pursuit we are engaged in has any claim at all to the title of science. If science requires the certainty we possess about the sum of two and two or the rising of the sun on the morrow, then obviously we are not being scientific. If, on the other hand, science means the orderly and systematic collection of data with maximum effort to exclude the possibility of error and maximum honesty about where the analysis might be mistaken, then we would think that, for all its admitted weaknesses, survey research has some claim to the title. The study of human behavior is still imperfect, but until someone provides us with more accurate tools, the best must be made of what we have.

But more is at issue than merely the academic question of how accurate our data really are. We cannot ignore the fact that in this study, as in many others, there are policy-making implications. Are our data of such quality that the policy-makers can safely base their decisions on them? In a sense the policy-makers must decide this for themselves after they have heard us describe both our findings and how we arrived at them. However, it would seem that the question is not whether the data are of high quality or only of moderate quality; the question is whether there are any other data at all. The policy-maker must base his decision on an evaluation of a given situation and must make use of whatever descriptive material is available to him. If he has a choice of following his own limited impressions or tossing a coin, on the one hand, and giving some credence to evidence collected by the best methods currently available, on the other, then clearly he must carefully examine the evidence and give it substantial weight in making a decision. Rarely will the evidence be overwhelming enough to make further deliberation unnecessary (and, as will be obvious as this report proceeds, the Catholic school is not one of these rare cases); but equally rarely will the evidence be of such little import that it can be ignored.

Some remarks should be made about two of the statistical tools used in analyzing our data—tests of "significance" and coefficients of association. To say that a given finding is "significant" is not necessarily to say that it is "important." A "significant" finding is rather one in which there is a fair degree of probability that the sample with which we are working is not different, in the particular matter under consideration, from the population which the sample represents. Thus a "significance test" tells us how many times we can expect on the average to make a mistake if we accept the kind of evidence for a proposition that the sample provides. To say that a proposition is significant at the .05 level (the level used in this volume) is merely to say that the sample provides evidence for the proposition of sufficient magnitude that we could expect, on the basis of such evidence, to make accurate judgments about the general population from a sample nineteen times out of twenty.

But we are not interested merely in whether the relationship to be found in our sample between Catholic schooling and adult religious behavior can be said with some considerable degree of probability to be representative of the general Catholic population. We are also concerned with the strength of this relationship. How much influence does Catholic education have on adult behavior? Is it stronger for one social or demographic group than another? Is it more important than a person's sex or educational level? The coefficient of association is a measure of the magnitude of the relationship between one variable and another. It enables us to judge whether a relationship is "important"—although we must usually make an arbitrary decision about how high a coefficient must be before it is considered "important." In our study the coefficient used will be the "gamma" coefficient developed by Leo Goodman and William Kruskal (1954). In a later chapter the precise meaning of this coefficient will be explained.

In succeeding chapters we will make use of summary tables, relegating the more detailed tables from which the summaries are made to appendices. Such a strategy prevents the main line of analysis from being lost in a morass of tables and still enables the reader who is interested in a more detailed examination of the data to explore the questions which are of special concern to him.

In most tables the Catholic respondents will be divided into three categories—those who have had all their primary and secondary education in Catholic schools, those who have had some education in Catholic and some in public schools, and those who never attended Catholic schools. The middle category is a somewhat nominalistic one, but its use is not merely an arbitrary choice dictated by the size of the sample and the impossibility of subdividing the "Some Catholic" group. Westoff in his study (1963) found that such a trichotomy was extremely helpful. In some tables we will also present information on Catholic respondents who were converts (and did not attend Catholic schools) and on Protestants. This information is presented, not only for its intrinsic interest, but also because it will in some instances prove useful for comparative purposes. It should be emphasized that the Protestants are white and have the same proportional distribution in NORC's primary sampling units as does the Catholic population, so that a control for geographic and ecological distribution is built into the sample design.

PLAN OF THE REPORT

In the following chapter we will disclose who went to Catholic schools, both because it is of some inherent interest to know which social, ethnic, and demographic groups were more likely to have attended Catholic schools and because such information will be most useful in determining, in later chapters, whether apparent relationships between religious education and adult behavior can be explained away as the result of something other than the religious educational experience.

The next six chapters address themselves to the major questions with which we are concerned. Chapter 3 examines the religious behavior of Catholics; Chapter 4 seeks explanations for the differences in religious behavior between those who went to Catholic schools and those who did not; Chapter 5 considers their social attitudes and behavior; Chapter 6 attempts to determine whether Catholic education is an obstacle to social and economic success; Chapter 7 wrestles with the question of what level of Catholic education is the most effective in achieving its goals; Chapter 8 asks whether there is any indication, among the adolescents in our sample, that Catholic schools have the same impact today that they had on our adult respondents in years gone by; Chapter 9 tries to see what hints can be gleaned from our data about the future of Catholic schools. Finally, Chapter 10 concludes with a summary of the major findings of the report and a discussion of the implications of these findings.

2

Attendance at Catholic Schools

The Third Plenary Council of the American hierarchy held in Baltimore in 1884 directed each parish to set up a parish school and each Catholic parent to send his children to these schools. The goal of a school in every parish and every child in a Catholic school has never been fully met. In 1964, for example, only 58 per cent of the parishes in the country had elementary schools, and in 1961, 45 per cent of the Catholic children in elementary school and 31 per cent of the Catholic children in high school were attending Catholic schools.

Looking back over the fragmentary (and somewhat untrustworthy) educational statistics of the twentieth century, it is apparent that the proportion of parishes with schools never rose higher than three out of five. In short, regardless of the desire of Catholics to attend parish and diocesan schools, for a good many, schools were not available. In addition, for a variety of reasons—some financial, others ideological—not all Catholics who had the opportunity took advantage of the existence of parish schools either to send their children or to attend themselves. As Table 2.1 indicates, 54 per cent of our sample of born Catholics between the ages of twenty-three and fifty-seven attended Catholic elementary schools, either wholly or in part. Of this group, 33 per cent had all their education in such schools, while the remaining 21 per cent had educational experiences involving a mixture of Catholic and other (usually public) schools.

Our problems of analysis would be relatively simple if there were only two groups of Catholics—those who went to Catholic schools and those who did not—but, as Table 2.1 shows, a fair number of Catholics (about one-fifth) had some of their elementary education in Catholic schools but not all of it. Nor did everyone who went to Catholic primary schools also attend Catholic high schools. Finally, approximately one-fifth of the sample did not attend secondary school at all.

About 13 per cent of all those who were born Catholic attended Catholic primary and secondary schools exclusively (Table 2.2). Another 32 per cent had some of their education in Catholic primary and/or secondary schools, while 33 per cent of those who went to primary and secondary schools never set foot inside a Catholic school. If we distribute the one-fifth of the population that did not attend high school according to their elementary school attendance, we raise the "All Catholic" group to 19 per cent, the "Some Catholic" group to 38 per cent, and the "No Catholic" group to 43 per cent. It is these three analytic categories which we will use throughout the report.

There are, of course, difficulties involved in lumping those who did not go to high school with those who did. But controls for level of education, which we will use in later chapters, will filter out whatever differences there are among the three groups that might be attributed to the varying proportions of those who did not go to high school. We are thus spared the necessity of reducing an already small case base even further.

Table 2.1 School Attendance at Elementary and Secondary Levels, by Amount of Catholic Education (Per Cent in Each Category)

Amount of Catholic Education	Level of Education	
	Primary	Secondary
All Catholic	33	22
Some Catholic	21	6
No Catholic	46	72
Total	100	100
N	1,809	1,408
NA	13	13
No schooling at this level	5	406
Total N	1,827	1,827

Since the number of parishes with schools has remained fairly constant over the past half-century, we can expect that a good number who did not go to Catholic schools did not go because there were no schools available in their particular parish at the time. Although one could wish for a more objective measure, some fix on the availability of Catholic schools (particularly at the elementary level) can be obtained from the respondents' accounts of whether there was a school available at the time they were going to school (see Table 2.3). Almost one-half of our

Table 2.2 Percentage Distribution of Adult Catholic Sample (Classed by Amount of Catholic School Attendance) According to Elementary School and Secondary School Attendance

Elementary School Attendance	Secondary School Attendance			No High School	Total
	All Catholic	Some Catholic	No Catholic		
All Catholic	13[a]	2[b]	12[b]	6[a]	33
Some Catholic	2[b]	2[b]	12[b]	5[b]	21
No Catholic	1[b]	2[b]	33[c]	10[c]	46
Total	16	6	57	21	100

[a] "All Catholic" elementary and secondary (if secondary attended): 19 per cent.
[b] "Some Catholic" elementary and/or secondary (if secondary attended): 38 per cent.
[c] "No Catholic" (i.e., all public) elementary and secondary (if secondary attended): 43 per cent.

Table 2.3 Availability of Catholic Schools for Those Who Attended Public Schools at Elementary and Secondary Levels (Per Cent for Whom Available)

Availability	Level of Education	
	Elementary	Secondary
Most of the time	47	47
Some of the time	10	7
None of the time	43	46
Total	100	100
N	1,403	1,302
NA	45	42
No school	5	21
Catholic school	618	243
Total N	2,071	1,608

respondents who attended public primary schools had to do so if they were to attend school at all. Only for the remainder was attending Catholic schools a possible alternative. When offered a choice, more than seven out of ten of our respondents chose to attend Catholic schools (Table 2.4).

If attending Catholic schools were purely a matter of their availability, the task of analyzing our data would be eased considerably. But this is not the case. Some of our respondents' parents chose to send them to Catholic schools; others apparently preferred the public schools. Still others sent their children to public schools because that alternative was the only one available to them.

The question of the availability of schools is important theoretically, because it enables us to approximate, in a rough fashion, a controlled experiment. In such a design the crucial respondents are not those who could have gone to Catholic schools and did not, but rather those who could not attend but who came from the kind of religious background which would have made them select Catholic education if it were available. If the apparent consequences of Catholic education are in reality consequences of the proclivity of those from highly religious backgrounds to go to Catholic schools, then persons from very religious families who could not go to Catholic schools ought to be very little different from those from the same kind of families who did attend a Catholic school. At a minimum we would expect the fervent families who could not send their children to Catholic schools to develop, if they possibly could, some compensating mechanisms which would produce the same effect as the schools.

Table 2.4 Per Cent Attending Catholic Schools (Primary and Secondary), with Availability Controlled

All Catholic	19
Some Catholic	38
No Catholic (school not available)	22
No Catholic (school available)	21
Total	100
N	2,065

If such compensating mechanisms do not in fact appear, we may conclude with somewhat more confidence that an observed relationship between Catholic education and adult behavior is an educational consequence and not a cryptofamilial consequence.

The task of analysis is complicated by the socio-economic heterogeneity of the American Catholic population. Furthermore, the nature of the American Catholic population was shifting rapidly during the very period in which most of our respondents obtained their primary and secondary education. Because of the spread in age represented in our sample,[1] our respondents can have attended school any time between the end of the second and the end of the fifth decades of the twentieth century. The year 1910 marked the peak of immigration from southern and eastern Europe, and the next decade was perhaps the point at which the American Catholic population was at the lowest level of the socio-economic hierarchy in the heavily urbanized areas of the Northeast and Midwest. The latter part of this half-century found American Catholics more closely integrated into the American middle class. These trends are easily discernible in Table 2.5, which examines, for different age groups, the occupational attainment of our respondents and of their fathers. It was during this

[1] Persons in the sample were between the ages of twenty-three and fifty-seven. For details, see the sampling description in Appendix 1, entitled "A Methodological Note on Sampling and Fieldwork."

Table 2.5 Socio-economic Status (SES) of Respondents[a] and Their Parents, by Age and Religion (Mean Score on Duncan Index)[b]

Religion	Age of Respondent			
	23–29	30–39	40–49	50–57
Parental generation:				
Catholic	$3.3_{(301)}$	$3.4_{(558)}$	$3.2_{(600)}$	$3.2_{(310)}$
Protestant	$3.9_{(90)}$	$3.8_{(167)}$	$3.5_{(170)}$	$3.6_{(100)}$
Respondent's generation:				
Catholic	$4.8_{(301)}$	$4.7_{(558)}$	$5.0_{(600)}$	$4.3_{(310)}$
Protestant	$4.5_{(90)}$	$4.5_{(167)}$	$5.5_{(170)}$	$5.0_{(100)}$

[a] Wives are assigned the social status of their husbands.
[b] See text for explanation.

period that the American population shifted from a predominantly rural to an overwhelmingly urban one, and increasing industrialization and mechanization of industry changed the kind of work demanded of the population from hard and heavy tasks to cleaner and less physical tasks, involving the manipulation of paper, typewriter, and people.

The measure of occupational prestige used in Table 2.5 is that developed by Duncan and his colleagues (Duncan, 1961). It divides the present population of the United States into ten roughly equal groups, according to the prestige of their occupations. Duncan measures occupational prestige basically by the average income derived from the occupation and the average amount of education needed for the job. Thus when we say that Catholics in their fifties have a mean occupational prestige score of 4.3, we indicate that the average Catholic in his fifties has a score slightly below the national average score of 5.0 (which is precisely the score for Protestants in their fifties).

The mean scores for respondents and parents—both Protestant and Catholic—in Table 2.5 first of all reflect the upward shift of the whole American population in the last half-century, which results from the decline in farming as the major occupational activity of most Americans and the rise of the technical and professional middle class that serves our urban industrial economy. Second, we note that, while Catholics lagged behind Protestants in occupational prestige through the entire parental generation, and among the older respondents in the present generation as well, the Catholics in their twenties and thirties have not only caught up with Protestants of the same age level but have actually forged ahead. While both religious groups have enjoyed the benefits of the last quarter-century of prosperity, it appears that Catholics have been able to use this period of time to achieve rough social and economic parity with Protestants, at least among those who are under forty. It should be emphasized that all the Protestants in our sample are white and are distributed in the same proportions in the NORC sampling units as are the Catholics. Thus there are built-in controls for region, size of city in which one is living, and race in Table 2.5.

While this marked upward shift in the social class of American

Catholics is interesting in itself, it creates new problems for our analysis. We must beware of the possibility that it may be the shifting socio-economic composition of the Catholic population which accounts for phenomena that we would be inclined on first reading to associate with Catholic education.

The socio-economic heterogeneity of the American Catholic population is further illustrated by its ethnic composition and dispersion among the various regions of the country, as shown in Tables 2.6 and 2.8. The Italians, Irish, German, Poles, and French (mostly French-Canadian) are the largest ethnic groups within the Catholic population, and each of these groups has brought with it a distinctive religious and cultural tradition. It

Table 2.6   Per Cent of Persons Born Catholic, by Ethnic Group[a]

Italian	20
Irish	18
German	17
Polish	10
French	10
Eastern European	9
English	6
Spanish	5
Other	5
Total	100
N	1,840

[a] Father's ethnicity.

Table 2.7   Per Cent of Persons Born Catholic, by Type of Hometown

Large city	35
Small city	25
Town	25
Farm or open country	15
Total	100
N	1,824
NA	16
Total N	1,840

would be reasonable to assume that religious practice in general, and Catholic school attendance in particular, will be affected by one's ethnic background; hence we must be aware of the possibility that something which looks like a correlate of attending a Catholic school may in reality be the result of overrepresentation of a devout ethnic group in these schools.

It is a sociological commonplace that Catholics are concentrated in the big cities north of the Ohio River and east of the Mississippi. But Tables 2.7 and 2.8 show how strong this concentration really is: 60 per cent of the Catholic population was born in cities and 77 per cent was born in the northeastern or north central regions.[2] When one adds the 10 per cent foreign born, it becomes clear that only a little more than one-tenth of the Catholic population is from the southern and western parts of the country. This concentration of Catholics has provided a population base which supports a complex organizational structure—including an extensive system of schools—but it has also reduced Catholicism, in the areas outside the concentration, to the status of a very small

[2] The states have been divided into the following four regions: *Northeastern states:* Connecticut, Maine, Massachusetts, New Hampshire, New Jersey, New York, Pennsylvania, Rhode Island, Vermont. *North central states:* Illinois, Indiana, Iowa, Kansas, Michigan, Minnesota, Missouri, Nebraska, North Dakota, Ohio, South Dakota, Wisconsin. *Southern states:* Alabama, Arkansas, Delaware, District of Columbia, Florida, Georgia, Kentucky, Louisiana, Maryland, Mississippi, North Carolina, Oklahoma, South Carolina, Tennessee, Texas, Virginia, West Virginia. *Western states:* Alaska, Arizona, California, Colorado, Hawaii, Idaho, Montana, Nevada, New Mexico, Oregon, Utah, Washington, Wyoming.

Table 2.8 Per Cent of Persons Born Catholic, by Region of Origin

Foreign	10
Northeastern states	45
North central states	32
Southern states	5
Western states	6
Other	2
Total	100
N	1,828
NA	12
Total N	1,840

denomination or even a sect. In these regions an extensive Catholic school system is most unlikely. Hence Catholic school attendance is found in precisely those regions where the strength of the Church enables the school to reinforce its norms most powerfully while nonattendance occurs in those regions where the Church is weak to begin with and where the temptation to depart from ecclesiastical norms in the face of a hostile majority could very well be strong.

From the preceding pages it should be abundantly clear that in our sample of Catholic adults is manifest a variety of social origins and historical experiences, each of which can be expected to play some role in attendance at Catholic schools. Catholic schools are more available in some regions than in others, a product of the history of those regions and the density and prosperity of the Catholic population therein. Some ethnic groups, having come from countries where the Roman Catholic Church was not the established church, had stronger attachments to its institutions than those who came from countries in which Catholics were more apathetic. The tuition costs for Catholic schooling, while nominal to upper-middle-class household budgets, can be burdens to the less affluent. Finally, Catholic parents who take the obligations of their faith more seriously (and hence provide a more religious family background) are probably more favorable to Catholic schools than those who are more relaxed about their canonical obligations.

It will be helpful to keep in mind, during this and subsequent chapters, the historical periods in which our respondents went to school. Respondents in their fifties would have been in high school during the 1920's and would have finished their secondary education before the great depression. Those in their forties would have spent the years of their young adulthood in the midst of the depression, and the males among them would have been likely to have served in World War II. Respondents in their late thirties would have finished high school in the early 1940's and would have been susceptible to the draft toward the end of the war, while those in their early thirties would have graduated from high school after the war and in time to be caught by the Korean War. Respondents in their twenties would have finished their secondary education during the last decade, when the forces of change within the Roman Catholic Church were stirring. Thus we are in effect studying the consequences of Catholic education over the half-century beginning just before 1910 and ending just before 1960. It is reasonable to assume that the atmosphere and goals of Catholic education have also changed in the course of this half-century and that different consequences may be expected among respondents of different age levels.

AGE AND SEX

Reflecting perhaps the fact that Catholic schooling has been available to the sample to about the same degree throughout the last fifty years, it is hard to discern any clear pattern in attendance that is dependent on age (see Table 2.9). Although respondents in their fifth decade were somewhat less likely than others to have had all their education in Catholic schools (perhaps a reflection of the great depression of the thirties) about one-fifth of all respondents did have all their schooling in Catholic schools.

Women respondents were more likely to have attended Catholic schools than men, although sex differences are not particularly striking (see Table 2.10). Catholic parents apparently thought it more important to send their daughters to Catholic schools than their sons, but this differential regard was not strong enough to produce striking differences between the sexes.

Table 2.9 Age and School Attendance of Respondent (Per Cent in Each Category)

School Attendance	Age of Respondent			
	23–29	30–39	40–49	50–57
All Catholic	19	20	15	21
Some Catholic	43	36	40	33
No Catholic	38	44	45	46
Total	100	100	100	100
N	309	579	615	316

N	1,819
NA	21
Converts	231
Total N	2,071

REGIONAL PATTERNS IN SCHOOL ATTENDANCE

As we saw earlier in this chapter, the Catholic population of the United States in the first half of the twentieth century was heavily concentrated in the northeast and north central states. The heavy Catholic immigration of the late nineteenth and early twentieth centuries produced streams which dumped their human cargoes into the industrial centers in those regions. Similarly, although some Catholics—particularly the early German immigrants—settled in rural areas, the vast majority settled in the cities. Obviously the density of Catholic settlements, as well as their prosperity and cultural composition, affected the ability of parishes to set up and maintain parochial schools and of dioceses to establish secondary schools.

Thus in Tables 2.11 and 2.12 we note that urban Catholics and those from the northeastern and north central regions are much more likely to go to Catholic schools than those from the rural and the southern and western regions. But this concentration of attendance does not appear—at least when our respondents were going to school—to be the result of differential attitudes toward Catholic schooling. When we control (Table 2.13) for the availability of the school during the respondent's youth we see that, with the single exception of respondents from the west, approximately 70 per cent of those for whom schools were available did in fact attend them, regardless of region or size of

Table 2.10 Sex and School Attendance (Per Cent in Each Category)

School Attendance	Respondent's Sex	
	Male	Female
All Catholic	16	21
Some Catholic	39	37
No Catholic	45	42
Total	100	100
N	817	1,002

N	1,840	
Converts	231	
Total N	2,071	

hometown. Residents of cities and those from the north central and southern states were slightly more likely to use Catholic schools if they were extant, but the differences are rather small and the important fact is that better than two-thirds of the Catholic population, no matter where its origin, did attend Catholic schools when possible.

Table 2.11 Size of Hometown and School Attendance of Respondent (Per Cent in Each Category)

School Attendance	Size of Hometown			
	Farm and Open Country	Small Town (Under 10,000)	Small City (10,000–500,000)	Large City or Suburb (Over 500,000)
All Catholic	12	11	25	23
Some Catholic	29	32	39	45
No Catholic	59	56	35	32
Total	100	99[a]	99[a]	100
N	272	471	474	607

N	1,824
NA	16
Converts	231
Total N	2,071

[a] Less than 100 per cent due to rounding.

Table 2.12 Place of Birth and School Attendance (Per Cent in Each Category)

School Attendance	Place of Birth					
	Foreign	Northeast	Central	South	West	Other
All Catholic	21	21	18	19	6	17
Some Catholic	21	37	47	42	23	38
No Catholic	59	42	35	39	72	45
Total	101	100	100	100	101	100
N	174	813	574	97	123	47

N	1,830
NA	10
Converts	231
Total N	2,071

ETHNICITY AND GENERATION

Ethnic traditions have a very powerful effect on Catholic school attendance (Table 2.14), as anyone familiar with American Catholicism and its vast internal pluralism would be prepared to expect. The French, Irish, and Polish are the most likely to have gone to Catholic schools, while the Spanish-speaking, the Italians, and the "other eastern Europeans"[3] are the least likely. The German and "English" groups occupy a middle position. A detailed explanation of these differential traditions will have to wait for a more definitive study of ethnicity in American culture. It suffices at the present to say that the strict loyalty to external religious practice seen in the French-Canadian, Irish, and Polish traditions is an adequate explanation for their inclination to go to Catholic schools, and the more relaxed attitude toward external practice (coupled with a possibly greater emphasis on certain spiritual values) held by the Latin groups is sufficient reason for their being less likely to attend a Catholic educational institution.

[3] A composite group which will undoubtedly lose us many friends among the Lithuanian, Slovak, Croat, Slovene, Hungarian, and Czech groups, but, alas, our sample is not big enough to give the diversity of these groups proper recognition.

Table 2.13 Per Cent Attending Catholic Schools When They Were Available, by Size of Hometown and Region of Origin (Persons Having at Least Some Catholic Education)

Size of hometown:	
Large city	74(554)
Small city	75(417)
Town	69(305)
Farm or open country	69(154)
Region of origin:	
Northeastern states	70(675)
North central states	76(464)
Southern states	76 (76)
Western states	48 (75)

Table 2.14 Ethnicity of Father and School Attendance (Per Cent in Each Category)

School Attendance	Father's Ethnicity								
	French	Irish	Polish	German	English	Eastern European	Italian	Spanish-speaking	Other
All Catholic	34	30	22	21	20	13	8	4	7
Some Catholic	44	47	51	43	37	39	23	18	38
No Catholic	22	23	27	36	43	48	69	77	55
Total	100	100	100	100	100	100	100	99[a]	100
N	185	318	186	318	109	178	363	137	58

N	1,852[b]
NA	52
Converts	231
Total N	2,135

[a] Less than 100 per cent due to rounding.
[b] Some respondents reported multiple ethnicity for their parents.

There is also a consistent association between generation and Catholic school attendance; third-generation respondents and those whose families have been here even longer than three generations are considerably more likely to have some Catholic education (Table 2.15) than those who are from the first or second generation. In Table 2.16 we investigate whether this is a real generational effect or is the result of somewhat more loyalty to Catholic schools in the ethnic groups that came earlier. It appears that generation and ethnicity have an effect. In both generational groups, the Irish, German, Polish, and French are more likely to go to Catholic schools than are the Italians or the Spanish-speaking, but in the later generations there is an increase in the proportion of these latter two groups going to Catholic schools. Germans also increase their proportion in Catholic schools in the later generations, and there is little change for the Polish. In the later generations there is a decline among the Irish in the proportion having exclusive Catholic education and a decline among the French both in those having exclusive Catholic education and those having some experience in Catholic schools. At least in part, this can be explained by the fact that later generations can be assumed to go farther in their education and thus be more likely to attend high school (which will more probably be public); thus the proportion of the mixed group will rise. However, the increase among the French-Canadians in those

Table 2.15 Generation and School Attendance (Per Cent in Each Category)

School Attendance	First Generation	Second Generation	Third or Later Generation
All Catholic	20	16	20
Some Catholic	21	34	47
No Catholic	59	50	33
Total	100	100	100
N	183	750	749

	N	1,682
	NA	158
	Converts	231
	Total N	2,071

Table 2.16 Catholic School Attendance by Generation and Ethnicity (Per Cent in Each Category)

School Attendance	First and Second Generation						Third or Later Generation					
	Irish	German	Italian	French	Polish	Spanish	Irish	German	Italian	French	Polish	Spanish
All Catholic	41	15	8	50	21	5	27	22	10	23	19	3
Some Catholic	39	34	22	37	51	16	49	52	32	48	50	35
No Catholic	20	50	70	13	28	79	24	26	58	29	31	65
Total	100	99[a]	100	100	100	100	100	100	100	100	100	103[a]
N	75	3	290	70	110	115	204	174	59	73	58	17

[a] Greater or less than 100 per cent due to rounding.

having no Catholic education at all is not so easy to explain. It may be a result of being another generation removed from the state-supported, comprehensive Catholic school system of Quebec and thus demonstrate a weakening of the tradition of Catholic education among this group, the only one to possess such a tradition before coming to the United States.

It is important to note that three of the groups which were less likely to have sent their children to Catholic schools notably increase in the proportion of their members in Catholic schools during later generations—the Italians, the Spanish-speaking, and the Germans. The implications seem to be that, as acculturation proceeds, the ethnic differences in Catholic school attendance are likely to decline, and the proportion having at least some Catholic education levels out around 50 per cent. The Irish and French groups have declined to that level and the Germans have risen to it. For the Poles such a proportion represents no change, and the other two groups seem to be rising toward 50 per cent although both still have a long way to go. On the other hand, most of the Latin groups would still be in the third generation (of the "Third or Later Generation" group), while many of the Irish and German respondents would have come from generations after the third. Hence the Italians and the Spanish-speaking may

Table 2.17 Father's Occupation[a] and School Attendance (Per Cent in Each Category)

School Attendance	Father's Occupation		
	Low (1–2)	Medium (3–5)	High (6–10)
All Catholic	17	20	21
Some Catholic	35	42	40
No Catholic	48	38	39
Total	100	100	100
N	908	544	327

N	1,780	
NA	14	
Not applicable	46	
Converts	231	
Total N	2,071	

[a] Ratings from Duncan scale (see text for explanation).

still have been "catching up" during the time that the respondents to our survey were in school.

SOCIAL CLASS

Table 2.17 and Tables 2.18 and 2.19 turn to the question of the social class of the families from which the respondents came and the probability of Catholic school attendance. Using the occupational prestige scale developed by Duncan and his colleagues, we observe that respondents whose fathers were in the lower half of the Catholic population were slightly less likely than others to have had exclusively Catholic education and 10 per cent less likely to have had any Catholic education. Father's occupation was clearly a less important predictor of Catholic school attendance than either the size of the hometown of the respondent or his ethnic background.

The same relationship between social class and Catholic school attendance can be seen when the measure of social class is the educational level of one's parent. The proportion of those who had ever attended Catholic schools increases from approximately one-half to over two-thirds when those whose parents did not

Table 2.18 Education of Father and School Attendance (Per Cent in Each Category)

School Attendance	Father's Education			
	Sixth Grade or Less	Seventh or Eighth Grade	At Least Some High School	At Least Some College
All Catholic	17	18	22	28
Some Catholic	31	47	44	41
No Catholic	52	35	34	32
Total	100	100	100	101[a]
N	609	440	298	116

N	1,463
NA	5
DK	372
Converts	231
Total N	2,071

[a] Greater than 100 per cent due to rounding.

graduate from grammar school are compared with those whose parents went to college, but the crucial cutting point seems to be between those who did not get beyond sixth grade and all others. Beyond sixth grade, differences in parental educational level do not appreciably affect Catholic school attendance. (We will note in a later chapter that this same cutting point seems to be relevant in predicting the Catholic school attendance of children at the present time.)

There was, then, a relationship between social class and Catholic school attendance, but after a certain level was reached (beyond the sixth grade and beyond the second Duncan decile level) this relationship apparently was not very important. It was the poor and the poorly educated who disproportionately did not send their children to Catholic schools. An eighth-grade education and a job which would put one in the lower middle class (Duncan scores 3–5, for our somewhat arbitrary purposes) were enough to bring one up to the average; beyond these levels there was little increase in the proportion going to Catholic schools.

The simplest explanation is, of course, financial. The very poor did not have or at least did not think they had the money

Table 2.19 Education of Mother and School Attendance (Per Cent in Each Category)

School Attendance	Mother's Education			
	Sixth Grade or Less	Seventh or Eighth Grade	At Least Some High School	At Least Some College
All Catholic	16	19	25	19
Some Catholic	30	44	41	54
No Catholic	54	36	35	26
Total	100	99[a]	101[a]	99[a]
N	552	500	399	57

N		1,508
NA		7
DK		325
Converts		231
Total N		2,071

[a] Greater or less than 100 per cent due to rounding.

necessary to pay even the rather small elementary school tuition (a dollar a month as recently as the 1930's). In addition, however, there is abundant evidence that, in Western urban society at least, religious activity increases with social class. Whatever its origins, Christianity has become a middle-class religion; the more middle class a person is, the more likely he is to engage in approved religious behavior, including—it is safe to assume—sending his children to religious schools, if this is the behavior approved by his Church. But in this fact lies a possible trap for our analysis. If the persons who send their children to religious schools are precisely those whose social class is most likely to incline them to higher levels of religious behavior, an apparent relationship between religious education and adult behavior may in reality be a phenomenon of social class rather than of religion.

In concluding these sections about the demographic and social backgrounds which lead to Catholic school attendance, we observe that while age and sex do not seem to be important enough as predictors to cause us any trouble in our analysis, the factors of ethnicity, social class, generation, and availability of schools (as mediated by the place where a person grew up) might influence both Catholic school attendance and adult religious behavior. Hence, we must be very wary of attributing adult behavior to religious education until we have excluded the influence of these potentially intervening variables. We must be on our guard against the possibility of a selective enrollment in Catholic schools of those who are inclined, for a variety of background reasons, to be more religious no matter what kind of school they went to.

RELIGIOUS BACKGROUND

While social and demographic variables may have some influence on both Catholic school attendance and adult religiousness, there can be no doubt that the most important background factor which we must take into account is the religiousness of the family from which a respondent came. As a matter of fact, the validity of our conclusions depends to a considerable extent on our ability to control for the religiousness of the home environment in which adult Catholics grew up. There is every reason to think that the most religious families would be the ones most inclined to send their children to Catholic schools and also the ones most likely to socialize their children in adherence to religious norms. Thus the family religious atmosphere may well be the real cause of any differences between Catholic school Catholics and other Catholics.

A religiousness index was prepared, based on the religion of the parents, their church attendance, and their reception of the sacraments.[4] Obviously the only way we could know this information about the parents of the respondents was to ask the respondents themselves; hence, information on which the religiousness index is based is retrospective and not as reliable as we might like to have it. There is a possibility that religious respondents tend to exaggerate the religiousness of their parents, and nonreligious respondents, to underestimate it.[5] However, whatever bias occurs would work against the hypothesis that Catholic schools affect the religious behavior of adults. That is, if religious respondents exaggerate the religiousness of their parents, this would lead to an association between respondents' behavior and their parents' behavior, rather than between respondents' behavior and Catholic education. Therefore, if there is a bias in our religiousness index, the bias is against Catholic schools and not in favor of them.

The relationship between the religious background of one's family and whether one went to Catholic schools turns out to be quite strong (Table 2.20): 75 per cent of those whose parents were very religious attended Catholic schools while only 42 per

---

[4] The composition of the religiousness index was as follows: *high:* both parents Catholic, both weekly Mass-goers, at least one received Communion weekly; *higher middle:* both parents Catholic, both weekly Mass-goers, but neither Communion weekly; *lower middle:* at least one parent a Catholic and a weekly Mass-goer; *low:* all others. The reader may observe that the difference between the "high" and the "higher middle" groups may seem rather slight—whether at least one parent receives Communion every week. However, it will be noted in succeeding chapters that the distinction is of considerable importance in predicting the effect of Catholic education. Indeed, Table 2.20 shows that it is quite important in predicting Catholic school attendance.

[5] A religiousness index similar to that developed for parents of respondents was constructed for respondents themselves and then associated with the Catholic school attendance of respondents' children. The parental religiousness index had a gamma association of .33 with respondents' Catholic schooling, and the respondents' index association with *their* children's schooling at .35. This gives us considerable confidence in the parental religiousness index.

Table 2.20 School Attendance and Religious Background (Per Cent in Each Category)

School Attendance of Respondent	Religiousness of Parents				Parental Religious Education			Marriage of Parents	
	High	Higher Middle	Lower Middle	Low	Both Parents in Catholic Schools	Mixed	Both Parents, No Catholic School	Catholic	Mixed
All Catholic	38	21	11	8	39	20	7	20	10
Some Catholic	37	43	34	34	50	48	29	38	37
No Catholic	25	36	55	58	11	32	64	42	53
Total	100	100	100	100	100	100	100	100	100
N	323	664	366	486	240	477	439	1,653	187

cent of those whose parents were at the lower end of the religiousness scale had any Catholic education. As a matter of fact, each level on the parental religiousness index predicts approximately a ten percentage point increase in the proportion going to Catholic schools. It can also be observed in Table 2.20 that parental attendance at Catholic schools is an extremely strong predictor of the Catholic education of the respondent. Almost nine-tenths of the respondents both of whose parents went entirely to Catholic schools attended Catholic schools themselves, while approximately one-third of those whose parents had no Catholic education attended Catholic schools. Thus it appears that Catholic education may very well be a matter of family tradition.

The question of family tradition raises an interesting point about the relationship between ethnicity and religiousness of parents. We suggested in the previous section that the various ethnic groups came to America with vastly different attitudes toward religious behavior. It is altogether possible that ethnicity and family religiousness are closely connected phenomena and that a joint control for these two variables will lead to no more of a diminution of the relationship between religious education and adult behavior than will separate controls for each. But this question must wait until later chapters.

There is finally some negative relationship between a religiously mixed marriage and Catholic school attendance, though almost one-half of those whose parents were in a religiously mixed marriage had at least some Catholic education.

The Catholics who went to Catholic schools therefore came from a family religious background in which the external norms of religious devotion were much more likely to be honored. Their parents went to Church more frequently, received the sacraments more regularly, were more likely to have gone to Catholic schools themselves, and were more inclined to marry other Catholics. Such influences could very well have shaped their adult attitudes and behavior so completely that there was little left for the Catholic school to do. Hence, in the case of those from the most religious backgrounds, it is quite possible that Catholic education will have made very little difference and that a control for religiousness will eliminate (at least among the very religious) any difference between those who went to Catholic schools and those who did not.

However, there is an alternative possibility to be reckoned with: it might be that a fervent religious atmosphere in the home environment, far from making the work of the school unnecessary, will in fact predispose the child for the influence of the school. If this alternative turns out to be true, we can expect that the principal differences between those who went to Catholic schools and those who did not will occur precisely among those from the most religious backgrounds, since the Catholics from less religious families will have little in the way of predisposition to prepare them for the influence of the Catholic school. The question, then, is whether the Catholic school simply duplicates the efforts of the family or whether the family and the school reinforce each other and accomplish in tandem more than each can individually. Only the data can answer this question definitely, but at this point it is worth noting that, while popular theorizing has tended to choose the first possibility, what little we know about the reinforcing effects of various agencies of socialization incline us to the second possibility. (Honesty—which occasionally rears its ugly head even among the best trained social scientists—compels us to admit that we were not prepared for the second alternative before we saw the data.)

There is another familial religiousness which must be considered in addition to that of the family in which the respondent was raised: the religiousness of his own family at the present time. If Catholic school Catholics are more inclined to marry other Catholics (and more devout Catholics at that) and if we can assume—as seems very reasonable—that one's own religious behavior is strongly influenced by that of one's wife or husband, then it is altogether possible that the apparent influences of Catholic education really result from the kind of wife or husband that this education has disposed one to marry. In Table 2.21 we note that, while Catholic school Catholics are only very slightly more likely to marry other Catholics, the spouses they do choose are considerably more likely to be weekly churchgoers, with 85 per cent of the mates of the "All Catholic" group going to church each week, as opposed to 65 per cent of the spouses of those who did not go to Catholic schools. What influence this choice of spouse may have remains to be seen. The same alternatives discussed in the previous paragraph are possible: marriage to a religious person may be the real "cause" of the apparent differences between those who went to Catholic schools and those who did not, or it may merely reinforce differences which exist independent of marriage.

PRESENT SOCIAL STATUS

Thus far in the chapter we have taken into account the various background factors of Catholic education which must be watched lest we attribute to Catholic schools an influence on adult life they do not actually have. By so doing we have also described who went to Catholic schools and what groups are most likely to be overrepresented among those who had Catholic education. There is, however, another kind of variable which must be taken into account: the present social class of our respondents. Since those who went to Catholic schools were of a somewhat higher family status than those who did not, it is possible that in their adult lives they will still enjoy this higher prestige. If they have not lengthened the social gap between themselves and public school Catholics, a control for parental social status will, in effect, control for the respondent's current social status. However, if Catholic school Catholics have moved farther ahead of public school Catholics, we must take into account the possibility that differences we might find in adult religious behavior result not so much from Catholic education as from the increment in social class.

Table 2.21 Per Cent of Respondents in Each School Attendance Category, by Religion of Spouse and Spouse's Religiousness

Spouse's Religion and Religiousness	School Attendance of Respondent		
	All Catholic	Some Catholic	No Catholic
Married to non-Catholic	10	15	13
Married to Catholic who goes to church every week	85	72	65

There is also the theoretical possibility that the public school Catholics may have narrowed the gap between themselves and Catholic school Catholics. But while this would be an interesting substantive finding which we would have to account for, it would not act as an intervening variable rendering a relationship between religious education and adult behavior spurious.

Table 2.22 indicates that the Catholic school Catholics have increased their social class margin over other Catholics. The occupational prestige of Catholic school Catholics (as measured by the mean Duncan score) shows an increase 50 per cent greater than the increase of the "Some Catholic" and "No Catholic" groups over the father's mean score. The "All Catholic" group, starting at the same level as the "Some Catholic," has managed to catch up with the Protestants in occupational prestige, while the other two groups lag behind. The slower progress of those who did not go to Catholic schools at all may be attributed to the fact that a lower position from which to begin prevented them from acquiring the momentum to scramble upward. However, the more impressive showing of the "All Catholic" group when compared to the "Some Catholic"—both of which have identical mean occupational scores for parents—is not so easily explained.

The same phenomenon is to be observed in studying the educational achievements of the respondents (Tables 2.23 and 2.24). Even under a control for parental educational level, those who went to Catholic primary schools were more likely to graduate from high school than those whose grammar-school education

Table 2.22 Mean Occupational Rating (Duncan Scale) and School Attendance for Respondent and Father

Mean Occupational Rating	School Attendance				
	All Catholic	Some Catholic	Public (Catholic)	Public (Convert)	Public (Protestant)
Father	3.5	3.5	3.1	3.4	3.8
Son (respondent)	5.0	4.5	4.1	4.8	4.9
Difference	1.5	1.0	1.0	1.4	1.1

was mixed or exclusively public. They were just about as likely to graduate from high school as were American Protestants. Furthermore, those who went to Catholic high schools (either exclusively or at least for a time) were more likely to go to college than were those (Protestant or Catholic) who went to public high school, with the exception of Protestants attending public school whose fathers had gone to college.

The magnitude of the Catholic school's effect on high-school graduation can be judged from the fact that the Catholic grammar-school respondents whose fathers' educational levels did not exceed high school were more likely to graduate from high school than the "Some Catholic" or "No Catholic" respondents whose fathers went to college. Indeed, they were almost as likely to graduate from high school as the Protestant respondents whose fathers went to college. Similarly, the respondents who attended Catholic high schools were as likely to go to college as the

Table 2.23 Per Cent of Respondents Who Graduated from High School, by Primary Educational Experience (Controlling for Father's Educational Level)

Father's Education	Primary Education of Respondent			
	All Catholic	Some Catholic	Public (Catholic)	Public (Protestant)
Primary	$60_{(346)}$	$47_{(215)}$	$50_{(484)}$	$51_{(256)}$
Secondary	$90_{(114)}$	$76_{(71)}$	$73_{(113)}$	$88_{(130)}$
Higher	$89_{(46)}$	$84_{(31)}$	$78_{(39)}$	$93_{(67)}$

Table 2.24 Per Cent of Respondents Who Attended College, by Secondary Educational Experience (Controlling for Father's Educational Level)

Father's Education	Secondary Education of Respondent			
	All Catholic	Some Catholic	Public (Catholic)	Public (Protestant)
Primary	$32_{(164)}$	$31_{(39)}$	$20_{(605)}$	$24_{(216)}$
Secondary	$51_{(82)}$	$44_{(28)}$	$32_{(177)}$	$37_{(128)}$
Higher	$58_{(38)}$	$67_{(9)}$	$52_{(64)}$	$75_{(66)}$

respondents who went to public high schools and whose fathers were one level higher in education. Thus one-third of the Catholic high-school group with grammar-school-educated fathers went to college, and one-third of the public high-school group with high-school-educated fathers went to college (the public school Protestants are not notably ahead of either of these groups); one-half of the Catholic high-school group with high-school-educated fathers went to college, as did one-half of the public high-school group with college-educated fathers. Indeed, if anything, the magnitude of the differences is understated by Tables 2.23 and 2.24, since women are overrepresented in the "All Catholic" group, and women were less likely to pursue further education. Part of the explanation for this phenomenon may be that at least some Catholic high schools, especially in the years when our respondents were in school, have been essentially college-preparatory schools and may well recruit students with college intentions—or perhaps develop college plans among those who did not have them.

These rather dramatic associations between Catholic education and upward mobility are presented in this chapter mainly to develop a rationale for multivariate analysis in succeeding chapters. However, they clearly have major substantive implications, to which we will return in further analysis. There are at least two general explanations to be investigated. The first would try to find within Catholic education itself a cause for mobility; the other would try to determine if there were a factor in the family background of those who went to Catholic schools which would explain why those families whose children were more predisposed to upward mobility would send their children to Catholic schools. It may well be that some combination of both possibilities will provide a tentative explanation. However, our main purpose at present is not to explain this curious phenomenon but to establish that Catholic education associates with higher SES of respondents and that this association must be kept in mind in any consideration of differences in religious behavior.

CONCLUSION

In this chapter we have tried to describe which subgroups of

American Catholics were most likely to have gone to Catholic schools and hence to chart out for ourselves the pitfalls we are likely to encounter in our analysis. As Table 2.25 shows, the background factors which most strongly associate with Catholic school attendance are ethnicity and parental religiousness, while hometown size (in reality a manifestation of the availability of Catholic schools), parental and respondent's social class (as measured by occupational prestige and education), and the religiousness of one's spouse are also factors to be reckoned with. There is some reason to think that each of these variables might influence both Catholic school attendance and adult religious behavior and hence be the intervening variable that would render spurious any relationship between Catholic education and adult behavior we might discover. To say that religiousness, ethnicity, and social class might behave in this fashion is not to say that they will. As we noted in the body of the chapter, some or all might behave in the exact opposite way and reinforce the differences between Catholic school Catholics and those who did not go to Catholic schools. But before we determine how these control variables do in fact operate, we must first discover whether there are any differences at all to be observed among the three groups of Catholics we are studying.

Table 2.25 Background Gamma Associations[a] with Catholic Education

Parental religiousness	+.33
Ethnicity (northern and western European)	+.31
Hometown size	+.27
Generation	+.20
Mother's education	+.20
Father's education	+.16
Respondent's socio-economic status	+.14
Spouse's religiousness	+.12
Sex (female)	+.14
Father's socio-economic status	+.07
Age	−.05

[a] Goodman and Kruskal's gamma—see Chapter 4 for explanation.

3

Religious Consequences of Catholic Education

Our first key question is obviously the most crucial that can be asked: Are those who went to Catholic schools "better" Catholics? The whole *raison d'être* of a separate religious school system lies in its presumed ability to produce adults who are more likely to adhere to the norms of the religious group. If Catholic school graduates are better Catholics, then, at least from the viewpoint of the Roman Church, the schools have been a success. If on the other hand they are not better Catholics, then the schools have failed in their primary purpose, and there is no point in their continued existence.

Unfortunately the question of the success or failure of Catholic education is not a simple one even to ask, much less to answer. For it is not at all clear what sort of "payoff" would be necessary to consider the schools successful. If there were no differences in adult religious behavior and attitudes between those who went to Catholic schools and those who did not, then we could rather easily write off Catholic education as a failure. But if there are differences, how big must they be before we can safely say that the schools have accomplished their purposes?

Much of the discussion within the Roman Church about its schools seems to center on whether the philosophical goals of Catholic education—especially as set down in papal or episcopal documents—have been achieved. But such discussion is not very realistic; the ultimate philosophical goals of any educational system are just that: goals to be striven for, not objectives to be reasonably expected. The goals of Catholic education are anything but modest: they envision an adult who, if he were not a candidate for canonization, would surely be thought a rather remarkable human being. Christians who adequately reflect the model of behavior presented in the Gospels have been something of a rarity in the last two millennia, and to expect Catholic schools to accomplish on a large scale what the Church has not been able to during the first two thousand years of its history is somewhat naïve. In other words, if what is demanded of Catholic schools is that they produce an overwhelming number of model Christians (which, we gather, means the same thing as "saints"), then there would be no need of this study. As sociologists we might be hard put to devise a precise measure of sanctity, but it seems fairly clear that there are not too many saints around.

Thus one cannot say, for example, "Do Catholic schools take young people who come from families and neighborhoods where there is a long tradition of racial prejudice and turn all of these young people into staunch integrationists?" The answer to that question is clear: they do not and cannot, and neither can any other human institution of which we are aware. The relevant questions, to our way of thinking, are rather the following: Is there any difference at all in the racial attitudes of those who went to Catholic schools and those who did not? If there is a difference, is it big enough to be worth the effort to produce it, considering the immense difficulty experienced in changing human attitudes? Are there any other institutions that have done a better job in changing such attitudes?

It is only the first question, and the first half of the second, that we are in a position to answer in the present study. We can say whether there are differences between those who had Catholic education and those who did not, and we can say how big the differences are. Whether the differences are big enough to justify the effort is more difficult to specify. At the conclusion of this chapter we express the opinion that, considering the immense difficulty to be expected in modifying human behavior, the differences between Catholics who attended Catholic schools and those who did not are reasonably impressive. But such an opinion is based on a profound sociological skepticism about the possibility of changing human attitudes and values through formal education alone. Those who expect more from formal education (rather unrealistically, it seems to us) may be inclined to a different opinion.

Thus in this chapter we ask whether there are any religious differences between those who went to Catholic schools and those who did not, and, if there are differences, how big they are. Further, in our attempts to measure differences we split the Christian life into its various component parts and try to answer the following specific questions.

1. Are Catholics who went to Catholic schools more likely to engage in approved formal religious behavior? Do they go to Mass, receive Communion, and go to Confession more frequently?
2. Are the Catholic-educated more inclined to acknowledge the teaching authority of the Church and to recognize the right of religious leaders to indicate the appropriate stand for Catholics on controversial issues?
3. Are the doctrinal and ethical attitudes of those who went to Catholic schools more orthodox?
4. Do they have a more accurate knowledge of the formal teachings of their religion?
5. Are they more inclined to participate in the organizational activities of the Catholic Church?
6. Are they more dedicated in their practice of the virtue of charity?

The answer to most of these questions, it will turn out, is a qualified "yes." We will find statistically significant differences, many of which would be considered substantial in other sociological analysis, but the differences will not be great enough to end the debate about whether the schools have succeeded. (We should add, however, that in a later chapter we will discover differences of notable magnitude.)

CHURCH ATTENDANCE AND RECEPTION OF THE SACRAMENTS

Participation in church services has been a classic measure of religious behavior in both European and American studies. Even though it is a relatively easy measure about which to collect data (especially given the survey researcher's faith in the honesty of respondents), it is still considerably less than a satisfactory indicator. It might well be observed that church attendance has precious little to do with the essentials of Christianity, that it represents merely a fulfillment of canonical obligations imposed in the Middle Ages, and that it may indeed be a substitute for authentic evangelical Christianity.

While such observations may be valid, they are at least to some extent beyond the perspective of this volume. We are concerned essentially with whether the Catholic school system has accomplished what it set out to do. Whatever may be the relevant importance in the Christian life of church attendance and reception of the sacraments, there can be no doubt that frequent church attendance was and is *one* of the principal goals of the Catholic schools. In the United States, assiduous weekly church attendance has a highly important symbolic value for Catholicism. It not only distinguishes the "practicing" Catholic from the "non-practicing," it also frequently distinguishes the Catholic from the non-Catholic. The question "Does he go to church?" is taken to be a crucial means of defining a person's religious status. Going to church may not be the essence of Christianity, but it is central to the concerns of American Catholics. A failure of Catholic schools to contribute even a margin of increment to church attendance would be a major failure indeed. If, on the other hand, education in the schools does lead to an increase in church attendance, there is an indication that the schools are able to do one of the things they have set out to do; it also suggests that if some other form of behavior should become of central symbolic importance for a value-oriented school, then such behavior might also, in time, be induced by value-oriented education.

An inspection of Table 3.1 leaves no doubt that there are differences in the sacramental activity of the three groups of Catholics. The "All Catholic" group is "significantly" more likely to go to Mass every week, to receive Communion several times a month, and to go to Confession once a month than are the other two groups. The "Some Catholic" group is more like those who had no Catholic education than those who had exclusively Catholic education, but nevertheless is "significantly" higher in its scores on church attendance and reception of Communion than the "No Catholic" group.

The differences to be observed in Table 3.1 present us with a neat rhetorical problem which will plague us throughout the entire report. There are two kinds of assertions we can make about the table. First of all, even without the benefit of any formal Catholic education, two-thirds of the "No Catholic" group still reports weekly church attendance, one-third reports monthly Confession, and one-sixth reports frequent reception of Communion. These are higher levels of religious behavior than those in any of the other major industrial nations of the Western world—including many countries which are thought of as "Catholic" countries. Thus the high level of religious devotion in American Catholics cannot be attributed—directly, at least—to the existence of Catholic schools in this country. On the other hand, differences of twenty percentage points are substantial indeed and would be considered exciting in most survey analysis; hence it seems to us that they cannot be written off as of minor impor-

Table 3.1   Per Cent Participating in Various Religious Activities, by School Attendance

Religious Activity	School Attendance		
	All Catholic	Some Catholic	No Catholic
Mass at least once a week	86	73[a]	64[b]
Communion at least several times a month	38	25[a]	17[b]
Confession at least once a month	51	38[a]	32[b]
N	345	699	796

[a] Significantly different from "All Catholic."
[b] Significantly different from "All Catholic" and "Some Catholic."

tance. In attempting to combine these two perspectives, we suggest that while American Catholicism would probably have a high level of observable religious practice even without its school system, the schools apparently add a substantial margin to this level and may increase the margin over generations (a possibility to which we will return in the next chapter).

ATTITUDE TOWARD CHURCH AUTHORITY

For Mass, Communion, and Confession, the Church has norms that are clearly defined. Acceptance of these norms indicates a more general acceptance of the authority of the Church as a definitive teacher in certain areas of human behavior. But it does not follow that Catholics will necessarily accept the Church as a guide in all areas of life, especially those which, for one reason or another, may be labeled controversial. Our respondents were given a chance to indicate whether they would accept the teaching authority of the Church in some such areas, with results that are rather interesting (see Table 3.2).

Table 3.2 Per Cent Agreeing That Church Has the Right To Teach What Stand Members Should Take on Certain Issues

Issues	Educational Background			Convert	Protestant
	All Catholic	Some Catholic	No Catholic		
What are immoral books or movies	91	87	82[a]	85	56
Proper means for family limitation	66	56[a]	46[b]	57	18
Racial integration	58	48[a]	46[a]	50	34
Federal aid to education	50	44[a]	42[a]	37	16
Communist infiltration into government	43	42	40	43	27
Whether the U.S. should recognize Red China	19	15	15	15	8
Government regulation of business and labor	16	11	10	7	4
N	345	699	796	231	530

[a] Significantly different from "All Catholic."
[b] Significantly different from "All Catholic" and "Some Catholic."

First of all, Catholics are most likely to concede the right of the Church to lay down norms on the immorality of books and movies, but the differences in this respect between those who went to Catholic schools and those who did not are not significant. Apparently agreement on this matter is so universal that Catholic education does not add a margin to acceptance of authority (a finding that is essentially curious in view of the rumored plans to abolish the *Index librorum prohibitorum*).

The next three items—family limitation, racial integration, and aid to education—are apparently more controversial among Catholics. Fewer people are willing to concede the Church's right to take an authoritative stand, and those who went exclusively to Catholic schools are somewhat more likely to agree with such authority than are others. Finally, on the last three items— Communist infiltration, recognition of the People's Republic of China, and regulation of business and labor[1]—only a minority of Catholics say that the Church has a right to teach a definite position, and the Catholic school group is no different from the others. The pattern displayed is very interesting: the "All Catholic" group differs most from the others in the middle range of items, where Catholics are most likely to disagree among themselves about the authority of the Church. Where virtually everyone or virtually no one concedes the right of the Church to take a stand, there are no differences that associate with educational background. Having gone exclusively to Catholic schools apparently has an effect only in those areas in which many Catholics have serious doubts about the right of the Church to teach.

Thus Catholics are more likely than are Protestants to grant their Church the right to take a public stand on moral questions, and those Catholics who attended Catholic schools exclusively are most likely to make this concession on the key subjects of race, birth control, and education. The implication of these find-

---

[1] The small proportion agreeing to the right of Church intervention in labor-management relations seems to indicate a rejection of the social teachings of the so-called labor encyclicals. However, it is possible that respondents consider labor-management relations so complex that they consider them a technical rather than a moral issue. Such a possibility is confirmed by respondents' acknowledgment of the Church's right to teach on race—currently a much more controversial subject.

ings is clear: Catholics who have gone to Catholic schools participate in religious activities to the extent described in the previous section precisely because they are more inclined to accept the legitimacy of the Church's claim to be the authentic teacher and guide. The Catholic schools seem to generate "loyalty" to the ecclesiastical system (one might almost say for weal or woe, since there are undoubtedly many who would applaud the Church's stand on race who would disagree with its stand on birth control; loyalty, however, is not a selective virtue).

RELIGIOUS KNOWLEDGE

Like most world religions, Catholicism has a highly developed theological system which attempts to organize and harmonize the doctrines contained in its sacred writings. This theological system, adjusted of course to the age level of the students, is the subject of several classes a week in all Catholic schools (usually daily at the primary level). Whether religion can be "taught" in school may be open to question, but theology as an organized discipline can surely be taught. It is therefore appropriate to wonder whether much of this theological knowledge survives into adult life.

A brief test of religious knowledge was included as part of the interview with the respondents. We selected and pretested some twenty-five items from a standardized test of religious knowledge administered to high-school freshmen.[2] From these twenty-five, we selected six items, not so much for their content value as for the distribution of correct responses, thus excluding items judged to be too easy or too difficult.

Table 3.3 presents the proportion of correct responses for each of the three categories analyzed. In all six instances those who had all their education in Catholic schools were more likely to answer correctly; in three instances the differences were "significant," and in two they were of the order of twenty percentage points. However, in only one case does more than one-half of the "All Catholic" group give the right answer. Thus those trained in Catholic schools are more likely to have accurate information,

[2] Thaddeus O'Brien of the Project Staff supervised this aspect of the study.

but they are still not very likely to be correct. It is also interesting to note that those who had some of their education in Catholic schools are generally closer to those who had none than to those who went exclusively to Catholic schools.[3]

The impact of Catholic education seems especially strong in precisely those items about which Catholics are the least likely to answer correctly. Thus the smaller the proportion of correct answers (and the more difficult the question), the more probable becomes a difference between those educated exclusively in Catholic schools and other respondents. Those trained in Catholic schools are apparently better informed on the "fine points" of religious knowledge.

[3] As something of a lark, a question was included about the name of the Pope. Of those who went exclusively to Catholic schools, 86 per cent knew his name, as opposed to 73 per cent of those who had some or no Catholic education and 50 per cent of the Protestants.

Table 3.3 Per Cent Giving Correct Answers to Questions Testing Religious Knowledge, by Educational Background

Religious Knowledge	Educational Background			Convert
	All Catholic	Some Catholic	No Catholic	
Uncharitable talk is forbidden by the eighth commandment	55	47[a]	44[a]	42
The word we use to describe the fact that the second person of the Trinity became man is "incarnation"	48	38[a]	35[a]	31
Supernatural life is sanctifying grace in our souls	46	34[a]	27[b]	33
A man is judged immediately after he dies. This judgment is called "particular judgment"	37	22[a]	14[b]	20
The encyclicals *Rerum novarum* of Leo XIII and *Quadragesimo anno* of Pius XI both deal with the condition of labor	34	17[a]	10[b]	16
The Mystical Body is Christ united with His followers	23	15[a]	9[b]	14
N	345	699	796	231

[a] Significantly different from "All Catholic."
[b] Significantly different from "All Catholic" and "Some Catholic."

If the primary purpose of formal education is the communication of knowledge, and the primary purpose of religious education is the communication of religious knowledge, evidence in Table 3.3 amply supports the argument that Catholic schools have achieved their primary purpose. Respondents educated in Catholic schools may not score very high on the religious-knowledge test, but they do much better than those who did not have such an educational background.

Having established that those who went to Catholic schools are more loyal and better informed, we are prepared for the finding that they are also more orthodox in their belief, though we are not in a position to say to what extent this orthodoxy is a result of superior knowledge and to what extent it is a matter of deeper loyalty. On four of the six items in our scale of doctrinal orthodoxy, the "All Catholic" group is significantly more ortho-

Table 3.4   Per Cent Giving Orthodox Response to Issues of Doctrine, by Educational Background

Doctrinal Orthodoxy	Educational Background			Convert	Protestant
	All Catholic	Some Catholic	No Catholic		
Jesus directly handed over the leadership of His Church to Peter and the popes	89	75[a]	61[b]	55	7
There is no definite proof that God exists	80	74	65[b]	72	55
Science proves that Christ's resurrection was impossible	73	66[a]	60[b]	68	51
God will punish the evil for all eternity	62	52[a]	49[b]	42	34
God doesn't really care how He is worshiped, so long as He is worshiped	31	25[a]	24[a]	33	31
A good man can earn heaven by his own efforts alone	37	35	28[a]	39	46
N	345	699	796	231	530

[a] Significantly different from "All Catholic."
[b] Significantly different from "All Catholic" and "Some Catholic."

dox than the "No Catholic," and on two items, significantly more orthodox than the "Some Catholic." This latter group once again more closely resembles those who did not go at all to Catholic schools. But one cannot escape the conclusion that the orthodoxy demonstrated in Table 3.4 is more the result of loyalty than of superior knowledge. The biggest differences are found in the item dealing with the primacy of the Pope, and no differences exist in items which measure other heretical but less symbolically important attitudes. The respondents were asked their opinions on two statements that are quite heretical in Catholic doctrine. One was the Pelagian theory that man can obtain salvation by his own efforts alone; the other, the Modernist proposition that the form of worship is irrelevant. Even though the "All Catholic" group was more likely to reject both of these propositions, only 31 per cent opposed the latter and 37 per cent the former.

Thus the "All Catholic" group was quite alert on the symbolically important matter of papal primacy but not nearly so alert on other propositions which, even though heretical, are part of the "religion of Americanism." Catholic schools apparently do make a difference in the orthodoxy of their graduates, but the effect is selective. On matters that have been strongly emphasized, such as the position of the Pope, the effect is very great. On other matters that are of less symbolic value but still the object of some emphasis (the existence of God, the punishment of evil, the resurrection) the schools have an effect but not such a notable one. Finally, on matters which are technically heretical but not considered very important, the schools do not keep a majority of their graduates from making erroneous responses.

MORAL ORTHODOXY

In Table 3.5 we turn to the question of moral orthodoxy. The respondents were asked their opinions on a number of propositions representing judgments about common moral problems. In only four instances (three of them dealing with sex and one with honesty) are there significant differences between those who went to Catholic schools and others. On other matters the Catholic groups do not differ among themselves. Nor are they different from American Protestants, except, by a rather small margin, on the item concerning premarital chastity. On subjects such as racial integration, honesty in income-tax reporting and insurance claims, doing an honest day's work, and holding grudges within the family, the reaction of those educated in Catholic schools is not distinctly different from that of other Americans—Catholic or Protestant. Note, however, that by and large the reactions are in keeping with traditional Christian morality; the schools have added little to the moral norms existing in the culture.

In other words, Catholic schools are having an impact only in those areas in which Catholics have a position quite distinct from that of other Americans. When moral standards meet with consensus across religious lines, Catholic schools do not produce any higher agreement with the consensus than do public schools. Some two-thirds of the American population feels that income tax ought to be paid, and Catholic school products are no more enthusiastic about mailing their April 15 check than anyone else. It is not difficult to understand the reason for this phenomenon. If a religious institution senses that a given ethical proposition is reinforced by the larger society, it sees no reason to emphasize such a proposition strongly; it is taught, of course, but it does not become a matter of grave concern. The proposition will be honored (more or less) even if it is not preached "in season and out of season." On the other hand, if a moral dictate is at odds with the cultural consensus, it will become a subject of considerable importance to the religious body, which realizes that it must fight tooth and nail to defend such ethical standards in an unfavorable milieu. To expect that American Catholicism would not place very heavy emphasis on its distinctive sexual ethic would be quite naïve. Neither is it particularly surprising that such emphasis would be felt by the graduates of Catholic schools. What is surprising is that the differences are not greater. The fact that 40 per cent of those who had all their education in Catholic schools see nothing wrong with remarriage after divorce indicates the immense difficulty of preserving an ethical position against a cultural consensus—and also demonstrates the obstacles to developing values contrary to the cultural consensus by formal education.

Table 3.5   Per Cent Agreeing with Orthodox Position on Ethical Matters, by Educational Background

Statement	Educational Background			Convert	Protestant
	All Catholic	Some Catholic	No Catholic		
It is not really wrong for an engaged couple to have some sexual relations before they are married	81	74[a]	71[a]	77	63
A married couple who feel they have as many children as they want are really not doing anything wrong when they use artificial means to prevent conception	68	52[a]	44[a]	53	8
If the government wastes tax money, people don't have to be too exact on their income tax returns	64	67	62	70	69
A salesman has the right to exaggerate how good his product is when a customer is too suspicious	57	52	52	56	57
Two people who are in love do not do anything wrong when they marry, even though one of them has been divorced	60	44[a]	41[a]	45	12
It is all right to refuse to talk to some member of the family after a disagreement, especially if the argument was the fault of the other	52	50	49	55	52
It would be wrong to take considerable time off while working for a large company, even though the company would not be hurt by it at all	49	50	50	50	50
Even though you find some people unpleasant, it is wrong to try to avoid them	55	59	59	55	59
There is an obligation to work for the end of racial segregation	47	47	43	51	45

[a] Significantly different from "All Catholic.

(Table 3.5   continued)

Table 3.5 Continued

Statement	Educational Background			Convert	Protestant
	All Catholic	Some Catholic	No Catholic		
Even though a person has a hard time making ends meet, he should still try to give some of his money to help the poor	44	41	41	47	37
It is all right to ask an insurance company for more money than you deserve after an auto accident if you think they might cut your claim	43	37	33[a]	49	47
N	345	699	796	231	530

CHARITY

The essence of Christianity, however, does not have to do with religious devotion or religious knowledge or religious orthodoxy, but with the practice of the virtue of charity. As St. Paul pointedly observed, in the absence of charity all other religious behavior is little more than sounding brass and clanging cymbals. From the religious point of view, the most important question that could be asked about Catholic schools is whether there is a relationship between their attendance and the relative degrees of charity in Catholics. We made two attempts to resolve this problem, neither of them particularly satisfactory. Several opinion-attitude items concerning social consciousness were included in the questionnaire, and, as a succeeding chapter will indicate, there were very few differences between the Catholics who went to Catholic schools and those who did not. The respondents were also asked two questions about whether they had helped anyone who needed help in recent months. As we can see in Table 3.6, there were no differences in the responses of members of the three categories to either of these questions. Graduates of the Catholic system were no more likely to say that someone had spoken to them about a problem recently or to report that they had spent time during recent months in helping someone who needed help. These findings are tenuous at best, since the measures are so dubious. All we can say is that if the Catholic schools are turning out people who are more diligent in the practice of love of neighbor, the fact is not confirmed by the evidence available to us. Any further conclusion would be dangerous, at least until more careful research is attempted.

MARRIAGE AND THE FAMILY

Previous studies by Freedman *et al.* (1959) and by Westoff *et al.* (1961, p. 180) lead us to expect that there are considerable differences between American Catholics and other Americans in values having to do with family life; the studies also suggest that Catholic school Catholics are rather substantially different from other Catholics in these family-life values. The sexual-morality item mentioned in a previous section indicates that Catholics show a fairly strong relationship between attendance at Catholic schools and attitudes toward sexual morality. We are therefore led to hypothesize that Catholic school Catholics are more likely to have large families and to consider marriage within the Church and to other Catholics a matter of considerable importance.

While we can find some confirmation of these expectations in Table 3.7, the differences are not particularly overwhelming.

Table 3.6 Measures of Charity, by School Attendance (Per Cent Attending Each Type

Questionnaire Item (Response in Parentheses)	School Attendance			Convert
	All Catholic	Some Catholic	No Catholic	
Have you spent any time in the past few months helping someone who needed help? (yes)	52	57	56	61
Has anyone talked to you about his personal problems in the last few months? (yes)	48	50	41[a]	55
N	345	699	796	231

[a] Significantly different from "All Catholic" and "Some Catholic."

Those who had had only Catholic education were significantly more likely to be married by a priest; nevertheless, seven-eighths of those who did not attend Catholic schools also were married by priests. There are no significant differences in the proportions who married other Catholics or in the number having three or more children in the family. Those who had had exclusively Catholic schooling are significantly more likely to expect more children and to think that four or more children would be an ideal family size, but the magnitude of the difference is not very great. Of those who do expect more children, there are no differences in the proportion expecting two or more.

Those who had all their education in Catholic schools are also significantly more likely than others to think that marriage to another Catholic is "very important." But once again the magnitude of the differences is not impressive, for more than one-half of those who never attended Catholic schools still think endogamy is very important. Those who attended Catholic schools entirely would be more opposed to mixed marriage for their children— significantly more opposed than those who had never attended Catholic schools—but the proportion of the "All Catholic" group

Table 3.7 Marriage and Family Values, by School Attendance
(Per Cent in Each Category)

Marriage and Family Values	School Attendance			Convert
	All Catholic	Some Catholic	No Catholic	
Married by priest	93	87[a]	85[a]	87
Mixed marriages	10	15	13	4
Have three or more children	53	56	52	56
Expect more children	31	24[a]	20[a]	25
Expect two more additional children (of those expecting additional children)	33	30	27	22
Consider four or more children ideal family size	69	66	57[a]	67
Consider endogamy very important	64	56[a]	53[a]	49
Would oppose mixed marriage of children	31	26	21[a]	18
Would disapprove of teenage child's dating non-Catholic	60	44[a]	43[a]	32
N	345	699	796	231

[a] Significantly different from "All Catholic."

opposing mixed marriage is only one-third. The "All Catholic" group, however, is substantially more likely to oppose a child's dating a non-Catholic.

Marriage and family values do show some relationship with Catholic education; however, the relationship is in most instances not a strong one. Catholics continue to marry other Catholics, and they continue to consider endogamy important; they are not eager to have their children date non-Catholics, though they would not strongly oppose intermarriage once they were faced with it in their family. They are also inclined to favor reasonably large families. But none of these attitudes seems to be strongly affected by whether they had attended Catholic schools. While there were differences among Catholics of different schooling in their general principles of sexual morality, the differences in opinions on marriage and family size do not seem to be quite so strong.

There are some reasons why we might expect this to be so. First of all, discrepancies between principles and practice are part of the human condition. Those who went to Catholic schools might be more aware of the principles, but their practice could fall short of the principles, even though it would be more consistent than the practice of those who did not go to Catholic schools. Second, there is no necessary connection between disapproving of birth control and wanting a large family. Previous population research of Westoff *et al.* (1961) has demonstrated that Catholics have a relatively sophisticated perception of the nuances of their Church's sexual morality. Apparently Catholics do not conclude from their Church's teaching on birth control that they are bound to have a large family (and indeed they are not so bound). Thus Catholic school Catholics who are more likely to disapprove of birth control and yet do not intend to have more children may be displaying a nuanced understanding of the teaching of their Church. The question remains, of course, whether the means they use to control the size of their families is in accord with the Church's moral system. Westoff's work suggests that, to some extent at least, it is.

More difficult to explain is the fact that while nine-tenths of the "All Catholic" group members are married to other Catholics and two-thirds think marriage within a religious group is important, only one-third would oppose a mixed marriage for one of their children. Perhaps the cultural consensus which holds that the selection of a marriage partner is a matter of free choice overrides the religious disapproval of such a marriage. It might be suspected that in the long run this cultural consensus would lead to a marked increase in the proportion of mixed marriages even among those who had received all their education in Catholic schools. However, there is some research (Greeley, 1964) which indicates that there has been little increase in the proportion of mixed marriages for the last half-century. Whether there will be a change in years to come remains to be seen.

ORGANIZATIONAL ACTIVITY

Are Catholics who went to Catholic schools more likely to participate in the organizational activities of the Church? At first blush this question seems almost rhetorical. Those who attend Catholic schools would be in frequent contact with the parish church and with religious functionaries and would therefore have a tradition of Catholic activity which would continue in their adult life. One could very reasonably expect that being closely

Table 3.8 Organizational Participation, by School Attendance (Per Cent in Each Category)

Organizational Participation	School Attendance			Convert
	All Catholic	Some Catholic	No Catholic	
Belong to church organization	41	33[a]	29[a]	40
"Active" in church organization	26	22[a]	18[a]	37
Contribute more than $200 a year	44	36[a]	29[a]	37
Report recent visit by clergy	64	57	53[a]	64
Have talked to clergy about personal problems	31	23[a]	19[a]	28
Think their names are known by clergy	62	58	55	59
Have made a "mission" recently	44	34[a]	31[a]	31
Read Catholic journals regularly	73	62[a]	55[b]	60
N	345	699	796	231

[a] Significantly different from "All Catholic."
[b] Significantly different from "All Catholic" and "Some Catholic."

integrated with the Church during the years of childhood and adolescence would help to maintain an interest in the parish community (and other organizational activities) in later years.

Table 3.8 shows that those with all their primary and secondary education in Catholic schools are indeed more likely than others to belong to Church organizations and are also more likely than those with no Catholic education to be active members of these organizations. They are also somewhat more likely to contribute more than $200 a year to the support of their parish. Further, those who attended Catholic schools exclusively were more inclined than those who had no Catholic education to report a visit by a member of the clergy to their home in recent months. They were also more inclined than the other two groups to report that they had a serious conversation with a clergyman about some kind of personal problem. Finally, those with exclusively Catholic education were significantly, though not overwhelmingly, more likely to say that they read Catholic magazines and newspapers and had made a "mission"[4] recently. However, in no instance are the relationships between Catholic schooling and these ecclesiastical activities particularly strong. Since in American society there is a strong association between social class and organizational activities, there is some reason to believe that the differences we have noted will diminish or perhaps even disappear when social class is held constant, as it will be in subsequent chapters. The truth seems to be that most American Catholics, regardless of their education, are reasonably active in their church organizations, but organizational membership is only moderately related to the kinds of education the Catholic has had.

It must be confessed that the failure of Catholic school Catholics to be more tightly integrated into the Catholic community than they are is somewhat surprising. However, one of the authors, in reflecting on his experience in a Roman Catholic parish, remembered that it often seemed that there were some families who viewed the school as a place of education and not a community center. When the children of these families were no longer in the school, the families' commitment to other parish activities became minimal; indeed; their children themselves became quite

[4] A "mission" is a voluntary week of evening prayer and devotions.

passive members of the parish after they had graduated. What we might realistically expect, therefore, is that Catholic schooling will lead to a greater organizational commitment only if there is already family behavior which reinforces such a commitment. We shall turn to this possibility in the next chapter.

SUMMARY AND CONCLUSION

In answer to the six specific questions with which we began this chapter, we may say the following.

1. Catholics who went to Catholic schools do score considerably higher on measures of sacramental behavior, but even those who did not go to Catholic schools score relatively high on such measures.

2. Catholic school Catholics are no more likely to concede teaching authority to the Church in matters in which most people agree that the Church has a right to teach and in matters in which most say the Church has no right; but in areas of disagreement, such as race, sex, and education, those who went exclusively to Catholic schools are more likely to grant the Church teaching authority.

3. In doctrinal and ethical matters, the Catholic school Catholic is somewhat more orthodox, especially in matters such as sexual morality and papal primacy, which have been of considerable symbolic importance in recent Catholic history. There are also moderate differences in attitudes on family size and mixed marriages.

4. Catholic school Catholics are much better informed on the doctrinal fine points of their religion.

5. They also participate more in church activities, but not as much as might have been reasonably expected; we suggest that family behavior might be more important than schooling in producing organizational commitment.

6. With our admittedly limited tools, we could not discover any relationship between Catholic school attendance and disposition to help others.

Thus it appears that Catholic schools can lay legitimate claim to some important accomplishments, though in other areas (such as racial attitudes) they have not been as successful as they might have hoped. In at least some of the matters under consideration (i.e., participation in church organizations) the schools have had surprisingly little impact. Is it possible to find some pattern in these findings which would enable us to understand them in their historical context?

For most of the present century, the Roman Catholic Church in the United States has been involved in an acculturation process. Only one-tenth of our respondents were foreign-born, but almost one-half were immigrants or the children of immigrants. At the risk of oversimplifying a historical epoch, one could say that the Church's concern during the years when the respondents were in school was almost entirely focused on protecting the faith of its people. Certain elements of Catholic creed, code, and cult took on major importance as symbols of the faith which was to be preserved. Regular church attendance was a manifestation of loyalty to the Church of one's ancestors; acceptance of Church authority distinguished one from other Americans who did not vest their church with very much authority. Strict sexual morality not only preserved the rigorous morals of the Old World, it also marked Catholics as different from other Americans, whose sexual morality was thought to be undergoing a "revolution" with the increase in birth control and divorce.

By emphasizing external devotion, authority, and chasity, the Church not only preserved its distinctiveness but also defended its members from what it took to be the most serious threats of the New World culture—moral, doctrinal, and cultic indifferentism.

To achieve these goals of "pattern maintenance" was certainly one of the principal reasons for establishing a separate school system (though as Cross [1965] has shown, there were many other reasons too). No school can hope to inculcate all the values in the world view to which it subscribes. Some choice must be made, and the choice is very likely to be made in terms of those values which, for historical and social reasons, seem at a given time to be most important or most threatened.

Sunday Mass, monthly Communion, Confession several times a year, Catholic education of children, financial contribution to the Church, acceptance of the Church as an authoritative teacher, acknowledgment of papal and hierarchal authority, informality with the clergy, strict sexual morality, more detailed knowledge about one's religion—these are not only the apparent effects of Catholic education, they comprise as well a reasonable description of what the American Church has expected from its laity during the years when it was still concentrating on preserving the faith of the immigrant and his children and his grandchildren. If they indeed represented the goals of American Catholicism for the first half of this century, there does not seem to be much doubt that the schools have made a contribution to the achievement of these goals, a contribution we could term substantial, though not overwhelming. In this perspective we could say the Catholic experiment in value-oriented education has been a moderate (though expensive) success, giving us some reason to think that value-oriented education can affect human behavior and attitudes in matters that are invested with heavy symbolic importance.

From the experience of the Catholic schools we would expect the impact of a value-oriented education to be neither very small nor very large. The difference often seems to be in the neighborhood of twenty percentage points on crucial matters—a difference which could be termed substantial enough. The differences would rarely be expected to exceed twenty-five percentage points and would quite frequently remain around ten percentage points. It must be noted that this influence is most marked among those whose education has been entirely within the value-oriented system. Those who have had only part of their education in the system are, more often than not, closer to those who have no value-oriented education.

From a statistical point of view, American Catholics are now little different from other Americans in their income, education, and occupation. The social and economic basis for a "ghetto" Church seems to have been eliminated; the immigrant, the son of the immigrant, and the grandson of the immigrant have kept the faith (and probably would have to a considerable degree even if there had been no Catholic schools). With the "modernization" and ecumenism of Pope John and the Vatican Council, the theological basis for separatism also seems to be vanishing. At least some American Catholic theoreticians are arguing that, whatever is to be said of the goals of the past decades, they are no longer relevant today. From this argument it is a short step to contend that if the Catholic schools can do no more than turn out the Catholic described in the previous paragraphs, there is no point in having the schools. Others would argue that, just as the schools reflected the values of the Church when it was the Church of the immigrant and his offspring (even though, ironically, the immigrant was less likely to go to the Catholic school than the native-born), so they can come to reflect the values of the Church in the age of ecumenism and *aggiornamento.* Whether they can and whether they will belongs to a study of the future and not of the past.

It may be possible for Catholic schools to shift their emphasis. While taking the goals of past decades for granted, the schools may be able to emphasize new values, such as intellectual and civic competence and excellence, understanding of worship, the struggle for interracial and international justice, the quest for religious cooperation and unity. As one kind of value was taught in the past with some success, so a new kind of value could be taught in the future.

Whether these new values will be taught in the schools remains to be seen. They are less concrete and of much less symbolic importance than going to Mass on Sunday and not practicing birth control. It might be argued that the Church's teaching on race makes less demands on human nature than do its strictures on sexual morality and that therefore the Catholic schools could, if they are of such a mind, develop educational methods that would inculcate convictions on racial justice much more easily than convictions on birth control. However, it must be admitted that sex is an area in which Catholics have felt the Church could take a legitimate interest; family and Church have always been closely connected. The relationship between social justice and religion has not always been so obvious (even though the graduates of Catholic schools proved to be more likely to see the relationship—at least in theory). Furthermore, the Church's teaching on sex has been insisted upon with a persistence and a vigor which has not always existed in the past in its racial teaching. Nor is the search for unity nearly as simple and intelligible a matter as the primacy of the Pope. The values of a church which for the most part was turned in upon itself can be more readily reduced to educational goals and methods than the values of a church which seems to be opening up to the rest of the country. It is altogether possible that the expanded values of American Catholicism (if they are really expanding) could be taught in schools, but it certainly will be far more difficult, and the success may be even more moderate than that reported in this chapter.

4

The Search for an Explanation

In the last chapter we concluded that Catholic schools had some moderate success in achieving the goals for which they exist, but our conclusion must be very tentative until we make sure that the apparent relationship between Catholic education and adult religious behavior is not the result of the work of some factor other than Catholic schooling. We know, for example, that those who went to Catholic schools are more likely to be more successful economically than those who did not. We also know from the work of other sociologists that, in the American society, the higher one's income the more likely he is to take part in religious activity. So it might well be that the real explanation for the greater religious activity of Catholic school Catholics lies not in their religious education but in their social class. Until we can exclude the possible influence of this and other variables, we cannot back up the generalizations made in the previous chapter with any degree of confidence.

But even if we can decide that the relationship between Catholic education and adult behavior persists after the influence of other variables has been taken into account, we are still faced with the question of how important the relationship is. As we noted in the last chapter, the absolute importance of religious education in affecting adult behavior depends to a considerable extent on what one thinks can be legitimately demanded of a formal educational system. But apart from the stand one takes on this point, there is a question of relative importance. We could ask where religious education ranks among those variables which we know have some influence on religious behavior in American society. Is it as important as the religiousness of one's parents? Is it as important as one's sex? Is it as important as the amount of education a person has had?

Another way of approaching the problem of relative importance is to ask what the American Catholic Church would be like if it had never had a separate school system. Obviously when the question is stated that simply it is virtually unanswerable; the historical "might-have-beens" make for interesting speculation but can be neither proved nor disproved. What one can do, however, is compare behavior which is the result of several generations of Catholic education with the behavior of those whose family traditions involve no Catholic education to see whether a tradition of Catholic education has produced an elite group and a tradition of non-Catholic education has produced Catholics whose loyalty to the Church has become marginal. If it should turn out that those with no Catholic education in their family background are still "practicing" Catholics, it would appear that Catholic education is not directly[1] responsible for the vigorous religious practice to be observed in the American Church.

Thus our main concerns in this chapter will be *(a)* the persistence of the relationship in the face of our attempts to take into account the action of intervening variables and *(b)* the relative importance of Catholic schooling. We will find that the intervening variables do not notably affect the conclusions we drew in the previous chapter and that Catholic education is less important than the religiousness of parents and the amount of education one has had, but more important than one's sex. We will conclude by observing that, while there is little evidence that Catholic schools are directly responsible for the vigor of basic religious observance in American Catholicism, they do seem to have produced, through several generations, an elite group whose religious activity is considerably in excess of the basic minimum.

A NOTE ON STRATEGY

We must indicate for the nonsociological reader the strategy we intend to follow in this chapter. For the sake of simplicity

---

[1] Whether the schools have a strong indirect effect because they are sources of recruitment for priests and nuns is a question we are not able to answer with our data.

(and also to prevent the anguished reader from tossing the volume in the direction of the nearest wastebasket) we will combine the measures used in Chapter 3 into six summary indices. In addition we will state the relationship between Catholic education and scores on these indices in a single statistic, called the gamma coefficient,[2] instead of using an elaborate table. We will then ask whether any of the intervening attributes decrease the size of the relationship. If there is a decrease, we will look more closely at the process which seems to be going on. We will also, in two instances (availability of school and spouse's religious behavior), investigate in detail the absence of a decrease in the gamma coefficient when we would have some theoretical grounds to

[2] While the percentage distribution tables are to be found in the Appendices, the text of this and succeeding chapters consists of commentary on tables presenting coefficients of association that indicate the strength of the relationship between Catholic education and adult behavior and attitudes. If, for example, one presented the percentage distribution for the sacramental index in the three groups under analysis, the following table would be necessary.

Adults' Religious Behavior and Attitudes	Per Cent in Each School Category		
	All Catholic	Some Catholic	No Catholic
High	37	24	14
	21	17	17
	28	32	33
	8	12	17
Low	6	15	19
Total	100	100	100

After inspecting the table we would conclude that there was a relationship between attendance at Catholic schools and the score on the sacramental index. The coefficient of association gives us the same information in a single figure instead of an entire table. Thus, the "zero-order" coefficient for the above table is .26. The particular coefficient used in this study to measure the strength of association between religious education and religious behavior is called the "gamma coefficient" and was developed by Professor Leo Goodman of the University of Chicago (cf. Goodman and Kruskal, 1954).

Readers interested in the mathematics of gamma should consult the Goodman article as well as Davis' (1964) unpublished manuscript which develops the notion of the net partial gamma also used in the present study.

For those less interested in the exact meaning of gamma, the following explanation may be helpful. The coefficient measures the strength of the relationship between Catholic education and religious behavior; the higher the gamma the stronger the relationship. Let us imagine that pairs of randomly selected individuals are brought to us, and we are told that the members of each pair

expect a decrease. In some instances we will shift from the gamma coefficient to multivariate tables in order to look at an important finding from a slightly different perspective. The reader who wishes to investigate the data summarized by the gamma coefficients more closely may consult the appendices.

have different scores on the sacramental index and that we are to guess which one is higher. If we merely flipped a coin we would be right half the time. Now let us further imagine that we are given an additional piece of information: we are told that one respondent had a Catholic education and the other did not. We would expect that if Catholic education and frequency of receiving the sacraments were related to each other, our knowledge of whether the respondent had gone to a Catholic school would improve the accuracy of our predictions in choosing between the members of the pairs. Following this expectation, we would decide always to predict that the member of the pair who went to a Catholic school will be higher on the sacramental index than the other member. We must then ask how much better our accuracy will be if we follow this strategy rather than the coin-flipping one. The gamma coefficient indicates the nature of the improvement of our power to predict. Thus, if we always predict that the member of the pair who went to a Catholic school will score higher on the index than the one who did not go to a Catholic school, we will be correct 26 per cent more of the time than if we had relied on the flip of a coin. A gamma of 1.00 would mean that we would be accurate all the time, and a gamma of .00 would mean that our predictions would not rise beyond the level of chance.

A partial coefficient tells us the strength of the relationship within subclasses of the population. Thus, let us imagine that our pairs continue to differ in the two variables—religious education and sacramental activity—but we are informed that their parents have the same position on the index of parental religiousness. The partial gamma of .34 for those whose parents were highly religious indicates that our accuracy will be one-third better than chance if we predict sacramental activity from Catholic school attendance for each pair chosen from among those whose parents were themselves frequent receivers of the sacraments. On the other hand, the partial gamma of .10 for those whose parents did not receive communion once a week would tell us that if our random pairs were chosen from those whose parental religiousness was low, our accuracy would be one-tenth better than chance if we always predicted that the member of the pair who attended a Catholic school would score higher on the sacramental index.

The net partial gamma tells us how much our prediction accuracy is improved or hindered by dealing only with pairs matched on some third variable. Thus the net partial gamma of .14 for the relationship between sacramental activity and Catholic education when pairs are selected from within parental-religiousness groups indicates that a control for parental religiousness decreases the accuracy of our predictions, because a control for religiousness weakens the relationship between religious education and adult religious behavior. In other words, despite the stronger connection between Catholic education and sacramental activity for those from highly religious Catholic families, the very weak connection for those from other Catholic families leads to a net relationship less powerful than it had originally appeared. If the net partial should descend toward .00, it would indicate that the relationship was spurious and that Catholic schooling did not

INDICES AND CONTROLS

The relationships between Catholic education and adult religious behavior described in the previous chapter are summarized in Table 4.1 in two ways. The proportion of each of the three groups under analysis scoring high on each index is presented in the first three columns, and the coefficient of association between Catholic education and score on the index appears in the fourth column. The strongest associations are with religious knowledge and sacramental behavior, and the weakest, with accepting the Church as a teacher and the ethical orthodoxy index. However, virtually all the differences in the proportion scoring high are statistically significant. Thus we can say at the beginning of this section that we are dealing with relationships that run from relatively weak to moderate but which are, in all but one

---

affect adult behavior, but that the real correlate was parental religiousness. However, in the present instance we have, rather, a specification of the relationship; it is strongest among those from very religious backgrounds and much less strong among those from less religious backgrounds.

The net partial gamma therefore could be said to "filter out" the possible influence of an intervening variable to determine the actual nature of the relationship between the independent variable (Catholic education) and the dependent variable (sacramental activity).

Table 4.1 Religious Behavior and Per Cent Attending Each School Category

Religious Behavior	School Attendance			Gamma Association
	All Catholic	Some Catholic	No Catholic	
High on sacramental index[c]	37	24[a]	14[b]	.26
High on accepting Church as teacher[d]	46	35[a]	31[a]	.15
High in doctrinal orthodoxy[e]	33	24[a]	17[b]	.19
High in ethical orthodoxy[f]	35	28	23[a]	.12
High on religious knowledge index[g]	36	22[a]	13[b]	.30
N	345	699	796	

[a] Significantly different from "All Catholic."
[b] Significantly different from "All Catholic" and "Some Catholic."
[c] Mass every week, Communion several times a month.
[d] Accepting Church's teaching authority in four or more areas.
[e] Four or more orthodox responses.
[f] Eight or more orthodox answers.
[g] Three or more correct answers.

instance,[3] significant. The crucial question is whether the relationships survive when control is applied for potentially intervening variables.

Three different kinds of intervening influences might be relevant. First, there are the demographic factors, such as age, sex, ethnic background, and place of origin, which might predispose some of those who went to Catholic schools to more intense religious behavior. Second, there are social-class variables (occupation and education both of the respondent and his parents) which are known to correlate with religious behavior and with Catholic school attendance. Finally, there are factors which are essentially religious and would affect adult behavior insofar as those who went to Catholic schools might be more religious to begin with and, because of this basic "religiousness," would be more inclined to choose Catholic schools and to engage in a higher level of religious activity after they had left school.

In Table 4.2 we investigate the possibility that any of fifteen attributes may render the apparent relationship between Catholic education and adult behavior spurious. Since the table summarizes an immense amount of information, we will describe how it should be interpreted. The first row presents the gamma associations between Catholic education and six dependent variables. Each of the following rows presents the gamma coefficient after the influence of the given control variable has been "filtered out." If there is a notable decline in any row from the zero-order gamma to the net partial gamma, then we conclude that the relationship between Catholic education and adult behavior is affected by the operation of this control variable and that the matter must be inspected more closely.[4]

Actually the associations between Catholic school attendance and the six measures of religious behavior are almost completely

---

[3] The reader will realize that the net partial gamma may mask "interactions"—an increase in association among one subgroup and a decrease in another subgroup. None of sufficient importance was found to merit its discussion in the text. However, the reader who is interested in inspecting more closely the partial associations from which the table was prepared will find the tables in Appendix 4 helpful.

[4] The difference between the "Some Catholic" and "All Catholic" groups on the ethical orthodoxy scale is not significant.

Table 4.2 Zero-Order and Net Partial Gamma Associations between Catholic Education and Adult Religious Behavior

Religious Behavior	Sacramental Index	Church-as-Teacher Index	Doctrinal Orthodoxy Index	Religious Knowledge Index	Ethical Orthodoxy Index	Organizational Membership[a]
Zero-order coefficient	.26	.15	.19	.30	.12	.15
Net partial coefficients—control for:						
Sex	.26	.15	.19	.31	.12	.16
Age	.27	.16	.20	.32	.12	.18
Size of hometown	.27	.15	.20	.30	.14	.19
Generation in U.S.	.24	.14	.17	.30	.11	.19
Ethnic background	.19	.13	.15	.26	.08	.08
Size of present town	.28	.14	.19	.30	.15	.18
Region of country	.23	.16	.19	.30	.23	.13
Father's occupation (Duncan index)	.24	.15	.18	.30	.12	.15
Father's education	.25	.14	.15	.28	.12	.14
Mother's education	.24	.13	.16	.29	.13	.17
Respondent's occupation (Duncan index)	.23	.15	.17	.28	.11	.14
Respondent's education	.24	.15	.18	.29	.11	.13
Religiousness of spouse	.23	.14	.17	.26	.10	.13
Religiousness of parents	.14	.12	.14	.26	.07	.04
Availability of school[b]	.21	.16	.18	.30	.12	.09

[a] Membership in at least one Church-related organization.
[b] Based on response to the question of whether there was a Catholic elementary school available in the respondent's youth.

unaffected by the different intervening variables under consideration. We find notable differences between the zero-order coefficients and the partial coefficients in only two rows of the table, the rows controlling for the religiousness of parents and for ethnic background. A control for ethnicity diminishes the association between Catholic education and adult behavior only for the sacramental index and the ethical orthodoxy index, although it does have some slight effect on the relationship with the doctrinal and ethical orthodoxy scales. The religiousness of parents, however, does account for a weakening of virtually all gamma coefficients, but the effect is rather slight for the Church-as-teacher and religious knowledge indices. On the other hand, this control almost eliminates the relationship between Catholic education and membership in a Church organization.

Before we go on to inspect the two variables which seem to affect the strength of the relationship between Catholic education and religious activity in adult life (and also two variables which we might have strongly expected to diminish the relationship but which in fact do not), we must observe that the absence of variation in the stately rows of gamma coefficients is quite striking. Sociologists are accustomed to having differences persist in the face of social and demographic controls, but usually there is at least some diminution of the magnitude of differences. That no such diminution occurs under almost all the controls implies that the apparent consequences of Catholic education can be attributed to Catholic schools with some degree of confidence. It is especially interesting to note that the various social-class measures which we might reasonably have expected to intervene at least in some fashion have not the slightest effect on the relationship between Catholic education and adult behavior. Demography, social class, and, at least to some extent, religiousness of background are not the explanation. While we cannot reject out of hand the possibility that some other factor which we are unable to measure may be at work, such a factor is not, as far as we can see, discoverable by the usual methods of sociological analysis.

Table 4.2 makes our search for a variable that diminishes the connection between Catholic education and adult behavior much more simple: we can forget about most of the variables and focus on the respondents' ethnic background and the religiousness of their parents.

PARENTAL RELIGIOUSNESS

Two processes might be at work behind the decline in the coefficients of association when parental religiousness is taken into account. As we mentioned previously, it could be that the apparent effect of Catholic schooling is in reality the result of the family environment in which the child grew up: devout Catholic families send their children to Catholic schools, and the children are devout not because of the schools but because of the family. If this were what was happening, the decline in the gamma coefficient should take place in each of the subgroups based on parental religiousness. A second possibility is that the religiousness of the family reinforces the impact of the school and that it is only among those from highly religious families that one can expect the school to have much influence. In such a case the differences between those who went to Catholic schools and those who did not would be limited to respondents from highly religious backgrounds. In these circumstances, the gamma would rise for the respondents from very religious backgrounds and decline for those with less religious backgrounds.

It is the latter process which seems to be at work in Table 4.3. Not only are the relationships not diminished among those respondents one of whose parents went to Communion every week; they are, in fact, substantially strengthened. We can go so far as to say that, for all practical purposes, the religious impact of Catholic education is limited to those who come from highly religious families. With the exception of the relationship between Catholic education and religious knowledge, only one gamma coefficient in the lower three parental-religiousness groups is above .11. But among those from highly religious backgrounds, all gamma coefficients are above .2, four of them are above .3, and one (religious knowledge) is .4.

Thus the impact of Catholic education on the religious behavior of adults coming from families who were not highly religious is limited to their religious knowledge, and even on this index the

The Education of Catholic Americans

relationship is virtually twice as strong among those from highly religious backgrounds. In all other instances the strength of the relationship between Catholic education and adult religious behavior among those from highly religious families is close to, or in excess of, three times as great as it is among the next most religious group.

The magnitude of these differences in gamma coefficients is even more surprising when one remembers that the only difference between the highest group and the second highest in family religious background is that the former had at least one parent who went to Communion every week; in both groups both parents

Table 4.3 Zero-Order, Partial, and Net Partial Gamma Associations between Catholic Education and Adult Religious Behavior, with Parental Religiousness Controlled

Religious Behavior	Zero-Order	Partial (Parental Religiousness)				Net Partial
		High	Higher Middle	Lower Middle	Low	
Sacramental index	.26	.34	.11	.09	.10	.14
Church-as-teacher index	.15	.22	.03	.15	.12	.12
Religious knowledge index	.30	.40	.26	.20	.22	.26
Doctrinal orthodoxy index	.19	.34	.11	.09	.10	.14
Ethical orthodoxy index	.12	.20	.05	.07	.01	.07
Sexual mores index	.19	.21	.08	.09	.11	.12
Organizational membership[a]	.15	.34	.11	−.08	−.10	.04

[a] Membership in at least one Church-related organization.

Table 4.4 Per Cent High on Sacramental Index, by School Attendance

Score on Parental Religiousness Index	School Attendance		
	All Catholic	Some Catholic	No Catholic
High	55(118)	34(113)	21(75)
Higher middle	28(130)	28(269)	23(215)
Lower middle	20(39)	21(122)	9(186)
Low	24(37)	14(161)	10(269)

were Catholic and both went to church every Sunday. Since this finding is of extreme importance for our study (and not without interesting implications for the more general interests of the sociology of religion), it is advisable to look at it in the slightly different perspective which a multivariate table provides (Table 4.4). Three important comments can be made regarding this table. (1) While there is a difference of only fourteen percentage points between the "All Catholic" and the "No Catholic" groups among those from the lowest religious-background category, there is a difference of thirty-four percentage points in the highest category. (2) An increase in the religiousness of parents does not affect the sacramental index score of those respondents in the three lowest categories of parental religious behavior who went to Catholic schools exclusively. But the proportion of those in the highest category scoring high on the sacramental index is almost twice the proportion in the second highest category. (3) With the exception of their confreres who had some Catholic education, those respondents who came from highly religious backgrounds and went to Catholic schools are at least twice as likely (55 per cent) to score high on the sacramental index as are members of any other group. A combination of Catholic education and parental devotion produces a remarkably high level of religious behavior in adult life. The conclusion seems inescapable: Catholic schools had an impact only on those who came from families in which one parent received Communion every week. Their "success" is almost limited to these families, but among such families it is quite impressive.

Before we attempted a complete explanation of the phenomenon described in this section we would have to know much more about the dynamics of religious socialization. The school apparently reinforces the work of the home after the devotional level of the home reaches a certain point. Or, to view the matter from the other direction, unless religious devotion in the home reaches a certain level, value-oriented schooling will have little or no effect on adult behavior; but once the religiousness of the home reaches a critical point, the additional effect of the school will grow very rapidly. A "multiplier effect" seems to be at work— religiousness of home and school reinforce each other, and when they are working in concert, the level of religious behavior increases in some sort of exponential fashion.

It appears that a school cannot be expected to carry out effectively a religious socialization process for which there is little sympathy at home; if a child is not in a religiously concerned environment when he is with his family, it would be naïve to think that a rather brief interlude of formal education would create religious concern. On the other hand, if religion is considered important by the primary socializing force, he will approach formal education well disposed to the reinforcement of the basic religious values he already has.

But we still lack explanations for the dramatic increase in effectiveness of the schools at the point between those who had one parent who went to Communion every week and those who did not. While the magnitude of the impact can be attributed only to some yet to be understood "multiplier effect," it might be possible to suggest reasons for the breaking point's being where it is. Within American Catholicism for the last forty years, the weekly reception of Holy Communion has been considered the sign of the "fervent" Catholic, as opposed to the mere "practicing" Catholic. (As we noted previously, the basic differences on the sacramental indices among the three categories of respondents analyzed have to do with frequency of reception of Communion.) Thus the weekly reception of Communion by at least one member of the respondent's family would show that in this family there was one parent who took his religion seriously enough to live up to what had been presented to him as an ideal course of action. In other words, a high parental sacramental score meant that Catholic schooling would notably increase the probability of a respondent's having a high sacramental score (as well as all other scores), precisely because the home was already following the ideals which the school was promoting. If the ideal was not observed at home, it would not have been taken too seriously at school either, and the probability of the school's increasing a respondent's sacramental score (and all other scores) was minimal.

In summary, far from reducing the influence of Catholic education on adult religious behavior, a control for religiousness specifies a rather strong influence among those respondents who came from highly religious families. Only on the purely cognitional effect of the religious-knowledge scale is there much of a relationship among those from less religious backgrounds. Catholic school administrators could reasonably assume that, at least in the past, they were wasting their time with the vast majority of their students. Without the predispositions created by a religious family, the school was not likely to accomplish very much. In theory at least, there was not much point in admitting children who were not from very devout families.

ETHNIC BACKGROUND

The same possibilities we described at the beginning of the previous section might be at work in the reduction of the gamma coefficients when ethnic background is controlled. It could be that the apparent relationship between Catholic education and adult behavior is the result of the fact that traditionally devout ethnic groups are overrepresented in Catholic schools, or it might be that the relationship between Catholic education and adult behavior is intensified in the devout groups and diminished in the less devout. While the pattern is less clear in this section than it was in the last, it is still generally true that Catholic schools are more likely to have their strongest impact on the devout groups. There are, however, some unexplained variations from this pattern which give hints of further research possibilities (Table 4.5).

For those Catholics of Anglo-Saxon background, associations between Catholic education and adult religious behavior are very weak, except in the matter of religious knowledge; for those of Irish descent, the relationships are consistently strong (except for organizational membership) but not much stronger than the zero-order relationships. Among those with Germanic background, the pattern is curious; relationships are stronger than the zero order in the sacramental index, the religious knowledge index, and the organizational membership index, but weaker in the doctrinal orthodoxy index and the Church-as-teacher index. With Italian respondents the impact of Catholic schooling seems to be stronger than the zero-order relationships on matters of ethical attitudes but weaker in the sacramental index, the doctrinal

Table 4.5 Zero-Order, Partial, and Net Partial Gamma Associations between Catholic Education and Adult Religious Behavior, with Ethnic Background (Father's Ethnicity) Controlled

Religious Behavior	Zero-Order	Partial (Father's Ethnicity)								Net Partial
		English	Irish	German	Italian	French	Polish	Eastern European	Spanish	
Sacramental index	.26	.03	.25	.33	.16	.24	.25	.05	.13	.19
Church-as-teacher index	.15	.06	.20	.08	.15	.12	.03	.16	.19	.13
Religious knowledge index	.30	.16	.31	.35	.20	.30	.16	.38	.33	.26
Doctrinal orthodoxy index	.19	.04	.25	.13	.16	.23	.08	.26	.02	.15
Ethical orthodoxy index	.09	.04	.08	.09	.24	.01	.06	.02	.04	.08
Sexual mores index	.19	.01	.12	.13	.18	.25	.08	.22	.13	.14
Organizational membership[a]	.15	.05	.05	.21	.05	.02	.23	.19	.55	.08

[a] Membership in at least one Church-related organization.

orthodoxy index, and the organizational membership index. The gamma coefficients among French respondents are higher on most items but lower on organizational membership and ethical orthodoxy. For the Poles, on the other hand, the coefficients are stronger than the zero order on organizational membership and weaker on the doctrinal orthodoxy, religious knowledge, and Church-as-teacher indices. The Eastern Europeans and the Spanish-speaking are both less likely than the average to be influenced by Catholic schools on the sacramental and the ethical orthodoxy indices but more likely to be influenced in religious knowledge. The Spanish-speaking are much less influenced in doctrinal orthodoxy, and the Eastern Europeans are more likely to display a very strong relationship (based on a very few cases) between Catholic schooling and organizational activity.

What do all these patterns mean? Is it possible that the Irish and the French are so committed to organizational activity that Catholic schooling has little effect on the level of such activity? But then why do the Poles show low relationships on the three knowledge-related items (the religious knowledge, doctrinal orthodoxy, and Church-as-teacher indices)? The traditional casual approach of Italians to religious practice may explain the weaker relationship between their Catholic school attendance and performance on the sacramental index, but why in the world would Italians demonstrate the strongest relationship on the ethical orthodoxy index? Why would the Germans be similar to the Poles in low relationships for the Church-as-teacher and the doctrinal orthodoxy indices but differ from the Poles in having a high gamma coefficient for religious knowledge? There are no obvious answers to these questions, and until much more is known about the sociology of American ethnic groups, there is no point in speculating. The temptation to probe deeper into these mysteries at the present time must be resisted, since it would take us too far from the main direction of the analysis with which this volume must be concerned, and especially since the limited number of cases within each group reduces the opportunities for more detailed analysis. In any event, while ethnic controls create many puzzles, they do not alter the basic fact of the relationship between Catholic education and adult religious behavior.

RELIGIOUSNESS AND ETHNICITY

Thus far in the present chapter we have treated two of the control variables separately. At this point it is necessary to ask whether a combination of parental religiousness and ethnicity might even further diminish the strength of the relationship between education and religious behavior. In Table 4.6 two sets of partial associations are presented. The first column gives the partial association between religious education in Catholic schools and religious behavior in adult life, with parental religiousness controlled. In the second column are the partial associations with both religiousness and ethnicity controlled. It is clear that the addition of an ethnic control affects the strength of the association only very slightly. Despite the puzzling behavior of the "ethnic factor," ethnicity appears to influence the religious behavior of our respondents through the religiousness of their parents. Certain ethnic groups have a tradition of fervent religious behavior and others do not. A control for ethnic background becomes, for all practical purposes, a control for parental religiousness. It is not necessary, therefore, to worry about the possibility that a joint control for the two factors would substantially alter the findings already reported.

We have established that the basic relationship between Catholic education and adult religious behavior is not reduced any more by a combination of controls for parental religiousness and

Table 4.6 Association between Catholic Education and Religious Behavior, with Controls for Parental Religiousness and for Religiousness and Ethnicity

Religious Behavior	Partial Association (Parental Religiousness Controlled)	Partial Association (Religiousness and Ethnicity Controlled)
Sacramental index	.14	.17
Church-as-teacher index	.12	.10
Religious knowledge index	.26	.23
Doctrinal orthodoxy index	.14	.15
Ethical orthodoxy index	.07	.03
Sexual mores index	.12	.10
Organizational membership[a]	.04	.03

[a] Membership in at least one Church-related organization.

ethnicity. Even so, it is still of some interest to inspect in greater detail the interactions among these variables to ascertain whether Catholic schools may have a greater effect on some ethnic groups than on others. Unfortunately, such an inspection is not so easy in practice; the peculiar historical backgrounds and religious traditions of the various ethnic groups make comparisons when controlling for religiousness of background and Catholic education very difficult. Most Italian respondents fall in the category of low parental religiousness and no Catholic education, while the Irish respondents for the most part have highly religious backgrounds and have had Catholic education. Thus the case bases are bound to be thin for one group or the other, no matter where cutting-points are set.

With this difficulty in mind we can essay a tentative interpretation of Table 4.7. Several points are to be noted. (1) A control for religiousness and ethnicity does not eliminate the relationship between Catholic education and adult behavior. (2) However, ethnicity does make some contribution independent of religiousness and Catholic education. The Irish and Germans in the upper half of the parental religiousness scale who went to Catholic schools score higher on the sacramental index than do the Italians or the Poles. (3) The group most likely to be affected by Catholic education is the Germans. (4) Neither Catholic education nor parental religiousness has much impact on the religious behavior of those from the Polish ethnic group. (5) To a considerable

Table 4.7 Per Cent High on Sacramental Index, by School Attendance, with Control for Parental Religiousness and Ethnicity

Parental Religiousness and Respondent's Schooling	Ethnicity			
	Irish	German	Italian	Polish
In upper half of parental religiousness index:				
All or some Catholic	40 (153)	60 (125)	30 (41)	20 (98)
No Catholic	30 (37)	33 (45)	14 (74)	14 (22)
In lower half of parental religiousness index:				
All or some Catholic	30 (57)	23 (52)	15 (63)	10 (33)
No Catholic	10 (31)	15 (47)	14 (171)	20 (26)

extent, the very high level of religious practice which seems to be a consequence of Catholic education is found mainly in the German and Irish ethnic groups.

There is no trouble in explaining the first two findings. We would have expected considerable overlap between religiousness of parents and ethnic background, so that a combination of the two was unlikely to reduce the relationship much more than either would independently. Furthermore the historical backgrounds of the Irish and German immigrants are such that they presuppose a receptive attitude toward the workings of religious education.

But the last three findings tax our ingenuity more than somewhat. Why do the Germans react so very favorably to Catholic education? And why are the Poles apparently unaffected either by Catholic education or by parental religiousness? There surely must be something very interesting at work within their ethnic traditions to account for this phenomenon, and though we can lay some claim to knowledge about the Italian and Irish ethnic groups, we are loath at present to attempt an answer to the questions about the other two groups. The long tradition of strict religious observance among the Irish (at least in part due to the perennial difficulties between the Irish and their British rulers), and the equally long tradition of a somewhat more relaxed approach to religion among the Italians, will explain why, among those from highly religious backgrounds, the Irish who did not go to Catholic schools and the Italians who did both have about the same level of religious devotion. But why the Poles are completely unaffected by Catholic education, and the Germans quite spectacularly affected by it, is a subject which we will discreetly leave to German and Polish sociologists—if we can call sociologists of German or Polish descent "German sociologists" or "Polish sociologists."

But undue modesty will not prevent us from making a suggestion. Might it be that the German and Irish ethnic groups are strongly oriented toward cross-generational influences, and Polish and Italians are oriented more toward intragenerational influences? Thus the latter two groups are not so much affected either by the religiousness of their parents or by religious education but rather by the religious level of their peer groups (often made up of relatives of the same generation). The former groups, on the other hand, are more disposed to being influenced by both parents and educators and are less likely to be swayed by peer groups. We would have to know much more about the sociology of American ethnic groups to be able to say, though popular impressions would confirm these hunches, as would Gans's (1963) study of Italians in Boston.

To summarize our investigation of control variables thus far, we can say that the relationship between Catholic education and adult religious behavior does not appear to be the result of any extraneous factors. Only the religiousness of parents—representing in many instances the religious traditions of ethnic groups—affects the relationship, and it does so only by intensifying the impact of Catholic schools on those from very religious backgrounds.

If we might be excused for temporarily putting off the mantles of sociologists and donning somewhat more pontifical garb, we will offer unsolicited advice to religious educators—and perhaps to all concerned with the development of values through formal education. The school, it appears, can indeed make a substantial contribution to the development of value-oriented behavior patterns, but it can do so only when the values of the school are reinforced in the family environment. The school can add an impressive margin to the work of the home, but only when the work of the home has been well done. In the absence of reinforcement from the family, there is no reason to expect that the school will modify values and value-oriented behavior. Whether it is possible for religious education—or any value-oriented education—also to have an impact on the family environment of its students remains to be seen. On the basis of our data, however, it seems fairly clear that if Catholic education wishes to influence those who come from relatively nonreligious families, it must strive to modify the religiousness of the family. That will not be an easy task.

We now turn to two control variables which do not in fact diminish the strength of the association between religious education and adult behavior but which are of such theoretical import that they must be examined in some detail: the availability of Catholic schools and the religiousness of one's spouse.

We mentioned in Chapter 2 that, from the viewpoint of approximating an experimental design in some crude fashion, the so-called availability factor was of considerable importance. A comparison between those from highly religious families who went to Catholic schools and those from similarly religious families who were prevented from going by the sheer physical impossibility of doing so would reveal whether those from highly religious families to whom schools were not available would develop compensating mechanisms for religious education. If such compensating mechanisms were in fact at work, we could conclude that the Catholic school was merely substituting for something that the parental family could provide itself, not making a unique contribution of its own. We would thus hold constant the religiousness of the family and vary the availability of the school to ascertain whether the school's contribution was in fact distinct from that of the family. To make such a test, we computed two sets of associations. The first group of associations involved the standard comparison between those who had had all their education in Catholic schools, those who had had some Catholic education, and those who had had none. In the second set of associations, the three groups that were compared were those who had had all their education in Catholic schools, those who had had some Catholic education, and those for whom no Catholic schools had been available. The associations are recorded in Table 4.8.

While a control for the availability of Catholic schools does slightly diminish the strength of the association between Catholic school attendance and adult religious behavior, the net effect is rather minor, even among those Catholics who come from highly religious backgrounds. The association of Catholic education with the sacramental index for those from highly religious backgrounds is diminished two points, the association with the ethical orthodoxy index three points, with organizational membership four points, and with the religious knowledge and sexual mores indices five points. Only the association with the doctrinal orthodoxy index is substantially reduced (fifteen points) for reasons that are not immediately clear. If availability of school is controlled, the association between Catholic schooling and doctrinal orthodoxy is as strong among those from less religious backgrounds as it is for those from highly religious backgrounds.

While Catholics from highly religious families who went to public schools when there were no Catholic schools available are slightly more likely to be similar in their religious behavior to those who went to Catholic schools, the change in associations introduced by making this comparision is not very great. Thus even those Catholics from very religious families for whom Catholic schools were not available would have apparently been notably

Table 4.8   Religious Behavior, by Catholic Education, Religiousness of Parents, and "Availability Factor" (Gamma Associations)

Religiousness of Parents	Association between Catholic Education and Religious Behavior			
	High	Higher Middle	Lower Middle	Low
Sacramental index				
"Availability" not controlled	.34	.11	.09	.10
"Availability" controlled	.32	.09	.06	.00
Church-as-teacher index:				
"Availability" not controlled	.22	.03	.13	.12
"Availability" controlled	.25	.05	.16	.14
Religious knowledge index:				
"Availability" not controlled	.40	.26	.20	.22
"Availability" controlled	.35	.24	.20	.23
Doctrinal orthodoxy index:				
"Availability" not controlled	.34	.11	.09	.10
"Availability" controlled	.19	.08	.12	.22
Ethical orthodoxy index:				
"Availability" not controlled	.20	.05	.07	.01
"Availability" controlled	.17	.03	.10	.03
Sexual mores index:				
"Availability" not controlled	.21	.08	.09	.11
"Availability" controlled	.16	.08	.12	.10
Organizational membership:[a]				
"Availability" not controlled	.21	.08	.08	.06
"Availability" controlled	.17	.05	.11	.04

[a] Membership in at least one Church-related organization.

influenced by religious education. The question of the "availability" of Catholic schools does not seem to be important in measuring the impact of Catholic education. There do not seem to be any important compensating measures which are used by those families who are very religious but for whom Catholic schools are not available.

We have already indicated in our discussion of Table 4.8 that a control for availability does not reduce the association between religious education and adult behavior. However, because of the importance of this factor from the point of view of scientific design, we must now take a closer look at the possible effect of non-availability of Catholic schools on adult behavior. In Table 4.9 we divide those who did not go to Catholic schools into two groups: those for whom a school was available and those for whom there was no possibility of attending such schools. We note that there is very little difference between the two groups. Those from very religious families for whom there was no school available are still less than half as likely to score high on the sacramental index as those from similar religious backgrounds who attended Catholic schools exclusively. Only four percentage points separate those from highly religious backgrounds who had schools available but did not go and those for whom no schools were available.

It might be argued that the important question is not so much whether a school was available but whether the parents would

Table 4.9 Per Cent High on Sacramental Index, by School Attendance, with Controls for Parental Religiousness and Availability of School

Rank on Sacramental Index	School Attendance			
	All Catholic	Some Catholic	None Available	Available but Did Not Attend
High	$56_{(118)}$	$35_{(113)}$	$23_{(39)}$	$19_{(33)}$
Higher middle	$29_{(130)}$	$28_{(269)}$	$23_{(120)}$	$23_{(92)}$
Lower middle	$21_{(39)}$	$21_{(122)}$	$11_{(82)}$	$8_{(104)}$
Low	$24_{(37)}$	$14_{(161)}$	$14_{(122)}$	$6_{(142)}$

have sent their children to such schools if in fact they were available. Such a measure is considerably less than satisfactory, since respondents who are now quite religious might be tempted to upgrade somewhat their parents' devotion to Catholic schools. Thus there would be a built-in bias in favor of a higher score on the sacramental index for those who claim their parents would have sent them to Catholic schools if they were available. We should point out, however, that the bias is against the hypothesis that Catholic schools make a unique contribution beyond that which family religious orientation provides.

Table 4.10 indicates that if there is a bias it is very small and that even reported parental disposition in favor of Catholic schools is no substitute for actually going to a Catholic school. Those from highly religious families who would-have-gone-if-they-could do score eight percentage points higher on the sacramental index than those who could-have-gone-and-did-not or those who would-not-have-gone-if-they-could (and any sociologist who thinks he can put this in a less complicated fashion is welcome to try, but after two years we fear that we are struck with these complicated labels). However, even the former group is still less than half as likely to have a high score on the sacramental index. In short, there is no evidence that religious families develop compensating mechanisms in the absence of Catholic schools, and we can now say with somewhat more confidence

Table 4.10 Per Cent High on Sacramental Index, by School Attendance, with Controls for Parental Religiousness and Disposition To Go to Schools if They Had Been Available

Rank on Sacramental Index	School Attendance			
	All Catholic	Some Catholic	Would Have Gone if Available	Would Not or Did Not
High	56(118)	35(113)	25 (36)	17 (39)
Higher middle	29(130)	28(269)	23(114)	23(101)
Lower middle	21 (39)	21(122)	11 (77)	8(109)
Low	24 (37)	14(161)	15(104)	6(165)

that the consequences we have been attributing to Catholic education do not arise from the family's religious background.

Nevertheless the failure of the "availability factor" to have any impact at all is rather surprising. It may well be that the decision of the American Church to have schools of its own has persuaded parents that religious education is essentially something to be left to the school; hence, those for whom no schools are available are excused from attempting to compensate for the absence of schools. If this be the case, then if there were no Catholic schools at all, the more religious parents might think differently about their responsibility and by their own efforts bring about the same kind of adult behavior in their children that the schools now apparently do. In the nature of things, this hypothesis cannot be proven or disproven, but we are inclined to think that it is a bit farfetched and that it attributes to parents a much more subtle and complex line of reasoning than can be legitimately postulated. A simple explanation is that, given the existing state of religious knowledge and understanding of religious pedagogy, the average parent—even if he is very devout in his own religious practices— can do just so much by way of religious education; anything beyond this parental effort will either be done by a Catholic school or will not be done at all.

RELIGIOUSNESS OF SPOUSE

In addition to parental religiousness, it is reasonable to assume that the religious behavior of one's spouse will influence his own religious behavior. It is therefore theoretically possible that, since those who went to Catholic schools are more likely to be married to persons whose devotion is high, the consequences of Catholic education that we have been predicating ought more properly to be attributed to the marriages that those who go to Catholic schools contract. In such an explanation Catholic schools make for marriages to people who are more religious, and these marriages in their turn make for higher levels of adult religious behavior.

Table 4.11 describes a phenomenon similar to the one we observed when we were considering the religiousness of parents. Even among respondents who have married persons who go to church every Sunday, those who went to Catholic schools score much higher on the sacramental index than those who did not. However, the difference between the Catholic-educated and the others is limited to those who are married to "practicing" Catholics. Catholic education, when combined with a marriage to a "lukewarm" Catholic, has precious little effect on adult religious behavior. On the other hand, when Catholic education is reinforced by marriage to a "practicing" Catholic, it produces very considerable differences. Just as parental religiousness does not eliminate the association between Catholic education and adult religious behavior but specifies that it occurs among those who come from the most religious backgrounds, so the spouse's religiousness does not eliminate the relationship but specifies that it occurs mostly among those who are married to the most religious spouses.

Something of a pattern begins to emerge: religious education does indeed have an impact on the adult lives of its students, but only when the social context of childhood or adulthood supports and emphasizes the values learned in the school. Religious education apparently works when there is constant reinforcement from outside the school. In the absence of such reinforcement, religious education tends to be a waste of time.

We now find ourselves faced with a very crucial question: What is the relationship between parental religiousness and the religiousness of spouses? Is it possible that the apparent specification

Table 4.11 Per Cent High on Sacramental Index, by School Attendance, with Control for Religiousness of Spouse (for Those Married to Catholics)

School Attendance	Religiousness of Spouse		
	Mass Weekly	Mass Monthly or Several Times a Month	Mass Rarely or Never
All Catholic	$40_{(220)}$	$9_{(11)}$	$0_{(27)}$
Some Catholic	$34_{(378)}$	$4_{(54)}$	$5_{(81)}$
No Catholic	$19_{(397)}$	$9_{(66)}$	$2_{(129)}$

of the impact of Catholic education, as it occurs among those from very religious families, is the result primarily of young people from those families being inclined to marry other devout Catholics? Table 4.12 provides the following helpful clues.

1. Both parental religiousness and the religiousness of the spouse have an impact on adult religious behavior.
2. But parental religiousness has no impact if it does not coincide with marriage to a spouse who goes to church weekly. A religious spouse apparently can compensate for a less religious family, but not vice versa.
3. Catholic schools have an impact only when there is at least one kind of religiousness, either a religious spouse or a religious spouse and religious parents. However, the schools have no effect when a respondent with religious parents marries an unreligious spouse.
4. The highest level of religiousness occurs when all three factors—school, parents, and mate—reinforce one another. While parental religiousness makes for higher levels of religious practice, the impact of one's religious *schooling* is

Table 4.12 Per Cent High on Sacramental Index, by School Attendance, with Controls for Religiousness of Parents and of Spouse (for Those Married to Catholics)

School Attendance	Religiousness of Parents					
	High[a]		Medium		Low[b]	
	Religiousness of Spouse					
	High[c]	Low[d]	High	Low	High	Low
All Catholic	59(81)	–[e] (7)	28 (89)	–[e] (1)	27 (36)	5 (19)
Some Catholic	43(79)	8(12)	36(168)	1(34)	26(115)	1 (81)
No Catholic	21(39)	11(18)	28(139)	3(33)	13(195)	4(128)

[a] Upper quarter.
[b] Lower quarter.
[c] Spouse goes to Mass weekly.
[d] Spouse goes to Mass less often than weekly.
[e] Number too few to percentage.

increased when he marries a religious person, especially if he comes from a religious background.

Thus a marriage to a devout Catholic can compensate for a less-than-devout family—both in the level of religious practice and in preserving the impact of Catholic schooling; but rearing in a devout family cannot offset the negative effects on religious practice and on the impact of Catholic education brought about by marriage to a less-than-devout spouse. It is not surprising that a marriage to someone who does not take religion so seriously can cancel out the effects of both parental family and schooling. What is surprising is that marriage to a devout Catholic can in a sense "resurrect" the impact of Catholic education for which there was no predisposition in the parental family. It appears that the parental family presupposes an impact by Catholic schooling, while the family of orientation preserves this impact. We will note later that there is some evidence that Catholic schools do have a short-run effect on all their students but that this effect is transitory for those whose family religious background does not reinforce the work of the school. It therefore seems that, to some extent, the role of the family in reinforcing the effect of the school consists in predisposing the respondent to marriage to a devout spouse and that the marriage itself is what preserves the effect of the school. In addition to its direct influence, religiousness of the family of origin therefore affects the impact of Catholic education by inclining a person to enter into a devout family of orientation. In other words, parental religiousness in part affects the impact of Catholic education through the mediation of the spouse's religiousness. The chain of influence is complicated: Catholic schools may well have a short-run impact on all students; whether this impact survives graduation depends on the kind of marriage one enters, but this in turn depends to a considerable extent on how religious one's parents were.

THE RELATIVE INFLUENCE OF CATHOLIC EDUCATION

We can now say with some degree of safety that Catholic education is related to adult religious behavior and that the relation is strongest among those from families in which the religious atmosphere is already rather devout. We must therefore proceed to the question of how "important" this relationship is. Rather than measure the influence of Catholic schools against abstract goals or against the expectations of the friends and foes of the schools, we will try to assess the relative impact of Catholic education compared with the influence of other known predictors of adult religious behavior.

The coefficients of association presented in Table 4.13 represent the relationship between the given predictor attribute and adult behavior or attitudes, with the other three predictor attributes held constant. Thus when we say that there is a net partial relationship of .34 between parental religiousness and the re-spondent's score on the sacramental index, we mean to indicate an association which exists when the respondent's educational level, sex, and Catholic schooling are held constant.

The first point to be made in Table 4.13 is that Catholic schooling is quite clearly not the most important predictor of adult religious behavior. Thus the association between attendance of Catholic schools and a high score on the sacramental index is half as strong as the relationship between parental religiousness and one's sacramental score. Nor is it nearly as important as how much education a respondent has had. A respondent who has had sixteen years of education, all of it in non-Catholic schools, will have a higher score on the sacramental index than a respondent who has had only eight years of school, all of which was Catholic. On the other hand, Catholic schools do have about the same impact on adult behavior as does sex, which is normally a very powerful predictor attribute and which traditionally has been taken to be a strong correlate of religiousness. To put the matter in a different perspective, as far as adult sacramental activity is concerned, going to a Catholic school makes about the same difference compared with not going to a Catholic school as being a woman does compared with being a man.

What conclusion one wishes to draw from this observation depends to a considerable extent on the rhetoric he wishes to use. One might say that Catholic schools are obviously not very important in the development of religious values, since level of education and family background are clearly much more important. Or one could say that such pervasive factors as social class (as represented by educational level) and family religious environment could be expected to have a strong influence on adult behavior and that formal education—which represents a rather small segment of life—does surprisingly well in being almost as

Table 4.13 Net Partial Associations between Predictor Attributes and Religious Behavior

Sacramental index:	
Religiousness of parents	.34[a]
Educational level	.28
Sex (female)	.20
Catholic school	.17
Church-as-teacher index:	
Educational level	.20
Catholic school	.12
Religiousness of parents	.06
Sex (female)	.04
Religious knowledge index:	
Educational level	.30
Catholic school	.27
Sex	.09
Religiousness of parents	.07
Doctrinal orthodoxy index:	
Educational level	.22
Religiousness of parents	.19
Catholic school	.14
Sex	.06
Ethical orthodoxy index:	
Educational level	.26
Sex	.17
Religiousness of parents	.14
Catholic school	.06
Organizational membership:	
Religiousness of parents	.39
Educational level	.18
Sex	.15
Catholic school	.04

[a] Coefficient represents degree of association, with influence of other three predictor variables held constant.

important a predictor as sex. Our own personal feeling is that it would be quite unrealistic to expect a school to be more important than family background or more important than social class. The crucial question continues to be: What institution would replace the school in having the influence it does have?

The second point to be noted concerning Table 4.13 is that on the next four items (Church-as-teacher, religious knowledge, doctrinal orthodoxy, and ethical orthodoxy indices) educational level is the strongest predictor of adult behavior, while Catholic education is in two instances (Church-as-teacher and religious knowledge) the second most important predictor, in one (doctrinal orthodoxy) the third most important, and in one (ethical orthodoxy) the least important. On only the ethical orthodoxy index, however, is the influence of Catholic schools quite weak. Catholic schooling in these four areas tends to be more important than family religious background and sex but less important than social class, as represented by educational level. Whether this demonstrates a clear future of schools to achieve their goals or simply shows what one can realistically expect from an educational institution depends on the rhetorical and ideological stance one wishes to take. Our own feeling continues to be that, considering the great difficulty of shaping human attitudes when they are in opposition to one's family environment and social class, Catholic schools have done reasonably well in the religious knowledge, doctrinal orthodoxy, and Church-as-teacher measures, though not quite so well in the area of ethical attitudes. We also note that the importance of educational level as a predictor may result from the fact that better-educated respondents are more sophisticated in test-taking and hence better able to guess the "right" answers in our survey questions.

A third observation to be drawn from Table 4.13 is that it seems abundantly clear that membership in Church organizations is primarily the result of family traditions and is only very marginally influenced by Catholic education. It is our impression that this finding may be something of a surprise. Many American Catholics have thought that those who go to Catholic schools are much more likely to be found in Church organizations than are those who do not. Such an impression is accurate, but the influence seems to be not from the schools but from the family background of the members. Involvement in the Church through the years of schooling does not lead to organizational membership in later life unless there is already a family tradition of religious devotion. And even in the absence of religious education, the Catholic from a devout family is very likely to participate in a formal religious organization in adult life.

As a final observation concerning Table 4.13, we should note that the present technology of the gamma coefficient does not enable us to add up the partial gammas to obtain a multiple gamma which would indicate the amount of variance that can be explained by a combination of the predicting attributes. We may, nevertheless, obtain some kind of idea from Table 4.14 of the strength of the four predictors of adult religious behavior when they are combined. Thus, of males with no Catholic education who did not graduate from high school and came from families with a relatively low religious background, only 11 per cent scored high on the sacramental index. On the other hand, of females who graduated from high school, came from relatively high religious backgrounds, and had all their primary and secondary education in Catholic schools, 55 per cent scored high on the sacramental index. The female respondent who had all the predictor attributes working for her was five times more likely

Table 4.14 Per Cent of Respondents High on Sacramental Index, by Religiousness of Parent, Sex, Educational Level, and School Attendance

| Religious-ness of Parent | Sex | School Attendance | | | | | |
| | | High School Graduate | | | Some High School or Less | | |
		All Catholic	Some Catholic	No Catholic	All Catholic	Some Catholic	No Catholic
High	Female	$55_{(56)}$	$20_{(114)}$	$18_{(68)}$	$33_{(58)}$	$29_{(70)}$	$27_{(60)}$
	Male	$39_{(95)}$	$20_{(127)}$	$20_{(93)}$	$26_{(35)}$	$21_{(66)}$	$8_{(63)}$
Low	Female	$44_{(25)}$	$27_{(84)}$	$12_{(114)}$	$15_{(20)}$	$14_{(70)}$	$11_{(124)}$
	Male	$20_{(15)}$	$17_{(71)}$	$10_{(108)}$	$13_{(16)}$	$17_{(55)}$	$11_{(99)}$

to score high on the sacramental scale than the male respondent who had no predictor attribute working for him.

PARENTAL CATHOLIC EDUCATION

One of the most effective arguments used in favor of the present system of Catholic education is that the European countries that do not have an extensive Catholic school system are precisely those countries where the people's religious practice and fervor are minimal. It would suggest that, should Catholic schools be abandoned in this country, the present rather high devotional levels would be substantially decreased in a generation or two. Such an argument is at best an oversimplification of complex social and historical realities, but it may conceivably have some truth in it. However, it is quite difficult to measure what the situation in the American Roman Catholic Church would be if there had been no Catholic school system and no other institution that could have accomplished the same effects. Ideally, we would have to know the religious level of a given family when it first came to the United States and then trace the descendants of the family who went to Catholic schools and compare them with those descendants who did not, holding all the variables constant. Such a design is, of course, out of the question. On the other hand, since what Catholic education does accomplish is to make the elite more elite, there seems to be some possibility that several generations of Catholic education would produce a body of Catholics whose level of religious behavior is substantially higher than the level of those families which over several generations have had no contact with Catholic schools. It is not clear whether the reverse proposition would be true—whether there would be a decline in religious practice in succeeding generations for those who did not attend Catholic schools.

Such questions are far too complicated to be answered definitively with the data available to us. However, since we do know whether the parents of our respondents went to Catholic schools, it is at least possible to see whether two generations of Catholic schooling notably increased the level of religious behavior in American Catholics.

The question, therefore, is whether the religious education of his parents notably strengthened the correlation between the respondent's Catholic education and his religious behavior in adult life. Table 4.15 suggests that, to some extent, the fact that a respondent's parents had Catholic education does increase the impact of Catholic education on the respondent himself. Those whose parents had at least some Catholic educational experience were more likely to be influenced by their own Catholic education as far as participation in the sacraments and religious knowledge are concerned, while those whose parents had an exclusively Catholic education were themselves more likely to be influenced by Catholic schooling in their scores on the Church-as-teacher index and the sexual mores index. Only on the index of doctrinal orthodoxy does there seem to be no intergenerational impact.

Thus, two generations of Catholic education do apparently produce a more devout Catholic group than one generation. To portray this intergenerational effect in a somewhat different fashion, Table 4.16 shows the proportion within the various groups scoring high on the sacramental index. Even though there is little relationship between parental education and respondent's score on the sacramental index for those respondents who had had some Catholic education and those who had had none, the relationship is very strong for those who had had only Catholic education. Of this group, those whose parents had attended Catholic schools were some 20 per cent more likely to score high on the index than were those whose parents had not.

Table 4.15 Associations between Religious Education and Religious Behavior, by Parental Attendance at Catholic Schools

Religious Behavior	Both Parents in Catholic Schools	Mixed	Neither Parent in Catholic Schools
Sacramental index	.31	.28	.09
Church-as-teacher index	.25	.10	.13
Religious knowledge index	.30	.34	.17
Doctrinal orthodoxy index	.16	.17	.18
Sexual mores index	.25	.12	.09

So there seems to be some reason to think that several generations of Catholic education do lead to the appearance of a more
fervent Catholic adult. However, it is to be remembered that
a high score on the sacramental index measures both attendance
of Mass and reception of the sacraments. If we are concerned
merely with the allegiance to the Church represented by attendance at Sunday Mass, then the intergenerational influence of
Catholic schools does not seem to be so overwhelming. Table 4.17
shows that, while almost nine-tenths of those who are the result
of two generations of Catholic education go to church every
Sunday, no less than two-thirds of the respondents in other groups
also go to church every Sunday. In the absence of any Catholic
education for two generations, American Catholics still achieve
a level of Church attendance which is far superior to that of
most of the industrial nations of the Western world. Thus we can
hazard the guess that while Catholic schools have produced a
more dedicated Catholic elite within the American Catholic population, they have not, by themselves, at least, been responsible
for the very high level of religious practice to be found among
all American Catholics.

To conclude sections of the relative importance of Catholic
education as an influence on adult religious behavior, we will
engage in a somewhat mad flight of fancy and imagine that a
committee of American Catholics—hierarchical, clerical, and lay,
and in this ecumenical age augmented by Protestant, Jewish, and
secularist advisers who as citizens are interested in Catholic
schools—came to us and asked whether the religious effects of

Table 4.16 Per Cent of Respondents High on Sacramental Index,
by Their Own School Attendance and That of Their Parents

Parent's School Attendance	Respondent's Own School Attendance		
	All Catholic	Some Catholic	No Catholic
Both exclusively in Catholic schools	45(108)	26(139)	9 (32)
Mixed	42(100)	28(228)	19(149)
Neither in Catholic schools	25 (32)	24(127)	17(280)

Catholic education as measured in this and the preceding chapters were worth the effort they have expended. We would at first modestly point out that such a judgment was far beyond our competence as social scientists and that policy decisions were theirs to make, not ours. However, under the pressure of cajolery, threats, and perhaps even bribery, we would finally be forced to express our "off the record" opinion. We would contend that, given the goals which were operative and the obstacles to value-change through formal education, Catholic schools were probably more worth the effort than not worth it—especially in the absence of any alternative institution which has proven itself to have the ability to accomplish the same effects. It seems to us that to criticize Catholic schools of the past for not producing graduates who were liturgically, ecumenically, and interracially oriented is to criticize the past for not being the present. We would further observe that, while Catholic education is not the most important influence on adult religious behavior, it is not an unimportant influence, and our hierarchical-clerical-lay commit-tee of policy-makers would, from the viewpoint of their religious goals, be poorly advised to contemplate abandoning their educa-tional system until, by careful experimentation, they had con-cluded that they had discovered an equally effective alternative. We would also comment that, while American Catholicism would probably have survived in reasonable health without its schools, the schools have nevertheless produced a rather fervent religious elite. We would conclude our "unofficial" advice by noting that, while religious training for those not in Catholic schools is an

Table 4.17 Per Cent of Respondents Attending Mass Weekly or More Often, by Their Own School Attendance and That of Their Parents

Parent's School Attendance	Respondent's Own School Attendance		
	All Catholic	Some Catholic	No Catholic
Both exclusively in Catholic schools	88 (108)	79 (139)	75 (32)
Mixed	91 (100)	77 (227)	67 (148)
Neither in Catholic schools	81 (31)	67 (127)	70 (279)

important problem, it might not in the long run be as crucial as discovering means to increase the effectiveness of formal religious education for those who attend Catholic schools but whose parents' religious performance does not adequately reinforce the work of the school. If our data from the past are any indication of the present situation, Catholic education is virtually wasted on three-fourths of those in Catholic schools because of the absence of a sufficiently religious family milieu.

If one of the members of our mythical, but by now perhaps bored, committee (maybe an editor of *The Commonweal*) should ask whether the price paid for these religious gains from Catholic education is worth the isolation of Catholic school Catholics from Americans of other religious faiths, we would be forced to suggest that the committee return to discuss this question at the end of the next chapter.

CONCLUSION

This chapter began with two main queries. (1) Does the relationship between Catholic education and adult religious behavior noted in the previous chapter persist when we take into account the influence of intervening attributes? (2) What is the relative importance of Catholic education when compared to other predictors of religious behavior?

To the first question we replied that the relationship is affected only by controls for ethnicity and parental religiousness, which seem actually to be part of the same dimension, and that parental religiousness reinforces the effect of religious education among those from very religious families. We also noted that, contrary to certain theoretical expectations, those highly religious Catholic families for whom no Catholic schools were available did not develop compensatory mechanisms of religious instruction which were as effective as Catholic schools. We also noted that there was some evidence to suggest that the reinforcement attributed to parental religiousness was to some extent the result of the fact that those from religious families marry religious people, and such marriages preserve the impact of Catholic education.

To the second question we responded that Catholic education was not as important as either the religiousness of parents or

the social class of the respondent (as represented by his education), but it was more important as a predictor of religious behavior than was sex and could not be written off as making
only a very minor contribution. Indeed it seems to us that, all
things considered, the schools had done a reasonably adequate
job at what they had set out to do.

In summary, we would observe that one of the consequences
of a religiously oriented school system is that those students
within the system who come from very religious backgrounds
become themselves even more fervent in their religious practice.
Those who come from moderately religious families or nonreligious families are only influenced in a minimal way by Catholic
education. On the other hand, those who did not attend Catholic
schools still seem to maintain a basic loyalty to and identification
with the Church. In answer to the question, "Have Catholic
schools worked?" we might respond that they have worked very
well for those who would already be part of the religious elite;
they have not worked so well for those whose religious backgrounds were less intense, and, apparently, Catholics who have
not attended them have not been appreciably harmed by their
nonattendance.

5

Are
Religious Schools
Divisive?

As we observed before, the sociologist is professionally skeptical about formal education as an institution of socialization in values. He is prepared to concede that skills and information can be imparted in schools, but he suspects that the influence of schools on value formation is much weaker than that of other institutions, such as the family and the local community (not to mention the culture of urban industrial society), in which the young person is immersed not for a few hours each day but for every second of his life. Just as he is not prepared to concede that religious values can be developed in schools until he sees definite proof that they are, he is also inclined to doubt that schools can succeed in isolating members of one religious community from other Americans. While he will admit that religion as such is an extremely important factor in the choice of friends, companions, and marriage partners, he also suspects that the homogenizing forces within an industrial culture (the mass media, common life styles, frequent interaction in the work environment, breakdown of immigrant ghettos) ought to be strong enough to overcome whatever "divisive" influence a separate school system might have.

But there can be no question that there is a good deal of popular opinion to the contrary. Perhaps the most frequent criticisms leveled at Catholic schools—both by Catholics and by non-Catholics are that they do restrict interaction between Catholics and adults of other religious faiths, that they lead Catholics to a noninvolvement in community activities, that they develop rigid and intolerant attitudes among their students, and that they cultivate social and economic attitudes which impede success in the occupational world.

If such impressions are at all valid, they consitute a serious objection to the separate Catholic school system and strongly suggest that the achievements of Catholic education reported in the last two chapters have been obtained at a very heavy price indeed. On the other hand, there is precious little evidence available to sustain the impressions which seem so widespread; in fact it is altogether possible that some of the impressions have to do with behavior which results not so much from Catholic education as from the more general tendency of the American to reserve certain portions of his life for interaction with his "own kind." We are therefore forced to ask whether we can find any evidence for a "divisive" effect in adult life which can be attributed to one's having attended a Catholic school.

To accomplish the goals of this chapter will require four steps. (1) We will attempt to determine whether Catholic school Catholics are less likely to have non-Catholics as friends, neighbors, and co-workers and whether they are any less inclined to engage in community activities and be well informed in matters of "secular" knowledge. (2) We will ask whether in their cultural attitudes Catholic school Catholics are any more intolerant or rigid than those who did not go to Catholic schools. It should be noted that the absence of differences on such items may satisfy those critics of Catholic schools who think that the schools are divisive, but it will not satisfy those critics within the Church who argue that Catholic schools—if they are effective in teaching the social doctrine of the Church—should produce adults who are more tolerant and more socially conscious. (3) If we can find no trace of "divisive" effects of Catholic education itself, we must ask whether there is anything in the social or demographic backgrounds of Catholic school Catholics that would mask differences that might actually exist between them and public school Catholics. (4) Finally, we must give some consideration to the contention of the defenders of Catholic schools that in recent years there has been an increased stress on social consciousness and that the youngest Catholic school respondents will be more socially conscious and more tolerant than their elders.

To summarize our answers to these four questions briefly, we will find no trace of a "divisive" effect of Catholic education, nor will control variables produce any such trace. On the contrary, there will be some indication that among the youngest graduates of Catholic schools there is more tolerance rather than less.

DIVISIVENESS

As we pointed out in Chapter 1, one of the crucial questions about any system of separate education concerns the extent to which the particular school system isolates Americans of one religious belief from their fellow citizens. It is true, of course, that all religion is to some extent divisive; people with different faiths and different moral codes are more likely to choose as their role opposites people of their own denomination. Hence the crucial question for this study is not whether Catholics associate with Protestants, but rather whether Catholic school Catholics are any less likely to do so. It seems possible to argue that if during their formative years young people do not get to know members of other religious groups, they will not be inclined to associate with members of other faiths in their adult life and will, in fact, tend to have rather unfavorable attitudes about such people. If one assumes that healthy relationships across religious lines in pluralistic societies depend on members of one group knowing members of another, it would seem quite clear that Catholic education ought to be divisive.

"Divisiveness," however, is not a particularly easy matter to measure, especially since it is used in many different senses by various authors who have made the word popular. However, several hypotheses were formed at the beginning of our research that were thought to operationalize, at least in some fashion, the divisiveness theory. The hypotheses were as follows.

1. Children in Catholic schools are less likely than Catholics attending public schools to have close contact with non-Catholics.

2. Adults who went to Catholic schools are less likely than other Catholics to interact with non-Catholics.
3. Adults who went to Catholic schools are less likely than other Catholics to be involved in the general "secular" community.
4. Adults who went to Catholic schools are more likely than other Catholics to emphasize obedience and less likely to accept independent initiative.
5. Catholics who went to Catholic schools are more likely than other Catholics to hold attitudes, values, and beliefs that are productive of interreligious conflict and are less likely to defend the civil liberties of others.
6. Catholics who went to Catholic schools are more likely than other Catholics to hold critical views of Protestants and Jews.

The crucial assumption in the divisiveness theory is that if young people are put into a school with members of other religious denominations, the probability of their associating on a fairly intimate basis with these members of other faiths is increased. The data presented in Table 5.1 suggest that there is some element of truth in this assumption. Two-thirds of those who attended exclusively Catholic schools reported that more than one-half of their friends at the age of seventeen were Catholic, and about one-half of the members of the other two groups were able to report that more than one-half of their friends at the age of seventeen were Catholic. While there is, therefore, support for the idea that religious mingling at the high-school level will increase friendship ties across religious lines, the rather surprising aspect of the first item in Table 5.1 is that one-half of those who had not attended Catholic high schools still reported that more than one-half of their friends at seventeen were Catholic. Thus, public schooling did increase somewhat the interaction across religious lines, but the tendency for Catholics to choose other Catholics as their best friends remains strong even in public high schools. Part of the explanation may be that in many of the immigrant neighborhoods in large metropolitan areas most of the young people attending public high schools were Catholics too.

The Education of Catholic Americans

However, at least at the time when our respondents were in high school, it would seem that the divisiveness which existed in American society on religious lines was divisiveness resulting not so much from religious education as from religion itself.

But one is still permitted to wonder whether this divisiveness, even though it is relatively minor, has persisted into adult life. The next two items in Table 5.1 address themselves to this question. The phenomenon reported here is quite interesting; in both instances there are only very minor differences between those who had had their education in Catholic schools and those who had not, while there is a statistically significant difference between these two groups and the group which had some Catholic education.

The "Some Catholic" group was significantly less likely than the "All Catholic" group to report that their three best friends were Catholic, though there is no significant difference between the "No Catholic" and the "All Catholic" groups. Although the differences between the "Some Catholic" and the "All Catho-

Table 5.1　"Divisiveness" and Per Cent Attending Each School Category

Divisiveness	School Attendance			Convert	Protestant
	All Catholic	Some Catholic	No Catholic		
More than one-half of friends at seventeen were Catholic	67	51[a]	49[a]	–	–
All three best friends Catholic today	51	43[a]	47	–	–
Community involvement index	33	42[a]	34	–	–
Almost all neighbors Catholic	27	23	24	14	–
More than one-half co-workers Catholic	24	20	24	9	–
Almost all visitors Catholic	31	27	28	14	–
Feel that it is very important to have Catholic friends	41	40	38	28	–
Scored high on general knowledge index (six or seven correct answers)	28	25	16[a]	28	28
N	345	699	796	231	530

[a] Significantly different from "All Catholic."

lic" groups are statistically significant, they are not very impressive. We are led to conclude, therefore, that while in adult life religion is extremely important in forming friendship cliques, just as it was in adolescent life, the kind of school one attended seems to have only marginal effects on one's choice of adult friends.

Nor does the kind of school one attended seem to have any great effect on one's involvement in the "secular" community.[1] Here, again, those who attended public high schools and Catholic grammar schools were more likely to score high on the community involvement index than were the other two groups. But there is no difference between those who had had all Catholic education and those who had none, and the difference between the "All Catholic" and the "Some Catholic" groups, while intriguing, is not nearly as large as the divisiveness theory led us to expect. It is quite possible that both age and social class will have some effect on this finding. Nevertheless, the differences reported in these two items in Table 5.1 are hardly great enough to confirm the suspicion that separate educational systems present major social problems in the adult life of people who have attended these schools.

Furthermore, religious education does not seem to be divisive in one's choice of neighbors, co-workers, or visitors or in one's feeling about how important it is to have friends in the same religious group. As the next four items in Table 5.1 show, not only are there no significant differences in the three groups of Catholic respondents on these matters, but virtually no differences at all. About one-quarter of each group reported that almost all their neighbors were Catholic, that more than one-half of their co-workers were Catholic, and that almost all their visitors were

[1] The community involvement index is composed of the following items: (1) How many organizations do you belong to besides religious ones—such as unions, professional organizations, clubs, neighborhood organizations, etc.? (2) In general, would you say you are very active in these organizations, fairly active, or inactive? (3) Do you read any non-religious magazines regularly? (4) How interested are you in what goes on in the world today? For instance, do you follow the international news very closely, fairly closely, or not too closely? (5) What about the local news—the things that happen here in your [town] [area]? Do you follow local news very closely, fairly closely, or not too closely? (6) Do you ever get as worked up by something that happens in the news as you do by something that happens in your personal life?

Catholic; about two-fifths of each group felt that it was very important to have Catholic friends. It might well be argued that, in an open and democratic society, such proportions are rather high, although on the other hand they might seem quite low in view of the fact that America is still a society engaged in assimilating immigrants and children of immigrants. In any case, there is no evidence in these four items for the suspicion that Catholic schools have either impeded or accelerated the process of assimilation.

Finally, we should pay at least some attention to the widespread notion that the concern of Catholic education for "otherworldly" values, and the emphasis on the importance of the next life in preference to this, impedes the pursuit of academic knowledge in Catholic schools and thus badly equips graduates of such schools for successful economic endeavor. As we saw in Chapter 2, there was no evidence that graduates of Catholic schools were any less successful economically than Catholics who had not attended these schools, and, as a matter of fact, the contrary seemed to be the case (though this surprising finding clearly needs to be studied further in the following chapters). The last item in Table 5.1 certainly does not indicate any lack of academic concern among Catholics who went to Catholic schools. While the brief general knowledge test[2] used in the survey can hardly be taken as a conclusive measure of the academic attainments of the respondents, the fact that the "All Catholic" group scored significantly higher on this index than the "No Catholic" group scarcely confirms the notion that Catholic schools were academically inferior when our respondents were attending them. Further, this finding, when coupled with the superior economic and social achievements described in Chapter 2, raises considerable question as to how "otherworldly" Catholic schools really are.

As we suggested in the beginning of this chapter, a considerable

---

[2] The general knowledge index is composed of the following items: (1) What ocean would one cross in going from the United States to England? (2) Could you tell me who Billy Graham is? (3) What mineral or metal is important in the making of the atomic bomb? (4) Will you tell me who Plato was? (5) Will you tell me who Robert McNamara is? (6) How about Charles Lindbergh—can you tell me what he was famous for? (7) Who wrote *War and Peace?* (8) What is the name of the Pope?

amount of popular opinion runs against the data reported in Table 5.1. One of the authors of this volume was told by a Catholic lay woman in a panel discussion that, despite the data cited, she knew from her own experience that Catholic schools did isolate Catholics from other Americans. When empirical data disagree with very strong impressions, the sociologist is cautious about asserting flatly that the impressions are wrong. Yet it seems to us that it is hard to dispute the evidence we have presented in Table 5.1—especially since there is ample reason in social theory to expect that, just as schools produce different values only with great difficulty, so they will separate peoples only with great difficulty. Catholic school Catholics do interact less with other Americans while they are in school. But when they are out of school and have entered into the work force and settled in their own neighborhoods to raise their families, they are no more or less susceptible to the cultural forces which make for conflict and consensus, for integration and isolation in American society than are Catholics who did not attend Catholic schools. We do not contend that there is no divisiveness along religious lines in the United States, nor do we argue that there is no divisive behavior on the part of American Catholics (and non-Catholics, for that matter). But the evidence available to us at the present time does not indicate that the formal educational experience of those who went to Catholic schools makes any more than a marginal contribution to divisiveness. The systematic data do indeed disagree with popular impressions, but one of the reasons for having social science is that it examines popular impressions to determine whether they are accurate. In many cases, all research does is to reinforce such impressions, but in this instance we must report that the impressions are not sustained. The burden of proof for the theory that Catholic education isolates its graduates from other Americans now seems to rest with those who support the theory.

INTERGROUP ATTITUDES

The second question with which we began the chapter was whether Catholic education develops rigid and intolerant attitudes toward members of other groups. Underlying the suspicion that they might is the assumption that, if one does not get to know members of other groups when he is going to school, then he will be intolerant of them. Such a notion is of course rather naïve from the point of view of those who have studied the psychodynamics of prejudice; but even those who understand that prejudice is a personality problem, rather than merely the result of ignorance, might be tempted to think that the "authoritarian" nature of the Catholic Church would lead to prejudiced personality orientations in those whose formal education was under Church auspices.

With the data available to us in this chapter we cannot say definitively whether such intolerant attitudes were developed in our respondents by Catholic schools (though in a later chapter, when we look at adolescents in Catholic high schools, we will be able to comment on this question). But we can at least decide whether at the present time in their adult lives Catholic school Catholics demonstrate more prejudice toward members of other groups than do Catholics who did not go to Catholic schools. We should note in passing that most of the opinion items used in this and the following section have been part of the collective preconscious of survey research for some time and are not original to this study. How accurately they get at underlying values and personality dimensions may be open to question, but they have been used often enough in the past to justify their inclusion in this study at least as indicators of a respondent's verbal reaction to statements calculated to measure prejudice. The cautious reader may well want to suspend judgment on whether deeper feelings are measured. However, the similarity between the results found from the opinion and attitude questions in this section and the behavioral items in the last section suggests that whatever subconscious mechanisms Catholic school Catholics may have developed for hiding their prejudice from an interviewer are not notably different from the mechanisms devised by Catholics who did not go to Catholic schools.

If Catholic school Catholics are less tolerant of members of other groups, such intolerance is not evident in Table 5.2. They are no more likely to think Jews have too much power or are dishonest. Nor are they any less likely to approve of Negroes'

"pushing" or moving in next door. They are not any more inclined to attribute race problems to troublemakers or to defend
all-white neighborhoods. Finally, they are just as likely to contend
that Protestants take their religion seriously and are fair to Catholics. From the point of view of the Catholic who demands that
his schools produce a much higher level of social awareness and
tolerance, Table 5.2 will be a harsh disappointment; but it will
also be a disappointment to the opponent of Catholic schools
who expected them to produce a less tolerant graduate. The
former will be unhappy that the schools have not produced better

Table 5.2 School Attendance and Per Cent Expressing Tolerant
Attitudes toward Other Groups

Item and Response	School Attendance			Convert	Protestant
	All Catholic	Some Catholic	No Catholic		
Jews have too much power in the United States (disagree strongly)	45	42	37[a]	48	41
Jewish businessmen are about as honest as other businessmen (agree strongly)	41	41	38	41	39
Negroes shouldn't push themselves where they are not wanted (disagree)	37	38	38	39	35
White people have a right to live in an all-white neighborhood if they want to, and Negroes should respect this right (disagree)	24	26	26	26	24
I would strongly disapprove if a Negro moved next door to me (disagree strongly)	24	22	22	19	23
Negroes would be satisfied if it were not for a few people who stir up trouble (disagree)	21	21	18	23	24
Most Protestants are inclined to discriminate against Catholics (disagree)	70	73	67	70	–
Protestants don't really take their religion seriously compared to Catholics (disagree)	34	38	33	40	–
N	345	699	796	231	530

[a] Significantly different from "All Catholic."

Catholics, and the latter will be unhappy that they have not produced poorer Americans. The wise researcher gets out of the way before the bricks start flying.

But it still might be pertinent to ask why Catholic schools— which clearly do inculcate some values—have not been successful in developing more enlightened racial attitudes. One suspects that, to paraphrase Chesterton, it is not that education for racial justice was tried and found wanting, but that it was found hard and not tried (at least while our respondents were in school).

We might make an interesting comparison between the attitudes of Catholics on racial justice and on sexual morality. About both, the Church has clear teachings; both are important parts of the Christian moral system; the graduates of Catholic schools are willing to admit that the Church has a right to teach authoritatively on both subjects. Yet there are no differences between Catholic graduates and others in their attitudes on racial justice and considerable differences in attitudes on sexual morality. The conclusion is hard to escape: for complicated historical and social reasons, the school have invested sexual morality with an important symbolical value and by this emphasis have produced an influence in the attitudes of their students, but the same value has not been assigned (or at least not nearly so forcefully) to racial morality, and hence the racial teachings of the Church have had no more impact on the graduates of Catholic schools than on Catholics who went to public schools.

This observation is hardly startling. Not even the most ardent proponents of Catholic education would claim that much emphasis was placed on racial justice (or at least emphasis comparable to that on, let us say, birth control) until very recently. However, if sexual morality can be taught in schools, so too should racial morality be teachable. We could even argue that the Church's teaching on race makes less demands on human nature than does its sexual code and that therefore the Catholic schools could, if they are of such a mind, develop educational methods which would inculcate convictions on racial justice much more easily than convictions on birth control. On the other hand, it must be admitted that sex is an area in which Catholics have traditionally felt that the Church could take a legitimate interest; family and Church have always been closely connected. But the relation-ship between social justice and religion has not always been so obvious. Furthermore, the Church's teachings on sex have been maintained with a persistence and a vigor which has not always existed in its past racial teaching. It will be interesting to watch the Catholic schools in years to come to see if the increased stress on racial justice has an impact on the lives of future gradu-ates. Data on respondents in their twenties, to be presented later in the chapter, suggest that there might be such an impact.

CULTURAL ATTITUDES

Having found no trace of greater prejudice among Catholic school Catholics, we must now ask whether they display other cultural attitudes which might have a harmful effect on the larger society. Are they less likely to defend civil liberties? Are they more given to extremist religious attitudes? Do they distrust the world and worldly effort? Are they more rigid in their child-rearing practices?

Nothing much can be found in Table 5.3 to provide affirmative answers to these questions. While one or two statistically signifi-cant differences do occur on the opinion items which constitute the table, there is no pattern in the differences, and no differences are very large. The striking fact about Table 5.3 is its similarity to Table 5.2: Catholics who went to Catholic schools and Catho-lics who did not do so respond to most questions in very similar fashion. Thus in a cluster of items we have called the "Man-ichaean" index,[3] we find that Catholic school Catholics are just as likely to judge the material world as a good and gracious place in which to live and work as are other Catholics. If the "other-worldly" orientation of the Catholic schools at one time influenced their attitudes on these subjects, the influence has long since waned. It is also possible that those authors who thought they observed an otherworldly orientation in Roman Catholicism did

[3] The "Manichaean" index is composed of the following items: (1) Although Christ saved the spiritual world by his death and resurrection, the material world is under the control of the devil. (2) The world is basically a dangerous place where there is much evil and sin. (3) The Catholic Church teaches that a good Christian ought to think about the next life and not worry about fighting against poverty and injustice in this life.

Table 5.3 School Attendance and Cultural Attitudes (Per Cent Giving More "Enlightened" Response)

Questionnaire Items (by Index)	School Attendance			Convert	Protestant
	All Catholic	Some Catholic	No Catholic		
Anti-civil-liberties items:					
People who don't believe in God have as much right to freedom of speech as anyone else (agree)	59	62	52[c]	55	57
Books written by Communists should not be permitted in public libraries (disagree)	42	46	38[b]	55	47
Only people who believe in God can be good American citizens (disagree)	45	53[a]	59	66	55
Protestant ministers should not be permitted to teach publicly things which are opposed to Catholic doctrine (disagree)	63	56[a]	60	—	59
Religious extremism items:					
A family should have as many children as possible and God will provide for them (disagree)	44	58[a]	59[a]	66	55
Love of neighbor is more important than avoiding meat on Friday (agree)	53	54	61[c]	—	66
The Catholic Church teaches that large families are more Christian than small families (disagree strongly)	45	45	39	—	46
The Catholic Church teaches that if there is ever a majority of Catholics in this country, Catholicism must become the official religion of the United States (disagree strongly)	64	65	55[c]	—	66
Permissiveness items:					
When parents are wrong they should be willing to admit it to their children (agree)	49	49	52	59	54
It is as important for a child to think for himself as to be obedient to his parents (agree strongly)	54	57	53	60	55
Rules should never be relaxed, because children will take advantage of it (disagree)	37	34	31	39	34
"Manichaean" items:					
Although Christ saved the spiritual world by his death and resurrection, the material world is under the control of the Devil (disagree strongly)	54	54	48	51	53
The world is basically a dangerous place where there is much evil and sin (disagree)	49	50	48	51	48
The Catholic Church teaches that a good Christian ought to think about the next life and not worry about fighting poverty and injustice in this life (disagree)	60	61	56	69	69
N	345	699	796	231	530

[a] Significantly different from "All Catholic." [b] Significantly different from "Some Catholic." [c] Significantly different from "All Catholic" and "Some Catholic."

not completely understand the different emphases to be found within the Church and may have generalized from the behavior of one immigrant group (Italians in New Haven, for example) to all Catholic groups. Undoubtedly there is a strong otherworldly strain within Catholic teaching, but there is also a strain of profound respect for the world and worldly effort. It is hardly surprising that this element in Catholic doctrine should receive considerable emphasis in the American environment. Even Max Weber, unlike some of his contemporary disciples, recognized that much of his "Protestant ethic" was to be found in the Roman Church before Martin Luther and John Calvin.

On the civil-liberties items there are some differences, three of which are significant though not very large, but astonishingly enough all the differences indicate that those who have had Catholic education are more tolerant of the freedom of atheists, of the right of Communist authors to have their books in libraries, and of the right of Protestant ministers to oppose Catholic teaching. It would be a mistake to make too much of these differences; the important point for our present purposes is not that the Catholic school Catholics are less intolerant but that they are not more intolerant.

There is every reason to think that much more emphasis is placed in Catholic schools on the evils of communism and atheism; hence we are permitted to wonder why these subjects do not arouse more intense feeling in the adults who had attended such schools. It is possible, of course, that the passage of years has dulled the impact of the school on attitudes toward atheism and communism. Or it is possible that the denunciations of these evils were taken with more than a few grains of salt as *pro forma* condemnations which were not of much importance. (After all, there were not many Communists or atheists around in the neighborhoods in which our respondents grew up.) But a third possibility must not be ruled out. It would be a mistake to assume that the Bill of Rights or the American Creed are ignored in Catholic schools; as a matter of fact, it is altogether possible that in schools that made an effort to prove that the children of immigrants could be more American than anyone else, the ideas of tolerance and freedom would be pushed with somewhat more

vigor than elsewhere. Though it is to be doubted that such principles were explicitly extended to cover communists and atheists,
it is not out of the question that the students were capable of
making the extension themselves. Whatever the cause, however,
Catholic school Catholics are no less tolerant than other Catholics—at least if their responses to our opinion items are to be
believed.

Our findings on the cluster of items used to measure religious
extremism are somewhat more ambiguous than those reported
for the previous two clusters. Those who did not go to Catholic
schools are significantly less likely to think they must have as
many children as possible and also significantly more likely to
think love of neighbor is more important than not eating meat
on Friday. On the other hand, those educated in Catholic schools
are less likely to think that a Catholic majority would mean the
establishment of Catholicism as the official religion of the country. The items in this cluster are quite diverse and ambiguity is
to be expected. About all we can conclude is that on some matters
the Catholic school Catholic seems more sophisticated than his
confreres and on other matters less sophisticated but that there
is no clear tendency in either direction.

Nonetheless, the difference on love of neighbor versus meat
on Friday is intriguing. Our colleague Michael Schiltz offers a
plausible explanation. In the traditional Catholic catechisms, eating meat on Friday is always considered a "mortal" sin (i.e., a
serious sin), while uncharitableness may be either "mortal" or
"venial" and hence is not nearly so serious a matter. Such legalism
may well obscure the obvious intent of the Gospels, but it will
not be the first time that structures have gotten in the way of
the Sermon on the Mount. However, such a finding is an instruc-
tive indication of the kinds of problems that are encountered
in any attempt to make religious values the object of formal
instruction; on some occasions at least, the legalist will triumph
over the prophet.

Finally, in the cluster of responses to questions about child-
rearing attitudes, we can find no evidence that the Catholic school
graduates were any more *reluctant* to admit to their children
that they were wrong, to argue that thinking for oneself is more

important than obedience, or to approve of relaxing rules. If more rigid emphases on obedience were stressed in their education, the passage of time and the general American consensus on how children ought to be reared has erased any differences between Catholic school Catholics and other Americans, whatever their faith or education.

Table 5.4 presents in summary indices the data discussed in this section. The hypotheses which suggested that Catholics who went to Catholic schools would be more intolerant, more rigid, more prejudiced, more "otherworldly," and more "extreme" were not supported by the evidence at hand. As we observed in the previous section, it may be possible to uncover other proof that Catholic schools are in fact divisive, but the ordinary survey research indicators that we have used do not get at such differences. If there actually are differences, it seems fair to suggest that they are not of the most obvious and clear-cut variety.

THE EFFECTS OF CONTROLS

We are now in roughly the same position as we were at the beginning of the last chapter. We have a finding which, if it can be sustained, is of substantial importance in any consideration of Catholic schools. However, in this instance, the finding is in

Table 5.4   Zero-Order and Net Partial Gamma Associations between Religious Education and Adult Social Attitudes and Behavior

Behavior Variable	Zero-Order	Net Partial—Control for:		
		Hometown Size	Educational Level	Age
Catholic friendship clique[a]	+.03	+.06	+.05	+.02
Community involvement index	+.02	+.02	+.02	+.03
Religious extremism index	−.03	−.01	−.01	−.03
Racism index	.00	−.07	−.02	−.01
Anti-Semitism index	−.04	−.02	−.01	−.02
Anti-Protestant index	−.05	−.05	−.05	−.05
Anti-civil-liberties index	−.11	−.10	−.09	−.11
"Manichaean" index	−.07	−.06	−.03	−.06
Permissiveness index	+.01	+.01	+.01	+.01
General knowledge index	+.12	+.10	+.05	+.11

[a] All three closest friends Catholic.

reality a non-finding. Neither behavioral nor attitudinal questions have uncovered any trace of a "divisive" consequence of Catholic education. Hence, when we begin to hold control variables constant, we are in effect trying to make differences appear which we could not uncover in previous sections. We know, for example, that those who went to Catholic schools were more likely to have grown up in large cities (gamma = .27), but cities are more sophisticated than small towns. Therefore the performance of those who went to Catholic schools on measures of social sophistication could very likely result from their having been concentrated in cities during their early years. If we were to compare Catholic and public school graduates from similar hometowns we might find that the former were indeed more intolerant, less ambitious, and more isolated. Catholic schools may quite possibly be divisive, but this divisiveness may be hidden in an overview because of the greater urbanity of those who went to Catholic schools.

Similarly, we are aware that Catholics who went to Catholic schools are, for reasons we will attempt to discover in the next chapter, more likely to stay in school longer (gamma = .10). It is well known from sociological research that there is a positive association between educational level and tolerance; thus to be certain that Catholic schools do not promote intolerance and divisiveness, we must compare Catholic school graduates with public school graduates, holding their educational level constant. If differences would then appear, we would be forced to say that the Catholic schools were divisive but that this divisiveness was canceled out by the peculiar fact that Catholics who went to Catholic schools had more education than those who did not; that is, the Catholic schools would have simultaneously generated divisiveness and destroyed it.

Finally, we must consider the possibility that differences in the other direction might be discovered. Perhaps Catholic schools do produce more enlightened Catholics than public schools, but, if so, this effect has occurred only in recent years and will be observable only among those who are still relatively young. The defenders of Catholic education could argue that the increased emphasis on social consciousness during the last two decades of Catholic education ought to lead to a negative correlation of Catholic school attendance with prejudice and intolerance. Therefore the three groups of Catholics must be compared holding their age constant.

As in the last chapter we will use net partial gammas to determine whether the control variables have any effect. We will then look in closer detail at the effect of education and age on the relationship between Catholic education and social attitudes, because the partial relationships offer some intriguing suggestions about changes in American Catholicism. The three control variables we are using do not modify our judgment about the absence of a relationship (Table 5.4).[4] In fact, only three net partials in the whole table change the zero-order relationship by more than .03. A control for educational level reduces the gamma association between Catholic education and general knowledge from .12 to .05 and the negative gamma association between Catholic education and score on the "Manichaean" index from −.07 to −.03. A control for hometown size creates a negative association between Catholic education and racism of .07, where previously there had been no association either positive or negative. Only very, very weak associations exist between Catholic schooling and social attitudes and behavior. Catholic primary and secondary schools apparently do not have a divisive influence, but neither do they train more tolerant adults.

A HINT OF CHANGE?

Even though the coefficients in Table 5.4 give no evidence that the age factor might have some influence on the relationship between Catholic education and social attitudes, we must consider the partial associations between Catholic education and social attitudes for each age group, if only because of the contention of some Catholic educators that recent changes in curricular emphasis might be producing a more enlightened graduate.

The relationships remain weak even among the twenty-year-olds, but there is some sign of a change (Table 5.5). Thus the religious extremism index changes from a zero order of −.03 to

---

[4] Controls were also used for all the variables considered in the last chapter; however, no modifications of the findings presented in this chapter were indicated.

The Education of Catholic Americans

a partial for those in their twenties of −.19. The relationship
of Catholic education with racism changes from .00 to −.06,
with opposition to civil liberties from −.11 to −.16, and with
"Manichaeanism" from −.07 to −.12. None of these changes
can be taken to indicate an overwhelming improvement, but they
do suggest that something interesting may be going on.

It is possible that the change might result from the somewhat
better education of the Catholic school Catholics in their twenties
compared with public school Catholics in the same age group,
but Tables 5.6, 5.7, and 5.8 suggest that a different phenomenon
is occurring: a combination of youth and education is apparently
producing more tolerance among Catholic school Catholics.
Among the better-educated respondents (high-school graduate or
more) the only strong decrease with age in the proportion scoring
high on the anti-Semitism index is found among those educated
exclusively in Catholic schools, but here the change is quite dras-

Table 5.5 Zero-Order, Partial, and Net Partial Gamma Associations
between Religious Education and Adult Social Attitudes and Behavior,
with a Control for Respondent's Age

Behavior Variable	Zero-Order	Partial (Respondent's Age)				Net Partial
		20	30	40	50	
Catholic friendship clique[a]	+.03	+.09	−.03	−.04	+.13	+.02
Community involvement index	+.02	+.09	.00	+.07	−.07	+.03
Religious extremism index	−.03	−.19	−.06	+.02	+.11	+.03
Racism index	.00	−.06	+.02	+.04	−.09	+.01
Anti-Semitism index	−.04	−.11	−.04	+.04	−.15	+.02
Anti-Protestant index	−.05	−.05	−.04	−.01	−.15	+.05
Anti-civil-liberties index	−.11	−.16	−.07	−.15	−.02	−.11
"Manichaean" index	−.07	−.12	−.06	−.06	−.03	−.06
Permissiveness index	+.01	−.09	+.01	.00	+.09	+.01
General knowledge index	+.12	+.22	+.13	+.09	+.01	+.11

	Case Bases			
Religious Education	Respondent's Age			
	20	30	40	50
All Catholic	60	118	95	68
Some Catholic	133	208	243	110
No Catholic	116	253	277	148

[a] All three closest friends Catholic.

tic. While approximately a third of those in their forties and fifties (35 and 29 per cent, respectively) score high on this measure, only 14 per cent of those in their twenties score high. Exactly the same phenomenon occurs on the racism index. The proportion scoring high on this index decreases among the "All Catholic" group from 35 per cent among the fifty-year-olds to 12 per cent among the twenty-year-olds, while declines of 3 and 2 per cent, respectively, occur in comparable age levels of the "Some Catholic" and "No Catholic" groups. On the other hand, with only one exception the "All Catholic" group scores lower on the anti-civil-liberties scale at all levels of age and education than do the other two groups. Thus, with regard to attitudes toward civil liberties, the Catholic schools have shown their im-

Table 5.6 Per Cent High on Anti-Semitism Index, by Educational Level and School Attendance

Age	Some High School or Less			High-School Graduate or More		
	All Catholic	Some Catholic	No Catholic	All Catholic	Some Catholic	No Catholic
20	44 (9)	49 (41)	55 (38)	14 (51)	38[a] (92)	37[a] (78)
30	60 (42)	51 (69)	46 (93)	27 (76)	39 (139)	43 (160)
40	77 (43)	54 (105)	50 (147)	35 (52)	42 (137)	40 (130)
50	56 (39)	55 (56)	66 (94)	29 (21)	39 (44)	42 (41)

[a] Significant difference.

Table 5.7 Per Cent High on Racism Index, by Educational Level and School Attendance

Age	Some High School or Less			High-School Graduate or More		
	All Catholic	Some Catholic	No Catholic	All Catholic	Some Catholic	No Catholic
20	14 (7)	31 (38)	21 (34)	12 (49)	22 (88)	24 (70)
30	32 (38)	29 (62)	22 (77)	25 (75)	28 (130)	24 (149)
40	50 (40)	36 (93)	33 (131)	24 (50)	28 (127)	28 (119)
50	14 (42)	25 (61)	39 (105)	35 (23)	25 (44)	26 (41)

pact no matter what the age and education of respondents, while in the matter of racial attitudes the effects seem to be limited to the young, but at all levels of education. Anti-Semitism scores stand between the other two patterns: among the better educated, those who had only Catholic education are more enlightened than those who did not, but the most enlightened, regardless of religious education, are those who are in their twenties.

It would be a mistake to make too much out of differences which are based on fifty-one cases (the number of twenty-year-olds who went exclusively to Catholic schools and who graduated from high school), especially when the only statistically significant difference is the difference in the anti-Semitism scores of the "All Catholic" group from the other two groups among the twenty-year-olds. Nevertheless, Tables 5.6–5.8 do raise the possibility that, with change in the social and economic status of the Catholic population and change in the emphases of Catholic education, Catholic schools may have an effect on the social attitudes of their students similar to the effect they have had on religious behavior—an effect which is statistically significant, though not overwhelming. It should be noted, however, that the association between Catholic education and anti-Semitism among the better-educated twenty-year-olds is quite powerful (Q = .57).

There are many possible explanations for the patterns observed in Tables 5.6–5.8. Catholic schools may have become more concerned about social tolerance in recent years; the Catholic colleges may have influenced some of the twenty-year-old high-school

Table 5.8 Per Cent High on Anti-Civil-Liberties Index, by Educational Level and School Attendance

Age	Some High School or Less			High-School Graduate or More		
	All Catholic	Some Catholic	No Catholic	All Catholic	Some Catholic	No Catholic
20	27 (8)	34 (38)	40 (33)	20 (49)	25 (84)	28 (71)
30	43 (39)	56 (62)	47 (83)	29 (67)	18 (131)	40 (147)
40	44 (39)	45 (94)	55 (127)	19 (47)	29 (121)	36 (116)
50	46 (41)	56 (57)	49 (92)	30 (20)	48 (42)	44 (34)

graduates; the mere fact that twenty-year-olds now have more education may have enabled them to internalize norms taught in high school and grammar school. But one is still struck by the rather sharp differences in racism and anti-Semitism among the twenty-year-olds. One wonders, for example, whether even in the last ten years there has been such strong emphasis on the evils of anti-Semitism in Catholic high schools that it has produced a significant and powerful association between Catholic education and a low score on the anti-Semitism index. Gerhard Lenski (in personal conversation) has suggested an additional explanation. Those who have had many years in Catholic schools may well be more effectively plugged into the Catholic "communication network"—especially if they are young. Hence they may have been more likely to "receive" communications coming from the Vatican Council about the evils of anti-Semitism. Their Catholic education may have disposed them to learn more quickly about the dramatic shift in emphasis on this subject that has occurred in very recent years. Similarly, a more strategic place on the communication network would enable these respondents to learn about the recent strong teachings of the American hierarchy on racial justice.

If such an explanation is valid, it would imply not only a more strategic place on the communication network as a result of Catholic education but also a greater willingness to accept such a change in emphasis in Catholic teaching. Presumably the more youthful respondents, partly because of their youth and partly because of the teachings they had already received during their school years, would be better disposed to adjust to change. If such an explanation has any merit, it would raise the interesting possibility that a value-oriented school might not only change attitudes but also create a predisposition for more change in later life.

If our mythical committee of policy-makers should have the patience to return to hear our opinion on the "divisiveness" issue, we would probably reply in the following fashion: the accusation that Catholic education is "divisive" is so widespread and so serious that Catholic educators must lean over backward if they are to avoid giving substance to the accusation. It is most unlikely that the accusation will be silenced until those who went to Catholic schools are notably more tolerant and more active in the problems of the larger community than those who did not go to Catholic schools. While our failure to find any concrete evidence of "divisive" consequences of Catholic education ought to be encouraging to Catholics, they would be quite mistaken if they thought our data would settle the issue.

Nor should the fact that Catholic school Catholics are no more intolerant than other Catholics be a cause for anything more than very moderate rejoicing. If the social teachings of the Church mean anything, the goal of Catholic education ought to be a graduate who is considerably less intolerant than other Catholics. That this goal has not been achieved may be historically understandable (though hardly excusable), but at the present time the rationalizations of the past are no longer very convincing. The signs of greater social enlightenment among the very young graduates of Catholic schools are reassuring but not powerful enough to be grounds for relaxation of effort.

With all these qualifications in mind, if we are still asked, "Have Catholics had to pay a high price for their schools in terms of isolation from the rest of American society?" we must reply that our data strongly suggest that they have not.

CONCLUSION

We are now able to essay answers to the four questions posed at the beginning of the chapter.

1. Are Catholic school Catholics more isolated from non-Catholics than are coreligionists who did not go to Catholic schools? They were indeed less likely to associate with non-Catholics when they were in school (though the effect of the school was rather marginal compared with the isolating effect of religion itself), but at present there is no trace of any divisive influence. Catholic school Catholics are just as likely to be interested in community affairs and to have non-Catholic visitors, friends, neighbors, and co-workers as are public school Catholics. As a matter of fact, Catholics who have had a "mixed" educational experience are more likely to have non-Catholic friends

and to be involved in community affairs than either of the other two groups—though the difference is minor.

2. Are Catholic school Catholics more rigid and intolerant than those who did not go to Catholic schools? The answer once again is negative. Catholic school Catholics are actually more tolerant with regard to civil liberties and are no more anti-Negro, anti-Semitic, or anti-Protestant. Neither are there any differences on attitudinal measures of "Manichaeanism," religious extremism, and permissiveness. While there is no evidence of divisive attitudes among the Catholic-educated, neither is there any evidence (except in the matter of civil liberties) of more social consciousness.

3. Are there social or demographic variables which might mask a divisive effect of Catholic schools? We could find no control variables which altered the findings we reported in answer to the previous questions. The sophistication of better education and urbanism in those who went to Catholic schools did not hide any socially harmful results of Catholic schooling.

4. Is there any evidence of greater social consciousness in the younger Catholics who went to Catholic schools? There were some signs that the younger and better-educated Catholic school Catholics had greater social consciousness and greater tolerance than Catholics of the same age and educational level who had not gone to Catholic schools. Thus there was a statistically significant relationship between Catholic education and a low score on the anti-Semitism measure for those who had at least graduated from high school and were still in their twenties. While the evidence that Catholic schooling had a positive social effect on the younger and better educated was not conclusive, it was nonetheless suggestive.

It may well be that, on the basis of the answers to these four questions, we cannot yet bring in a "not guilty" verdict to the charge that Catholic schools have a harmful influence on the social consensus of the land. But surely it would not be an exaggeration to render the ancient Scotch verdict of "not proven."

6

Occupational and Educational Achievement

We now turn to the question whether Catholic schools impede the economic and educational achievement of those who have attended them. There are several reasons for thinking that there might be such impediments. First of all, sociologists have long suspected that the "otherworldly" emphases of Roman Catholicism hamper devout Catholics in the rough-and-tumble life of the marketplace. Presumably those who went to Catholic schools are the most devout, the most dedicated to the "Catholic ethic" of concern about the other life. Second, if it is true that, upon arrival in the United States, Catholics begin to assimilate the values of the host culture, the ones to assimilate most rapidly would be those who would break out of the Catholic ghetto and attend public schools. Third, the alleged academic deficiencies of Catholic schools—overcrowding, poor teacher training, absence of the most modern methods—could be expected to handicap, in their later life, those who attended Catholic schools. Finally, the alleged anti-intellectualism of American Catholics (described by O'Dea [1958] and others) ought to have led those trained in Catholic schools to place little value in higher educational pursuits.[1]

On the other hand, it is quite possible that the underachievement of Catholics has been exaggerated. National sample data concerning the McClelland measure of the need for achievement (cf. Veroff *et al.,* 1962) show that Catholics score somewhat higher on achievement need than do Protestants. In addition Bressler

[1] For examples of the literature on the underachievement of Catholics, see Lenski (1961, esp. pp. 76–102), McClelland (1961), Mack *et al.* (1956), Mayer and Sharp (1962), Rosen (1959), Veroff *et al.* (1962).

and Westoff (1963, p. 233) could find no difference in socio-economic values between Catholic school Catholics and other Catholics and concluded by remarking that "the available evidence fails to sustain those who either hope or fear that a Catholic education magnifies religious differentials in the economic sector or in other secular areas of American life."

Furthermore, as we have pointed out earlier, there are enough elements in the Roman Catholic tradition to justify this worldly effort, and it would not be terribly surprising if these strains received considerable emphasis in the American milieu. Finally there is what one of us calls the "John Ireland factor" (after the turn-of-the-century Archbishop of St. Paul), which describes the attitude of Catholics who are so determined to become completely American that they actually outdo the more native Americans in their enthusiasm for the culture and goals of American society. If such attitudes are at work in Catholic schools, it is at least possible that the graduates of these schools would have been under pressure for achievement which would not be found in public schools. Success in the occupational world thus becomes proof not only that there is no conflict between the Catholic Church and the United States but that Catholics are actually better Americans than anyone else. This line of theorizing is usually greeted with a polite smile in secular sociological circles and loud laughter among Catholic sociologists. But then most sociologists are usually free from the necessity of spending long periods of time talking to well-to-do Catholics.

We will therefore ask three questions in this chapter. (1) Are Catholics who attended Catholic schools less successful in the occupational and educational worlds than other Catholics? (2) If there is no sign of lower achievement, can we find among the standard battery of control variables an explanation for an unanticipated high achievement of Catholic school Catholics? (3) Finally, if the ordinary control variables do not provide an explanation, is there another possibility which might shed some light on the achievement of those who went to Catholic schools?

We find, first of all, that not only do Catholic school Catholics not underachieve; they in fact overachieve. None of the ordinary social or demographic explanations can account for this rather slight but persistent association between Catholic education and achievement, but there is apparently a connection between achievement and the consistency of one's relationship to the religio-ethnic community during adolescence.

OCCUPATIONAL AND EDUCATIONAL ACHIEVEMENT

Catholics who had had all their education in Catholic schools are almost a point higher on the Duncan occupational-prestige index[2] than those who went entirely to public schools, and they are also somewhat more likely to go to college. In both instances the differences are statistically significant. It is interesting to note that the "All-Catholic" group has about the same achievement levels as American Protestants. For reasons that are still unclear, Catholic school Catholics and public school Protestants resemble each other in academic and occupational achievement more than either of them resembles public school Catholics.

Our initial findings (Table 6.1) appear to support the "John Ireland" hypothesis rather than the "Protestant Ethic" theory. Not only is there not a negative relationship between Catholic

[2] Occupational achievement is measured by the Duncan decile scale. A married woman is assigned the occupational prestige of her husband unless she herself is working, in which case she receives the score of her own occupation. Tables were also prepared in which women received their husband's prestige score, even if the woman had an occupation of her own. No important differences were observed between those tables and the ones presented in this chapter. It will be noted later in the chapter (cf. Table 6.2) that a control for sex does not change the findings reported; thus the phenomenon described in the chapter does not result from a large number of Catholic school women's "marrying up."

Table 6.1 Occupational and Educational Achievement of Catholics, by Educational Background

Achievement	Educational Background			
	All Catholic	Some Catholic	No Catholic	Protestant
Mean occupational prestige (Duncan decile scale)	5.0	4.6	4.1[a]	4.9
Per cent who attended college	26	21	18[a]	30

[a] Significantly different from "All Catholic."

education and achievement in occupation (as measured by the Duncan index) and between Catholic education and educational level (as measured by the proportion going to college), there is in fact a positive relationship between Catholic schooling and these two measures of success.

A finding such as this, which goes against almost all previous theorizing, obviously cannot be permitted to stand without further questioning. It is surely possible that Catholic school Catholics have been more successful because they have entered the race for social status with a head start. Their parents had better jobs and better education; they came from ethnic groups which have been in the country longer and are more accepted. They are farther away in generations from the peasant farms of Europe. They have had better education themselves. They represent an intellectual elite which was able to get into Catholic schools. Their greater achievement therefore might be explained not by the schools they went to but by these intervening background variables.

However, none of these explanations seems to work. The positive relationship between Catholic education and achievement is rather weak, of course, but as Table 6.2 shows, it is also quite persistent. A control for parental socio-economic status (SES), and a joint control for parental SES and the standard battery of potentially intervening variables, leaves the relationship between Catholic education and occupational achievement intact,

Table 6.2 Zero-Order and Partial Associations between Catholic Education and Occupational and Educational Achievement

Attribute	Occupation	Education
Zero-order	.13	.10
Partial—control for:		
Parents' SES	.10	.05
Parents' SES and father's education	.12	.08
Parents' SES and mother's education	.11	.04
Parents' SES and respondent's education	.09	–
Parents' SES and ethnicity	.09	.11
Parents' SES and generation	.10	.02
Parents' SES and hometown	.14	.06
Parents' SES and sex	.10	.08

although the net partial gamma associations for educational achievement are diminished by a control for parental SES. Before searching for a further explanation we will pause to examine in detail some of the partial associations on which Table 6.2 is based.

When a sociologist is faced with a situation in which one group of people is more successful occupationally or educationally than another, he almost automatically seeks an explanation that will take into account the social status of the families from which the more successful group comes. Thus we assume that Catholic education leads to greater achievement because those who come from Catholic schools have a higher social status to start out with, since their parents were better educated and had more prestigious occupations.[3] So if we compare Catholic school Catholics and public school Catholics from the same social background, we may find the positive association disappears or even becomes negative.

However, the relationship between Catholic education and achievement is quite weak at the lower levels of parental occupation and increases as parental occupation increases (see Table 6.3).

[3] It should be noted that the term "high," as applied to parental occupation status in this chapter, is a relative term; it refers to that half of the respondents' parents whose occupational prestige was between 3 and 10 on the Duncan decile scale. The lower half of the parental population was concentrated in the first two deciles.

Table 6.3 Associations between Catholic Education and Occupational and Educational Achievement, with Control for SES of Respondents' Parents

Parents' SES (Duncan Score)	Occupational Achievement	Educational Achievement	Educational Background		
			All Catholic (N)	Some Catholic (N)	No Catholic (N)
1	.06	.07	(67)	(124)	(144)
2	.11	.09	(83)	(187)	(275)
3	.05	.08	(32)	(64)	(58)
4	.07	.08	(39)	(87)	(85)
5	.20	.16	(39)	(73)	(53)
6	.19	.31	(30)	(59)	(64)
7	.14	.26	(22)	(40)	(31)
8–10	.27	.22	(13)	(32)	(29)

Thus the strongest relation between Catholic education and achievement is precisely among those Catholics who are most well-to-do. Apparently a "multiplier effect" such as that mentioned in Chapter 4 is at work here too. Catholic schools have relatively little effect on achievement until a "breaking point" is reached, but when that point is reached (apparently at a Duncan rating of 5) there is a dramatic increase in the strength of the relationship of Catholic education to occupational and educational achievement. If this phenomenon continues, it could lead to a rapid improvement of the social status of the children of Catholic school respondents who themselves are sent to Catholic schools, since the Catholic school respondents now have a mean score which is precisely at the "breaking point."

We are faced, therefore, with the question of why something we will call the x factor (which provides Catholic school Catholics with a greater opportunity for achievement) is more likely to operate among those who came from families which were themselves relatively prosperous. Such a question is difficult to answer until we know what the x factor is, but it seems at least plausible to suspect that, like most other correlates of achievement, it would have its strongest effect on precisely those people who, because of their background and training, are the most disposed to achieve. Thus achievement is more likely to occur among those from fairly well-to-do and better-educated families and also among those who are more intelligent. The x factor simply reinforces this tendency.

Thus far we have treated occupational achievement and educational achievement as distinct variables, but it is clear that they are closely related. The occupational achievement of those educated in Catholic schools quite possibly may be explained by their greater educational achievement; if we were to compare Catholics who went to Catholic schools and who graduated from high school with Catholics who went to public schools and graduated from high school, the association might vanish. However, Table 6.4 suggests that, at least among those from backgrounds of higher parental socio-economic status (SES), the reverse is the case; the association between Catholic schooling and occupational achievement is highest for precisely those respondents who have had the most education. Social-class variables seem to have a consistent multiplier effect on the association between Catholic education and achievement.

But could it be that Catholics who went to Catholic schools are simply more intelligent? Since Catholic schools are not required by law to admit every applicant, and since they can get rid of their "problem cases," their student body may be composed of young people who are more intelligent and who will certainly do better both educationally and occupationally. We do not have IQ scores to test this hypothesis, but our general knowledge index may provide a crude measure of general intelligence. If the superior performance of Catholic school Catholics were the result of superior intelligence, we would expect the differences in achievement to disappear for those who score high on the intelligence indicator. But Table 6.5 does not confirm this expectation. Among high-school graduates from upper-SES backgrounds, the association between Catholic schooling and achievement is strongest precisely in the group scoring high on the general knowledge measure. "Intelligence" apparently reinforces the effect of Catholic schools on achievement. As we suggested before, the x factor is most likely to operate precisely among those who are already predisposed for achievement.

We are still faced with the question of the admissions policy

Table 6.4 Associations between Catholic Education and Occupational Achievement, with Controls for Parents' SES and Educational Level of Respondent

Parents' SES (Duncan Score) and Education of Respondent	Association	Occupational Achievement		
		Educational Background		
		All Catholic (N)	Some Catholic (N)	No Catholic (N)
Low (1–2):				
Some high school or less	.09	(86)	(165)	(241)
High-school graduate or more	.08	(64)	(146)	(178)
High (3–10):				
Some high school or less	.05	(42)	(102)	(105)
High-school graduate or more	.13	(133)	(252)	(215)

of Catholic schools. Since these non-public schools can admit whomever they want and get rid of their problem cases by expulsion, there is still the possibility that there are dimensions of ability not tapped by our crude intelligence measure which might explain the relationship between Catholic education and achievement.

Several comments are in order. First of all, if the cause of higher achievement is the ability of Catholic schools to get rid of problem students, we would expect those in the "Some Catholic" category to be the lowest achievers, because it is precisely in this group that those expelled would, by definition, be found. But while persons in the "Some Catholic" group achieve less than those in the "All Catholic" group, they are nevertheless more successful than the "No Catholic" group—in which, once again by definition, there are no "expellees." Thus the expulsion theory would not be a total solution to the problem. Second, we would have to know how many students are expelled each year for academic or disciplinary reasons. It is frequently repeated in discussion of Catholic schools that it is easy for them to turn their "problems" over to the public schools, but we do not know

Table 6.5 Associations between Catholic Education and Occupational and Educational Achievement, with Controls for Parents' SES and Respondent's Score on General Knowledge Scale

Parents' SES (Duncan Score) and Respondent's Knowledge Score	Occupational Achievement	Educational Achievement	Educational Background		
			All Catholic (N)	Some Catholic (N)	No Catholic (N)
Low parental Duncan score (1–2):					
Low general knowledge score	−.09	−.05	(109)	(207)	(308)
High general knowledge score	+.02	+.12	(39)	(98)	(103)
High parental Duncan score (3–10):					
Low general knowledge score	+.06	+.01	(76)	(181)	(186)
High general knowledge score	+.16	+.16	(93)	(164)	(129)

how much of this actually occurs, and we know even less about how much of it occurred in the past. A spot check in one very large diocesan school system revealed less than twenty such transfers in the course of one year. Much more information should be collected and made available on this subject; we trust that our make-believe committee of policy-makers will take note. Third, we have no evidence that there was a high rejection rate of potential students during the years when our respondents were in school. The increased demand for classroom space in Catholic schools is apparently a post–World War II phenomenon. While there are unfortunately no conclusive data available, the strong impression of most observers is that in the years before 1940 there was actually a lack of demand and that the annual Sunday sermon about attending Catholic schools reflected such a condition. Virtually no case of rejection (or expulsion) could be found among the reasons given by our respondents for not attending Catholic schools, but this fact is hardly conclusive evidence for their absence, because a respondent might be reluctant to admit that he was rejected or expelled.

In summary, we cannot conclusively rule out an explanation of the achievement of Catholic school Catholics which attributes the finding to the selective admission and retention policies of these schools, but neither can we adduce any proof that such an explanation might be valid. We will therefore turn to other explanations, but the reader must keep in the back of his head the observation that more detailed data on the admission-retention question are very much in order.

CATHOLIC FRIENDSHIP PATTERNS AND UPWARD MOBILITY

At this point, it might be quite legitimate to end the chapter. The major question with which we are concerned has been answered: even with control variables held constant, there is no evidence that Catholic education interferes with occupational or educational achievement. But the positive association between Catholic education and success is intriguing: it is not quite large enough to be really impressive, yet it runs against almost everything that has been written previously on the subject of Catholicism and worldly achievement. Therefore, in the concluding two sections of this chapter we will digress temporarily from our main line of analysis to see what we can make of this unexpected phenomenon. Our digression may be more interesting to the sociologist than to the general reader, who is much more concerned about the obvious consequences of Catholic education. Both the sociologist and the general reader will recognize that our discourse in the next two sections is of quite a different sort from that in previous chapters. Until now we could speak with some precision and confidence; but for the rest of this chapter our speculations will be very hesitant and tenuous. Nevertheless we feel that these speculations are worth the effort, because they contain some very interesting implications for our understanding of the role played by religion and religious institutions in American society.

None of the standard explanations for superior achievement available to us has weakened the persistent association between Catholic education and achievement. On the contrary, we have noted a multiplier effect: Catholic school Catholics from higher educational and occupational backgrounds display more notable achievement than public school Catholics from such backgrounds, and the degree of difference in their achievement is greater than that of Catholics from less privileged backgrounds.

We are therefore forced to look for another explanation of this unexpected association. Rosenberg (1964) has reported that growing up in a neighborhood where one was a member of a religious minority seems to lead to a higher level of emotional anxiety in later life. It could be that something similar is happening in the present situation. Catholic school Catholics presumably are in environments in which they are not members of a minority group; the "emotional well-being" of which Rosenberg speaks may give them somewhat more self-confidence and enable them to be more successful than Catholics who find themselves in a less secure and friendly atmosphere. In Table 6.6 we seek to learn whether having mostly Catholic friends during adolescence may be the factor which promotes achievement. The table gives a hint that this may be the case. In three out of four comparisons, the gamma association between Catholic education and achievement either vanishes or becomes negative for Catholics half or less than half of whose friends at age seventeen were Catholic.[4] In the fourth case (the occupational achievement of those from low-SES families) the association is twice as strong for Catholics more than half of whose friends were Catholic. Furthermore, at the upper-SES level the magnitude of the differences in associations is quite impressive—differences of .26 for occupational achievement and .34 for educational achievement. Apparently the multiplier effect of Catholic education on achievement is enhanced not only by the respondent's social class but also by the degree of his integration into the Catholic community.

It is worth noting in passing that the friendship-pattern variable behaves exactly as our *x* factor might be expected to behave: it has the strongest impact among those already disposed to mobility by the social class of their parents. Thus among those from the less well-to-do families, the differences between the respondents who had Catholic friends and those who did not are .07 for occupation and .19 for education, while among those from more well-to-do families the differences are .26 and .34,

[4] The question was worded thus: "When you were seventeen or so, how many of your friends were Catholic—more than half, about half, less than half, or none?"

Table 6.6 Associations between Catholic Education and Occupational and Educational Achievement, with Controls for Parents' SES and Proportion of Catholic Friends at Age Seventeen

Parents' SES (Duncan Score) and Proportion of Catholic Friends	Occupa-tional Achieve-ment	Educa-tional Achieve-ment	Educational Background		
			All Catholic (N)	Some Catholic (N)	No Catholic (N)
Low parental Duncan score (1–2):					
More than half of friends Catholic	+.13	+.12	(104)	(167)	(203)
Half or less than half	+.06	−.07	(45)	(142)	(210)
High parental Duncan score (3–10):					
More than half of friends Catholic	+.26	+.29	(120)	(164)	(141)
Half or less than half	.00	−.05	(54)	(185)	(175)

respectively. If Catholic friendship at seventeen does indeed lead to greater achievement, it does so with special vigor for those who are predisposed for achievement by the success of their parents.

Is it possible that the religious community plays the role of a sort of superethnic group which provides the emotional support a young person needs in order to develop motivation for achievement in his early years? Such a question must be asked in a very tentative fashion, and nothing in our data enables us to answer it definitively. However, we do have an anomie scale,[5] which may tell us something about the respondent's "morale" at the present time and the relationship between this morale and the effect of Catholic education on his achievement.

The next step, therefore, is to ascertain whether a joint control for social class of parents, anomie, and Catholic friends at seventeen contributes to our understanding of the problem. It might be that going to Catholic schools and being in a Catholic friendship clique at seventeen promotes a state of "well-being" (reflected in later life by one's lack of "anomie") which in turn leads to achievement. While Table 6.7 does not settle the question, it at least encourages us to think that this line of reasoning may merit further investigation in other research. Among those respondents more than half of whose friends at age seventeen were Catholic (in either SES category) it is precisely those with low anomie scores who demonstrate the strongest relationship between Catholic education and achievement. Table 6.6 specified that the achievement relationship existed principally among those whose friends were Catholic at adolescence, and Table 6.7 further specifies that it is strongest among those whose friends were Catholic and who scored low on the anomie scale.

The weak link in the line of reasoning, of course, is the anomie

---

[5] Items from which the scale was composed are the following. (1) Which of these opinions come closer to the way you feel? Some people feel that *other persons can be counted on* for important help in an emergency. Other people feel that these days *one never knows whom he can count on.* (2) Some people say that *anyone who looks for meaning in life is just kidding himself.* Other people say that *you don't have to look too hard* to find meaning in life. What do you think? (3) Some people say that for the average man things are getting worse. Other people say things are getting better. Would you say things are getting *better* or *worse?* A low score on the anomie scale required that answers to all three questions be "non-anomic."

scale. It may simply measure the result of achievement, rather than indicate a precondition for it. Instead of being the intervening variable between friendship patterns and achievement, it may rather be a consequence of economic success. But if such were the case, one would think that a low anomie score would have been a sign of success for all Catholics and that the difference in achievement between those who went to Catholic schools and those who did not would diminish in Catholics with low anomie scores.

The speculation in the last several paragraphs is obviously based on data which were not designed to support such speculation and from which we can theorize only with great reservations. Nevertheless we have established with some confidence that the explanation of the greater achievement by Catholic school Catholics is related, in some complicated fashion, to their integration into the Catholic religio-ethnic community during their adolescence. Catholic school Catholics who were not part of Catholic

Table 6.7 Associations between Catholic Education and Occupational Achievement, with Controls for Parents' SES, Proportion of Catholic Friends at Age Seventeen, and Anomie

Parents' SES (Duncan Score), Proportion of Catholic Friends, and Anomie	Occupational Achievement	Educational Achievement	Educational Background		
			All Catholic (N)	Some Catholic (N)	No Catholic (N)
Low parental Duncan score:					
More than half of friends Catholic					
Low anomie score	+.19	+.24	(38)	(71)	(81)
High anomie score	+.06	+.14	(57)	(80)	(98)
Half or less than half					
Low anomie score	+.09	−.09	(24)	(60)	(94)
High anomie score	.00	−.15	(17)	(72)	(90)
High parental Duncan score:					
More than half of friends Catholic					
Low anomie score	+.26	+.32	(68)	(87)	(53)
High anomie score	+.16	+.15	(39)	(70)	(62)
Half or less than half					
Low anomie score	−.02	+.03	(32)	(88)	(91)
High anomie score	+.09	+.06	(19)	(79)	(66)

friendship groups were no more successful than anyone else. As Table 6.8 demonstrates, public school Catholics who were not involved in strongly Catholic friendship patterns have *higher* occupational achievement scores than Catholic school Catholics who were similarly uninvolved.

Thus it appears that for Catholics there were two ways of achievement—either one went to a Catholic high school and remained in a heavily Catholic friendship pattern, or one went to a public high school and was much less involved in friendships with fellow Catholics. Those who were caught in between—public education with Catholic friends or Catholic education with largely non-Catholic friends—were less successful than the two extreme groups. One either cut himself off from the support of the religio-ethnic ghetto and tried to make it on his own, or he remained completely in the ghetto and relied on the emotional support the ghetto had to offer. Compromises between either course decreased his chances of success.

The notion that those who are caught in cross-pressures are somewhat more marginal than others is not a new one in sociology, but neither is it one that can be looked on as conclusively proven (few sociological theorems are, as a matter of fact). However it is perhaps a bit revolutionary to suggest that a lack of consistency between schooling and religion of friends in adoles-

---

Table 6.8 Occupational Achievement of Catholics, by Parents' SES, Friendship Patterns at Age Seventeen, and High-School Attendance (Mean Duncan Score)

Parents' SES and Proportion of Catholic Friends	Respondent's Occupational Achievement	
	Catholic High School	Public High School
Low parental SES:		
More than half of friends Catholic	4.2 (104)	3.6 (370)
Half or less than half	4.0 (46)	4.2 (359)
High parental SES:		
More than half of friends Catholic	6.0 (120)	4.7[a] (55)
Half or less than half	4.7 (54)	5.1 (370)

[a] Significantly different from "Catholic High School."

cence may affect one's later performance in the occupational world. Conversely, it is also rather startling to suggest that a consistency between the religious orientation of one's school and the religion of his friends during adolescence will make for somewhat greater achievement in both educational level and occupational success. A great deal more would have to be known about the psychodynamics of adolescence before such suggestions could be anything more than very tentative. Indeed, the phenomena we are hypothesizing might have been limited to immigrant and post-immigrant generations and hence no longer be observable. With all these qualifications in mind, we still assert that, while the explanation developed in the past several paragraphs may well be far out, it is not inconceivable.

Finally, there is the intriguing possibility that the secret of the success of those who were in Catholic friendship cliques at age seventeen is that they remained within the Catholic ghetto and created their occupational success by serving the Catholic subculture. If this were true, one would expect that their co-workers today would be Catholic and that the greatest success would be precisely among those Catholics the majority of whose friends at seventeen were Catholic and the majority of whose co-workers are Catholic today. Unfortunately (as Table 6.9 shows) this hunch is not substantiated. While the gamma associations are higher for those whose friends at seventeen were Catholic, the addition of a control for proportion of Catholic co-workers

Table 6.9 Associations between Catholic Education and Occupational Mobility, with Controls for Catholic Friends at Seventeen and Catholic Co-workers Today

Proportion of Catholic Co-workers Today	Proportion of Catholic Friends Today		Educational Background		
	More than Half	Half or Less	All Catholic (N)	Some Catholic (N)	No Catholic (N)
More than half	+.28	+.15	(35)	(58)	(76)
Half	+.37	−.12	(33)	(58)	(67)
Less than half	+.31	+.08	(44)	(76)	(58)

today does not notably affect the relationship between Catholic education and occupational achievement for those who grew up as members of Catholic friendship cliques.[6]

THE COSTS OF ALTERNATIVE PATHS TO ACHIEVEMENT

For the last several pages we have indulged in theorizing about the dynamics of the relationship of Catholic education to economic and educational achievement. Although the explanation we have developed is presented with considerable reservations, we may perhaps be excused for suggesting one more highly speculative question: If there are two courses to be followed by Catholics in order to succeed in American society, what are the costs of each course to the Catholic religious group and to the larger society? First, if an individual chooses the path of "assimilation" (public education and fewer Catholic friends) is he likely to be less involved in religious behavior which is desirable from the Church's viewpoint? On the other hand, is he more likely to engage in behavior which is desirable from the viewpoint of American society? Second, if an individual chooses the path of achievement through integration into the religious ghetto (Catholic education and Catholic friends) is he more likely to be a better Catholic but a "poorer American?"

Table 6.10 attempts to answer these questions by comparing two extreme groups: *(a)* those who had all their education in Catholic schools and reported that more than half of their friends at seventeen were Catholic and *(b)* those who did not attend Catholic schools and reported that half or less than half of their friends at seventeen were Catholic. For the Church, there are clear gains from an individual's following the "ghetto path." Those in this group are significantly different on the sacramental index and in their attitudes on being involved in a mixed marriage, on marriage by a priest, and on sending their children to Catholic schools. The costs to society of this path do not seem large. While the "ghetto" group scores somewhat lower on the com-

---

[6] The gammas are all somewhat higher in Table 6.9 because we are now dealing not with the general population but only with those who are employed. It is interesting to note, however, that the relationship between Catholic education and achievement is even greater for the employed.

munity involvement index and somewhat higher on the religious extremism index, the differences are not significant. On the other hand, the ghetto group is significantly lower on the anti-civil-liberties index and somewhat (though not significantly) lower on the anti-Semitism index. There is, therefore, some reason to think that the "ghetto path" produces a Catholic who is more tolerant than the "assimilated" Catholic. Perhaps the emotional well-being provided by the ghetto makes for a more relaxed and tolerant attitude toward others.

It ought to be clear that the suggestions made in the last paragraph call into serious question the assumption that it is necessary, for the health of society, that the religious and religio-ethnic ghettos be eliminated. Such subcultures do not apparently impede achievement; on the contrary, they may even promote it. Nor do they lead to attitudes and behavior which interfere with societal consensus. In the long run, they may even promote greater tolerance, because they give a person a relatively secure social location and a fairly clear answer to the difficult question, "Who am I?" Far from being divisive, it is possible that Catholic schools have accelerated the acculturation of the Catholic immigrant

Table 6.10 Catholic School Catholics in Catholic Friendship Cliques at Age Seventeen Compared with Public School Catholics Not Then in Such Cliques (Per Cent)

Attribute	Catholic School, More than Half of Friends Catholic	Public School, Half or Less than Half of Friends Catholic
High on sacramental index	80	16[a]
Married by priest	93	85[a]
Children attend Catholic schools	85	51[a]
High on community involvement index	32	40
Mixed marriage	7	19[a]
High on religious extremism index	29	20
High on racism index	25	25
High on anti-Semitism index	39	45
High on anti-civil-liberties index	29	43[a]
High on "Manichaean" index	20	16
N	216	363

[a] Significant difference.

groups—partly because they have consciously promoted "Americanization" in a fashion that public schools could not have done without stirring up trouble from the ethnic communities. Finally, Catholic school Catholics may have higher achievement scores because their teachers felt that occupational and educational achievement of the graduates of these schools was essential if Catholicism were to survive and grow in American society.[7] But proof for such a hypothesis is far from the purpose of this volume.

Let us reconvene our committee of policy-makers to force upon them our opinions about Catholic schooling and achievement. Should they ask us (under whatever duress we can apply to produce the question) whether there were anything in the quality of Catholic education which would interfere with the later occupational performance of Catholic school graduates or whether the emphasis on the spiritual to the exclusion of the secular impeded the acculturation of the children and grandchildren of immigrants, we would reply as follows. Our data do not allow us to generalize directly about the quality of Catholic education either in the past or the present. (As a matter of fact, we are rather suspicious about any association between what goes on in a school and occupational achievement; it seems to us that factors making for achievement are largely beyond the influence of the school.) But whatever the quality of education in the Catholic schools of the past half-century may have been, it surely did not impede the success of its students. For reasons which are not altogether clear, but which may have something to do with the emotional security that Catholic schools provided for young Catholics, those who went to Catholic schools are somewhat more successful both in their educational level and in their occupational achievements. We would urge our committee to continue to press for more and more academic improvement in Catholic schools but not to do so on the grounds that Catholic schools in the past have ill prepared their students for the world. Whether intentionally or unintentionally, the schools seem to have been quite successful in this area. Some Catholic critics may

---

[7] One of the authors (Greeley, 1963, pp. 94–98) discovered a similar mechanism at work in Catholic colleges, where pressure was apparently brought to bear on the most promising students to continue their education in graduate school.

be tempted to argue that the schools have in fact been too successful in developing positive attitudes toward worldly success—they would like to see Catholics a little bit less "worldly" than others. Whatever may be said about the theological assumptions of such an argument—and our impression is that they would be quite unfashionable among contemporary Catholic theologians—it is not relevant to our discussion of whether Catholic schools impede worldly success.

The initial purpose of this chapter was to learn whether Catholic education would lead to lower levels of educational and occupational achievement. Exactly the contrary finding emerged: Catholics who went to Catholic schools were more successful than Catholics who did not. Even though the association was rather weak, it stubbornly persisted in the face of a battery of controls. In fact, the association became stronger for Catholics who came from families of higher social class; it also became stronger for those respondents who had themselves had more education and made higher scores on the general knowledge index.

Taking a new analytical tack, we discovered that the association appeared specifically to occur principally among respondents who were part of heavily Catholic friendship groups when they were seventeen years old. We then specified even further that it happened among respondents whose friends were Catholic and who scored low on a measure of anomie. We very tentatively suggested that integration into the Catholic community by schooling and friendship provided the "emotional well-being" necessary for achievement. It then developed that there were groups of Catholics which were more successful than their coreligionists—those who went to Catholic schools and had mostly Catholic friends and those who went to public schools and had fewer Catholic friends. We hypothesized that there might be two paths to achievement—the way of the ghetto and the way of assimilation—and that, while the former had clear-cut advantages for the Church, it did not, as far as we could determine, involve any serious disadvantages for the larger society. In the matter of attitudes toward civil liberties, the way of the ghetto seems to have advantages for the larger society as well.

The concluding speculations were based on rather thin data and should not obscure the major finding of the chapter: Catholic education does not correlate negatively with achievement.

7

Grammar School versus High School versus College

We have answered the first five of our "key questions": there is an association between Catholic education and adult religious behavior; the relationship with associational activity, however, is very minimal; Catholic schools do not seem to isolate Catholics from other Americans, to develop intolerance, or to impede social and economic success. We must now turn to the fascinating question of the relative effectiveness of the various levels of Catholic education. Granted that Catholic schools do have an effect on adult religious behavior, is the most notable effect at the elementary school, the high-school, or the college level?

In Chapter 1 we commented on the theoretical implications of such a question. At issue is not only what kinds of socialization occur at what educational levels but also which kinds of socialization are most appropriate to produce the desired adult behavior. The defenders of the elementary school apparently argue that the "formation" of young minds is crucial; the proponents of high-school religious education contend that survival through the adolescent crisis is most important; while the supporters of Catholic colleges maintain that the development of an adult ideology is most likely to lead to the appropriate religious behavior after the end of formal education. It is quite possible, of course, that each school of thought has in mind somewhat different forms of adult behavior as the most desirable.

It is also possible that none of the three educational levels is superior to the others in leading to adult religious behavior but that a combination of them is much more effective than any one by itself. If this is true, it would mean that for religious education to be really effective it must occur at all educational levels.

The question, then, has theoretical moment both in understanding religious socialization and in exploring value socialization in general, but it also has immense practical implications. Is it possible for Roman Catholicism (or indeed any institution that is interested in value oriented education) to concentrate its efforts at one educational level and obtain results which would eliminate the necessity of maintaining schools at other levels?

The question is easier to ask than to answer—at least with the relatively limited number of cases available to us in this analysis. Ideally we should compare those who went only to Catholic grammar schools, those who went only to Catholic high schools, and those who went only to Catholic colleges. But for the comparisons to be of value we would have to consider only respondents who went to college, and the number of college-attenders who received Catholic education at only one level is far too small to make this strategy possible. Thus we must proceed in a somewhat less direct fashion.

First of all we will compare the effect of Catholic grammar schools with that of Catholic high schools—a task for which we have more respondents than if we were also to consider college education. Then we will turn to a comparison of those who went to Catholic colleges with those who went to non-Catholic colleges. In this latter comparison we will find the most striking differences we have yet observed, and we will have to spend some time trying to understand the implications of these differences. Finally we will inquire whether these impressive differences are the result merely of Catholic college education or of a cumulation of years in Catholic schools.

Thus the following questions must be answered in the present chapter.

1. Is the previously recorded difference in religious behavior between the "All Catholic" and the "Some Catholic" groups the result of the fact that the former went to Catholic high schools, or does it seem to come from a cumulation of years in Catholic schools?

2. Do those who went to college show any religious or social differences that are related to Catholic higher education?
3. Can these relationships between Catholic higher education and adult behavior and attitudes be diminished or eliminated by the use of control variables?
4. Are the differences at the college level the result of the college experience alone, or do they represent the effect of a cumulation of years in Catholic schools?

One answer can be given to all four questions: much to the dismay of school administrators who might be searching for *the* level, notable religious and social correlates of value-oriented education seem to result from a cumulation of religious education, rather than from the influence of any particular level. But when a cumulation of exclusively Catholic education, from first grade to college, exists, the relationships of religious devotion and social tolerance with Catholic education are quite strong.

GRAMMAR SCHOOL VERSUS HIGH SCHOOL

Since in most instances the differences between those who have had totally Catholic education and those who have had some Catholic education is the difference between attending Catholic secondary schools and attending public ones, there are two possible explanations for the phenomenon that those with exclusively Catholic education do notably better on measures of religious behavior than those with some Catholic education. The first explanation is that the high school has the major part in value formation. If this conclusion were true, it would suggest that elementary education has a much less decisive role in the school system's development of desired values. The second possible explanation is that, as we said above, the higher performance of those who had all their education in Catholic schools is not so much the result of the effect of the secondary school as the result of a cumulation of time in Catholic schools. In this explanation the important fact is not that someone had attended a Catholic high school but rather that he had spent twelve years in Catholic schools, during which time values might be more deeply instilled than in a mere eight years and also might be better protected from the countervalues of the non-Catholic world.

To determine which of these explanations is the more convincing, we need to compare three groups of people—those who had all their elementary and secondary education in Catholic schools, those who went to Catholic elementary schools and public secondary schools, and those who went to public elementary schools and Catholic secondary schools. If there were no differences between those who attended only Catholic high schools and those who attended both Catholic grammar schools and Catholic high schools, we could conclude that the principal institution of value formation was in fact the Catholic high school. If, on the other hand, there were only slight differences in the scores of those who went to Catholic elementary and public secondary schools and those who went to public elementary and Catholic secondary schools, while the third group—those who attended only Catholic schools—was considerably different from the first two, we could conclude that the effect reported in previous chapters was brought about not so much by the secondary school as by a cumulation of years in a Catholic educational system.

Unfortunately for the purposes of finding an answer to this question, only a small proportion of our sample went to public elementary schools and then changed to Catholic secondary schools. Because of the very small case base (sixty-four respondents), the findings reported in this section must be viewed with considerable reservation and looked upon as suggestive material which could pave the way for further research.

The data presented in Table 7.1 are not sufficient to enable us to make a conclusive choice between the alternative explanations discussed in the previous paragraphs; however, the data indicate fairly strongly that the major differences are cumulative, rather than being the result of Catholic secondary education. Thus, for example, while those who went only to Catholic high schools do score somewhat higher on the sacramental index than those who attended only Catholic elementary schools, persons who had all their education in Catholic schools score significantly higher than both of the other groups. Exactly the same phenomenon may be observed in the responses recorded on the Church-as-teacher in-

The Education of Catholic Americans

Table 7.1 Per Cent of Respondents Scoring High on Religious and Social Behavior Indices, by Level of Catholic Education

Index	Catholic Elementary and Secondary	Catholic Elementary, Public Secondary	Public Elementary, Catholic Secondary	All Public
Sacramental index	63	47[a]	52[a]	41
Church-as-teacher index	53	38[a]	47	35
Doctrinal orthodoxy index	40	32	38	23
Ethical orthodoxy index	41	39	34	32
Religious knowledge index	47	32[a]	34[a]	24
Community involvement index	40	47	46	46
Racism index	21	27	21	25
Anti-Semitism index	30	28	40	40
Anti-civil-liberties index	26	28	21	37
"Manichaean" index	24	33	24	26
Religious extremism index	17	15	15	19
N	245	149	64	558

[a] Significantly different from "Catholic Elementary and Secondary."

dex. On the other hand, while the differences are relatively small, it seems that the Catholic high school is the more decisive influence in the formation of doctrinal attitudes, and the Catholic grammar school plays the more important role in the formation of general ethical attitudes, as well as attitudes on sexual mores. Finally, it appears that a cumulation of grammar school and high school is the most influential in the development of religious knowledge. Thus in three areas—participation in the sacraments, acceptance of the Church as a teacher, and religious knowledge— the fact of having attended Catholic schools for twelve years is most important in affecting religious behavior. In ethical attitudes the grammar school seems to be more important, and in doctrinal orthodoxy the high school appears to be of decisive importance. It is worth noting, however, that the magnitude of the differences is great enough to be convincing only in the three areas in which cumulation of Catholic education seems to be the important variable. In the other areas, differences generally are so small that they cause us to be quite reserved in drawing conclusions.

Despite the fact that the cumulation of years in Catholic schools is apparently more important than Catholic secondary education in explaining the superior performance of the "All Catholic" group in religious behavior, the second half of Table 7.1 gives us some reason to think that social and cultural attitudes are more likely to be influenced by Catholic high schools. Although none of the differences is great enough to generate much confidence, it still appears that the scores on the racism index, the anti-civil-liberties index, and the "Manichaean" index are associated with having attended a Catholic high school. A high score on the community involvement index seems to be related to mixed education of any sort; those who attended Catholic grammar school and public high school or public grammar school and Catholic high school both scored somewhat higher on this measure than those who spent all their years in Catholic schools. For reasons that are not by any means obvious, a low score on the anti-Semitism scale is associated with having gone to Catholic grammar schools. Finally, there does not seem to be any relationship between one's score on the "extremist" measures and the kind of educational background he has had.

With the exception of the sacramental index, none of the percentage differences reported in this section is large enough to make an absolutely convincing case. Much further research is necessary before it can be said with any confidence whether one level of education is more influential than another. However, on the basis of the admittedly thin evidence available to us in this section, we might suggest as a hypothesis for further research that, as far as religious values are concerned, neither grammar school nor high school is as important as attending both grammar school and high school in a value-oriented system. Second, we might hazard the suggestion that the liberalizing of social attitudes, if it occurs at all in a religiously oriented school, is more likely to occur at the secondary level than at the elementary level. If this latter suggestion proved to have any merit, we might project a little further and say that social attitudes will be liberalized even more in a college atmosphere than in a high-school atmosphere. Thus we would hypothesize that, if we compare Catholics who went to Catholic colleges with Catholics who went to other colleges, there will be even greater differences in measures of political and social liberalism. It is to this question, among others, that we turn in the following section.

We still must face the question of why the cumulation of time in religiously oriented schools is more effective in leading to appropriate adult religious behavior than any single level of schooling. The simplest answer of course—and sociologists do not necessarily reject simple answers, especially when there aren't any others—is that the more input there is, the more impressive will be the output. Those who have had both grammar school and high school in the Catholic system have simply spent more time in Catholic schools and therefore will have been exposed to more religious influence (or indoctrination, if one wishes to be unpleasant). It is also quite possible that those who have argued in the *either*-elementary-*or*-secondary debate have overlooked the fact that both educational levels complement and reinforce each other. Perhaps a Catholic high school is more effective in guiding a young person through the adolescent religious and moral crisis if the grammar school has prepared the way for the high school's influence. And quite possibly the religious norms internalized during childhood will have more influence on adult behavior if they mature through adolescence as the personality matures and become something more than the pious beliefs of a little child. In the absence of formal religious socialization at both levels, the effectiveness of the process may be somewhat truncated.

COLLEGE AND *THE COMMONWEAL*

Thus far in our study we have been concerned with primary and secondary education. The reasons for this focus were dictated by the nature of the sample of respondents with which we were dealing. Since only a relatively small proportion of the American population has attended college, a national sample contains a rather small proportion of college graduates. Thus we do not have a sufficient number of collegians to provide case bases necessary for detailed analysis. Nevertheless, whether a value-oriented college, by itself or in association with a previous value-oriented education, does produce a different kind of person from that produced by a non-value-oriented college is a question of sufficient importance for us to explore it tentatively, even with a rather small number of respondents.

In this and following sections we will investigate the impact of the Catholic college, both on the general sample of American Catholics about whom we have been reporting, and on the random sample of Catholics who might be considered the liberal elite by virtue of their subscribing to *The Commonweal*.

The *Commonweal* sample was gathered essentially to see whether the members of the liberal elite had a view of the functions of Catholic education that was notably different from that of the general population of American Catholics. We will discuss this subject at greater length in Chapter 9, but it is still interesting now to ask whether Catholic colleges, if they have an effect on the general sample of college graduates who are Catholic, also have an effect even within the liberal elite who read *The Commonweal*.

Religious Behavior

We have been accustomed in earlier chapters to dealing with percentage differences which generally could be described as moderate—neither impressively large nor insignificant. We are thus rather unprepared for the magnitude of the differences found in Table 7.2. It should be remembered that in this table there is a built-in control for level of education, since all the respondents under consideration have attended college. The differences are quite striking. On all but one of our religious behavior indices, the respondent in the general sample who attended a Catholic college was significantly more likely to have high scores than was the respondent who did not attend a Catholic college. In some instances the differences are quite large: the respondent who attended a Catholic college is twice as likely to score high on the sacramental index; the difference on the doctrinal ortho-doxy index is thirty percentage points; on the religious knowledge index, thirty-nine percentage points. Finally, the graduate of a Catholic college is almost three times more likely to attend Mass more than once a week than the Catholic who did not attend a Catholic college. Even in the *Commonweal* sample, the dif-ferences are notable: eighteen percentage points on the Church-as-teacher index, twenty-five percentage points on the doctrinal orthodoxy index, fourteen percentage points on the religious knowledge index. More than one-third of the *Commonweal* Catho-lics who went to Catholic colleges go to Mass more than once a week. (The clergy and religious who are *Commonweal* readers have been excluded from the tables in this chapter; it is edifying to know that all forty-four of the clergy and religious in the sample report that they go to Mass every day.) It is also worth noting that the *Commonweal* Catholic, who has often been ac-cused of being somewhat rebellious against Church authority, is more likely than the Catholic in the general population to score high on the index which indicates willingness to accept the authority of the Church as a teacher. One might say almost face-tiously that, far from being anticlerical, it appears that the *Com-monweal* reader is a clericalist.

How can we explain these quite striking differences in religious behavior between persons who went to Catholic colleges and those who did not—especially since the differences at lower educational levels are not nearly so impressive? One possible explanation is that persons who go to Catholic colleges are predisposed to relatively high levels of religious behavior, or they would not choose to go to Catholic colleges in the first place. We can control for the predisposition that might arise from family religiousness, but we have no way of taking into account the religious concerns of the respondent himself in late adolescence which might have led him to make a commitment to the whole of Catholicism, including Catholic higher education. Such a commitment might well be the cause of Catholic college attendance, rather than the effect of it.

Against this explanation two phenomena might be cited. First of all, as we will note in the next section, those who went to Catholic colleges also have a much higher level of social enlightenment than do those who did not. It would be hard to link this set of attitudes to religious predispositions that would lead to choosing a Catholic college. If such social attitudes are apparently the consequence of going to a Catholic college, it is plausible to

Table 7.2 Religious Behavior of College Graduates, by Kind of College Attended for General Sample and for *Commonweal* Sample (Per Cent in Each Category)

Religious Behavior	College Attendance			
	General Sample		*Commonweal* Sample	
	Catholic	Non-Catholic	Catholic	Non-Catholic
High on sacramental index	49	24	76	70
High on Church-as-teacher index	44	34	44	26[a]
High on ethical orthodoxy index	44	33[a]	53	48
High on doctrinal orthodoxy index	56	26[a]	58	33[a]
High on religious knowledge index	65	26[a]	93	79[a]
Children in Catholic schools	73	69	95	84[a]
Mass more often than weekly	20	7[a]	36	16[a]
N	117	250	296	160

[a] Significantly different from "Catholic."

suspect that equally strong differences in religious behavior might also be linked to the college experience itself, rather than to predispositions.

Second, as we shall also note later in this chapter, the higher levels of religious practice seem to be limited to those who have gone to Catholic primary and secondary schools before going to Catholic colleges. Thus the mere choice of a Catholic college does not seem to be predisposition enough; what is required is the choice of a Catholic college after having gone to Catholic schools at lower levels. It seems reasonable to argue that we are observing a cumulation phenomenon resembling that which occurs at the secondary level, when the choice of the school one would attend was much less likely to be made by the student. By analogy we could argue that the cumulation of religious education is more likely to be the cause of higher levels of religious behavior than the predispositions which choosing Catholic college imply.

However, the matter is by no means certain: more research would be required before it could be argued conclusively that the observed higher level of religious behavior can be linked to experience in Catholic colleges. But there does seem to be reason to suspect that the college itself did play an important role in the process, probably by providing firmer ideological underpinning for the religious practices and attitudes which were internalized in earlier years.

Social and Cultural Attitudes

We suggested in the first section of this chapter that if it were true that Catholic high schools begin a liberalizing of their students' social attitudes, we could expect Catholic colleges to continue it. Table 7.3 confirms this suggestion. Those in the general-population sample who attended Catholic colleges have significantly lower scores on the indices for anti-Semitism, anti-civil-liberties attitudes, "Manichaeanism," and religious extremism. As in Table 7.2, one is impressed not merely by the significance of the difference but also by the magnitude of the differences—fifteen percentage points on anti-Semitism, thirteen percentage points on the anti-civil-liberties index, eighteen percentage points on the "Manichaean" index, and eleven percentage points on the religious extremism index. It appears that Catholic colleges are producing a graduate who is not only more devout but also more socially enlightened than the Catholic who has attended a non-Catholic college.

It should also be noted that in social-cultural attitudes there is no difference in the *Commonweal* sample between the respondent who went to a Catholic college and the one who did not, largely because all *Commonweal* readers scored uniformly low on measures of prejudice and cultural narrowness. The most obvious explanation for the greater social and cultural enlightenment seen in the general sample of Catholics who went to Catholic colleges is that at the college level they have learned a more sophisticated and mature approach to their religion. While there can be no doubt that the quality of theological and ethical instruction in Catholic colleges has not always been impressive, it remains possible that some kind of college-level religious instruction is much better than none and that even relatively poor theology classes will still produce a graduate who has a more adequate understanding of the social teachings and intellectual orientations of his religion. If the rather striking findings of

Table 7.3   Social and Cultural Attitudes and Behavior of College Graduates, by Kind of College Attended for General Sample and for *Commonweal* Sample (Per Cent in Each Category)

Social and Cultural Attitudes	College Attendance			
	General Sample		*Commonweal* Sample	
	Catholic	Non-Catholic	Catholic	Non-Catholic
High on community involvement index	43	41	59	63
High on racism index	19	20	5	5
High on anti-Semitism index	16	31[a]	7	6
High on anti-civil-liberties index	31	44[a]	7	6
High on "Manichaean" index	13	31[a]	9	9
High on religious-extremism index	18	29[a]	0	0
High on anti-Protestant index	39	42	33	33
N	117	250	296	160

[a] Significantly different from "Catholic."

Table 7.3 can be accomplished by a college theology which no one claims to have found very satisfactory, it seems reasonable to expect that the drastic modernization of theological curricula which is alleged to be currently taking place may produce even more dramatic results.

Changes in the Church

One of the demands that could be made on a higher educational institution with value orientations is that it produce a graduate who is sophisticated enough to have an intelligent understanding of the changes going on within his Church. Such a demand could be made on Catholic colleges with particular rigor now, when the Roman Catholic Church is going through a modernization process instituted by Pope John at the Second Vatican Council.

In Table 7.4 we inspect the responses of the general sample of those who attended college, as well as the *Commonweal* sample, to an open-ended question about what changes they would like to see in the Catholic Church.

Table 7.4 Changes in the Church Advocated by College Graduates, by Kind of College Attended for General Sample and for *Commonweal* Sample (Per Cent in Each Category)

| Changes in Church | College Attendance | | | |
| | General Sample | | Commonweal Sample | |
	Catholic	Non-Catholic	Catholic	Non-Catholic
Birth control	25	27	12	21
Liturgy	39	45	53	45
Confession	8	15	0	0
Marriage	11	21	3	4
Fasting	10	3	2	3
Position on social questions	2	3	11	17
Ecumenism	20	9[a]	22	22
Decentralization	6	5	11	10
More lay participation	22	7[a]	46	37
N	117	250	296	160

[a] Significantly different from "Catholic."

Two findings should be noted in this table. First, the only significant differences between those who went to Catholic colleges and those who did not are the result of a response indicating a need for more ecumenicity and more lay participation in the Catholic Church. In both instances, those who went to Catholic colleges are significantly more likely to demand a change. If the ecumenical movement and the development of the lay apostolate can be considered two of the most critical needs of present-day Catholicism, then we might well conclude, from the very substantial differences in the responses of those who went to Catholic colleges and those who did not, that the Catholic college has been able to produce a graduate who is more sensitive to the developments within Catholicism.

The second finding worth noting, for whatever implication it might have, is that the question of the changing attitude on birth control seems to be more important to the college-educated Catholic in the general sample than to the Catholic in the *Commonweal* sample. The change in the liturgy seems to be much more important to the *Commonweal* reader, no matter what his educational background, than the modification of the Church's position on birth control. Even though our data were collected in the spring of 1964, before discussion of the possible change in the Church's stand on birth control was so widespread, it is still somewhat surprising to find it of so little concern to the readers of a progressive journal such as *The Commonweal*.

It remains problematic whether very many of the respondents who attended Catholic colleges heard much about either the layman's role in the Church or the ecumenical movement during their college years. What seems more likely is that their college years may have linked them more closely to a communication network from which they could hear about these ideas in later life. Magazines like *America, The Commonweal,* and *The Critic,* book clubs, and the more liberal Catholic action organizations (such as the Christian Family Movement) would have been encountered in college, and these in turn would keep the graduate of a Catholic college better informed about the changes taking place in his Church. Almost three-fourths of the readers of *The Commonweal,* for example, went to Catholic colleges.

To summarize the last three sections of this chapter, we have noted very strong associations between attendance at Catholic colleges and religious devotion, enlightened social and cultural attitudes, and awareness of the changes in the Catholic Church. Most of the differences between those who attended Catholic colleges and those who did not were significant, and a good many of them were quite substantial. In the *Commonweal* sample, the difference between the Catholics who attended Catholic colleges and the ones who did not were limited to measures of religious behavior, although we did observe that the *Commonweal* readers showed no evidence of an anticlerical trend or a strong desire for a change in the Church's birth-control teaching and also that more than one-third of the readers of this journal attended Mass more than once a week.

The Effect of Controls

The rather surprising findings reported thus far cannot be permitted to stand without more careful scrutiny. While the differences are not great enough that they will disappear under social, religious, and demographic controls, we must nonetheless attempt such controls to see if we can find at least a partial explanation. Since we know that a person's social status influences both his social and his religious behavior, and since we also know that the religiousness of his background affects his own religious behavior, it is possible that a control for both these variables will reduce the magnitude of the relationship between attending a Catholic college and the religious concern and social enlightenment reported earlier in the chapter.

In Table 7.5 we present first the zero-order associations between the religious and social measures we have been using and then the net partial coefficients with controls for religiousness of parents and respondent's sex and socio-economic status.

It is not particularly surprising that neither sex nor social status leads to much of a change in the pattern of associations, since we have come to expect this phenomenon from previous chapters. But we have not been prepared for the relatively small effect on the strength of the gamma association produced by a control for parental religiousness. Apparently, religiousness of family background ceases to be an important intervening influence when young people get to the college level. The religious atmosphere of the home may predispose children for the effect of primary and secondary value-oriented education, but it does not notably add to the effectiveness of value-oriented higher education. As we shall discover in the next section, most of the variation we are now concerned with takes place among those who attended Catholic colleges and who also attended Catholic primary and secondary schools. Primary and secondary religious education may play the same predisposing role for the influence of higher education that family background plays for the influence of primary and secondary education.

We are inclined to suggest again that the principal contribution which the college makes is to assist in forming a relatively coherent system of religious ideology which enables the student to integrate the norms and habits learned at an earlier level into a more conscious and reflective world view. We are not arguing that all those who attend Catholic colleges emerge with such a world view or even that very many have a highly developed ideology. But we do suspect that the notable differences recorded in this chapter of those who went to Church-oriented colleges from those who did not can be attributed to their having a somewhat more mature and consistent religious outlook.

Table 7.5   Zero-Order and Partial Gamma Associations of Catholic College Attendance with Religious and Social Behavior and Attitudes

Variable	Zero-Order	Net Partials		
		Religiousness	Sex	SES
Sacramental index	+.49	+.44	+.48	+.50
Doctrinal orthodoxy index	+.43	+.39	+.44	+.43
Religious knowledge index	+.57	+.53	+.58	+.58
Ethical orthodoxy index	+.20	+.18	+.19	+.22
Attendance of Mass	+.70	+.69	+.68	+.67
Organizational membership	+.18	+.17	+.19	+.18
Religious extremism index	−.31	−.32	−.32	−.27
Racism index	−.13	−.09	−.15	−.10
Anti-Semitism index	−.24	−.18	−.25	−.25
Anti-civil-liberties index	−.23	−.22	−.26	−.21
"Manichaean" index	−.36	−.38	−.39	−.35

While an inspection of the tables of partial associations on which Table 7.5 is based revealed no interesting patterns when SES or religiousness were controlled, the partial associations with sex controlled (Table 7.6) are quite intriguing. On every item under consideration, the association between attendance of a Catholic college and adult behavior is much stronger for men than for women; in some instances the gamma for males is twice as large as that for females. Furthermore, the associations for men between Catholic education and attitudes of tolerance are higher than we have found anywhere else in the study: $-.23$ with racism, $-.29$ with anti-Semitism, and $-.37$ with the anti-civil-liberties index. Catholic colleges are not totally lacking in effect on women, but, rather surprisingly, they have their most powerful effect on Catholic men. Four of the gammas for males are .5 or higher.

To say that Catholic colleges have a stronger effect on men than on women does not mean that the men who went to Catholic colleges are more religious or more tolerant than the women who did so. On the contrary, it could mean that the men who went to non-Catholic colleges are considerably less religious and less tolerant than the women who attended non-Catholic col-

Table 7.6 Partial Gamma Associations between Catholic College Education and Religious and Social Behavior and Attitudes, with Sex Controlled

Variable	Partial (Catholic College Education)	
	Male	Female
Sacramental index	+.61	+.29
Doctrinal orthodoxy index	+.50	+.35
Religious knowledge index	+.64	+.46
Ethical orthodoxy index	+.21	+.16
Attendance of Mass	+.80	+.41
Religious extremism index	−.38	−.21
Racism index	−.23	.01
Anti-Semitism index	−.29	−.19
Anti-civil-liberties index	−.37	−.12
"Manichaean" index	−.39	−.33
N	60; 151	57; 104

leges. Table 7.7 (in which we turn from gamma coefficients to percentages) confirms this suspicion. There is little difference between the men and women educated in Catholic colleges in their scores on the various indicators, but the men who went to non-Catholic schools are less tolerant and considerably less religious than the women who attended these colleges. Thus Catholic colleges apparently bring men's levels of piety and tolerance up to the level of their female confreres. Perhaps the reason is that the more rational exposition of religion which is assumed to take place on the college level provides a basis for more intense religious behavior which men can accept. It is also possible that association with the clergy who are on the faculties at these schools has some influence on the male collegian's recognizing that masculinity and religion can be reconciled.

College or Cumulation

We must now face the same question we raised in the first section of this chapter, and with even fewer cases on which to base an answer: Is the very considerable effect of Catholic higher education that we have been describing the result of the college alone, or is it rather the result of a cumulation of Catholic education that now produces some kind of "multiplier effect"?

While any answer based on Table 7.8 must necessarily be very cautious because of the small number of cases, the direction of

Table 7.7   Selected Religious and Social Attitudes and Behavior, by College Attendance and Sex (Per Cent in Each Category)

Religious and Social Attitudes and Behavior	College Attendance			
	Male		Female	
	Catholic	Non-Catholic	Catholic	Non-Catholic
High on sacramental index	48	16	50	36
High on doctrinal orthodoxy index	55	21	51	38
High on racism index	19	24	18	16
High on anti-Semitism index	18	34	15	28
Mass more often than weekly	20	4	19	10
N	60	151	57	104

the answer is clear: those whose Catholic education was limited to college are, with the exception of their scores on the doctrinal orthodoxy index, much more like those who attended Catholic grammar schools and high schools but non-Catholic colleges than they are like those who had all their education in Catholic schools. Indeed, their Mass attendance and religious knowledge scores are lower than the scores of those who had Catholic primary and secondary education. Thus it appears from Table 7.8 that the quite powerful effect that Catholic colleges have on religious behavior and religious and social attitudes occurs in cumulation with the effects of Catholic grammar school and high school and not independent of them.

If we accept as plausible the implications of Table 7.8, then we seem to have another "breaking point" effect. We know from Chapter 4 that educational level is an extremely powerful predictor of religious behavior; when it is combined with cumulative religious education, it apparently produces quite a dramatic strengthening of the relationship between religious education and adult behavior, both religious and social. Thus the question raised in Chapter 5 about the strengthening of the relationship between religious education and adult behavior in those who went to college is answered. It is not merely going to college which accounts for the more powerful relationship. It is not even going to a Catholic college. It is, rather, *going to a Catholic college after going to Catholic grammar schools and high schools.*

From this point of view, if one wished to prevent American Catholicism from developing through its school system an elite which is both religious and socially rather impressive, one would do all in one's power to eliminate Catholic higher education. For while the colleges clearly do not do the job by themselves, they can, in cooperation with the earlier levels of schooling, produce results which by almost any standards are quite substantial. Indeed, should anyone desire to restrict the effectiveness of Catholic education severely, he could simply do all in his power to see that the current government aid to higher education does not help Catholic colleges. This would apparently deprive the Roman Church in America of many of its most fervent future leaders; it would also quite possibly deprive the larger society

Table 7.8 Religious and Social Behavior and Attitudes of College Graduates, by Level of Catholic Education (Per Cent in Each Category)

| Religious and Social Behavior and Attitudes | All Catholic | Level of Catholic Education | | | All Non-Catholic |
		Primary and Secondary Catholic	Primary Catholic	Catholic College Only	
High on sacramental index	59	42	23	43	26
High on ethical orthodoxy index	50	30	18	38	33
High on doctrinal orthodoxy index	66	33	31	52	26
High on religious knowledge index	74	32	23	30	11
Children in Catholic schools	100	71	85	46	68
Sunday Mass	98	82	85	65	64
High on community involvement index	37	39	38	43	36
High on honesty index	35	38	39	35	44
High on religious extremism index	17	29	36	30	33
High on racism index	19	19	29	23	22
High on anti-Semitism index	16	30	40	33	32
High on anti-civil-liberties index	12	10	17	20	32
High on "Manichaean" index	14	28	28	18	37
N	46	33	26	23	167

of a group of citizens who would be more socially conscious and enlightened than many. .

Perhaps the most basic question with which we began our research was whether a system of religiously oriented education produces an adult who is notably different from the adult of the same religious persuasion who did not go to religious schools. Until now the answer has been that the difference is quite moderate, except among the very young and the very well educated. But now we are able to say that substantial differences do appear when we consider individuals who have had their primary, secondary, and higher education in religious schools. Not only is this group much more religious than coreligionists who have not had such comprehensive training; it is also more socially enlightened and no less involved in community concerns. A denomination considering a religious school system must face the fact that, if it really wishes such a system to be effective, it will be forced to ponder the possibility of its having to be comprehensive —from first grade to college.

Individual Opinion Items

Throughout this report we have been relying on indices composed of various opinion items, because the index deals with patterns of responses rather than individual responses, which might be less accurate reflections of a respondent's opinions and values. In Table 7.9, however, we select certain opinion items out of the scales we have been using to illustrate more concretely the magnitude of the Catholic college's effect. Those who went to Catholic colleges are almost one-half as likely to approve of divorce, twelve percentage points less likely to object to a Negro as a next-door neighbor, eighteen percentage points less likely to think Jews have too much power, fifteen percentage points less likely to think they must have large families, twenty-three percentage points more likely to defend the right of a Protestant minister to teach things which are opposed to Catholic doctrine, and twenty percentage points more likely to reject an "otherworldly" approach to poverty and injustice. All these differences are statistically significant, as is the difference between Catholics from Catholic colleges and college-educated Protestants

Table 7.9 Comparisons of Opinions of Those Who Attended Catholic Colleges with Those Who Attended Other Colleges

Questionnaire Item (Response in Parentheses)	Catholics		Q^a	Protestants (Per Cent)
	Catholic College (Per Cent)	Other College (Per Cent)		
Two people who are in love do not do anything wrong when they marry, even though one of them is divorced (agree)	24	50[b]	−.52	87[c]
White people have a right to live in an all-white neighborhood, and Negroes should respect this right (disagree strongly)	40	30	−.22	31
I would strongly disapprove if a Negro family moved next door to me (disagree strongly)	36	24[b]	−.28	27
Jews have too much power in the United States (disagree strongly)	75	57[b]	−.43	54[b]
People who don't believe in God have as much right to freedom of speech as anyone else (agree)	74	63	+.25	—
The Catholic Church teaches that large families are more Christian than small families (agree)	12	27[b]	−.46	—
Protestant ministers should not be permitted to teach things publicly which are opposed to Catholic doctrine (disagree strongly)	67	44[b]	−.44	—
The Catholic Church teaches that a good Christian ought to think about the next life and not worry about fighting against poverty and injustice in this life (agree)	10	31[b]	−.60	—
Husband and wife may have sexual intercourse for pleasure alone (agree)	47	37	+.20	—
N	117	250	296	159

[a] Yule's Q is a form of the gamma association that is applied to two dichotomous variables.
[b] Significantly different from those who went to Catholic colleges.
[c] Significantly different from both Catholic groups.

on the anti-Semitic item. In addition there are differences in the same direction, though just short of statistical significance, on integrated neighborhoods, freedom of speech for atheists, and the legitimacy of sexual intercourse for pleasure alone.

There can be no doubt that the data presented in Table 7.9 run counter to many assumptions about the nature of Catholicism in general and American Catholicism in particular—assumptions which are as popular within the Church of Rome as outside it. Three explanations might be advanced for the discrepancy between assumptions and findings: (1) there is a "folk Catholicism" which corresponds to the assumptions but is quite different from the "elite Catholicism" of those who went to Catholic colleges; (2) there has been a dramatic change in the last decade and a half in the teachings of the Catholic Church and the attitudes of its better-educated members; and (3) the assumptions were based on information which, to put the matter charitably, was both inaccurate and inadequate.

It might be well to note that Catholic colleges are often, in discussion, compared with the best schools in the country (in certain Catholic circles, Harvard is apparently the only model to be considered). To those who are accustomed to such comparisons, the findings reported in this section will seem quite incredible. They may be tempted to dismiss the respondents as liars; Catholic colleges simply can't be that good. But they should not overlook the fact that, for most of our respondents, the choice was not between a Catholic college and Harvard but between a Catholic college and a public one which might have been no more excellent academically or enlightened intellectually than its Catholic counterpart. For all these weaknesses, Catholic colleges were apparently able to communicate enough of the social teachings of the Church and enough of a sophistication about the Catholic faith to make an important difference in the attitudes and behavior of their graduates. To put it somewhat differently, for the Catholic who went to a Catholic college (as opposed to a Catholic who went to another college), there was something more of a possibility that his religion would develop beyond the adolescent level.

CONCLUSION

Should we be able to call our committee of policy-makers back into session, and if they were then to ask us which level of Catholic education could be most profitably abandoned, we would be forced to tell them that there did not seem to be much of a future in such an approach: no particular level is more effective than any other. Catholic colleges do indeed have a very powerful impact both on religious behavior and social attitudes, but only among those who have already gone to Catholic primary and secondary schools. While the case base on which this advice rests is somewhat thin, we are not persuaded that further research will notably affect our findings. For formal religious education to be effective it must apparently be comprehensive, and it will have its most impressive impact on those who have gone to religious colleges.

In addition, we have found in this chapter, for the first time in the report, consistently strong and statistically significant relationships between Catholic education and adult behavior—relationships which are especially strong for males. Catholics who went to Catholic colleges not only were notably more religious, they were also notably more tolerant than Catholics who did not do so. The strength of these relationships was not diminished by controls for sex, SES, and parental religiousness in one's background. The failure of religiousness to have the impact we had come to expect led us to speculate that many different factors can produce the "breaking point" effect: what parental religiousness did for children who went to Catholic primary and elementary schools, primary and secondary religious education in its turn apparently does for young people who go to religious colleges. This hunch was confirmed by the fact that the powerful relationships between religious education and adult religious behavior for those who went to Catholic colleges existed only in persons who had also gone to Catholic grammar and high schools. The "multiplier effect" discovered in this chapter apparently results from a combination of educational level and cumulative religious education. It appears, therefore, that the most desirable effects of religious education (from the point of view of the sponsoring church) are produced principally in those who have had a *comprehensive* religious education. From the point of view of the larger society the effects are also desirable, since the product of the comprehensive religious educational experience is also significantly more tolerant and no less involved in community activities.

8

Catholic Education Today

In the previous chapters we have focused on the "past" of Catholic education. Our adult respondents had attended Catholic schools sometime between five and fifty years ago, and whatever influence Catholic schools finally had on them was of the sort which survives the erosion of time and aging. Two questions remain unanswered, however. First, have the schools changed in very recent years so that they produce different consequences? Second, how much of the influence of a religiously oriented school does in fact erode with the passage of time?

Both of these questions can, in theory, be answered by a study of persons currently in Catholic schools, but the answers will be a bit complicated. If we can detect no differences between the relationship of religious education with religious behavior among those still in school and the relationship among adults, we could conclude that there is little erosion of impact and also little change in the consequences of religious education. But if there is a stronger relationship among adolescents than there is among adults, we cannot be sure that the differences come from an increased effectiveness of the schools or from an erosion of influence among adults. We are inclined to think that both factors are at work, although the more powerful of the two would seem to be the very rapid erosion of the impact of religious education among those who do not come from very religious families.

In this chapter, therefore, we turn away from our adult respondents and focus rather on their adolescent children.[1] We shall

[1] Interviewers left 1,156 questionnaires in respondents' homes, 990 of which were returned. Of this sum, 256 respondents were not used in our analysis,

consider the religious behavior and social attitudes of Catholic teen-agers, their scholastic behavior and social activities, and finally their opinions on the "atmosphere" of their school.[2] In some instances we must ask whether social controls will eliminate the differences between those who go to Catholic schools and those who do not. We will also inquire whether religious instruction classes are a functional alternative to Catholic schools.

We continue, in this chapter, to use the "All Catholic," "Some Catholic," and "No Catholic" categories. Those in the first group are presently in Catholic high schools; those in the second group are not in Catholic high schools at present but were in Catholic schools (primary in most instances) at one time; the third group has never attended Catholic schools.

RELIGIOUS BEHAVIOR AND SOCIAL AND RELIGIOUS ATTITUDES

That Catholic education makes a very considerable difference in religious behavior and attitudes, at least in the short run, is quite clear from Table 8.1. Those currently in Catholic high schools are almost twice as likely to score high on the sacramental index[3] as are those who are not now in Catholic schools but were in the past, and they are four times as likely to score high as those who have never attended Catholic schools. Even greater differ-

---

because they were either still in grammar school or had left high school (through graduation or dropping out).

[2] All the adolescents in this analysis were in high school at the time of the survey.

[3] The indices used for the adolescent group were slightly different. The honesty index was composed of the following items, whose morality the adolescents were asked to evaluate: (1) helping another student during an exam; (2) handing in a school report which is not your own. The items on the sexual mores index were (1) heavy necking on a date; (2) sexual relations with the person you intend to marry. The items on the anti-civil-liberties index were (1) only people who believe in God can be good American citizens; (2) books written by Communists should not be permitted in public libraries. The items on the religious extremism index were (1) love of neighbor is more important than eating meat on Friday; (2) a family should have as many children as possible and God will provide for them. The items on the anti-Semitism index were (1) Jewish businessmen are about as honest as other businessmen; (2) (judge the morality of) having as little to do with Jews as possible. The items on the racism index were (1) Negroes would be satisfied if it were not for a few people who stir up trouble; (2) (judge the morality of) joining a protest against a Negro who moved into an all-white neighborhood.

ences occur on the religious knowledge index, while the associations on the doctrinal orthodoxy and sexual mores indices are quite strong (in excess of .3), if not so dramatic. Even the honesty index correlates with religious education for the adolescents. In virtually all instances the differences are statistically significant.

On the other hand, there are no significant relationships between religious education and scores on the tolerance indices, and the relationships in the religious extremism and anti-civil-liberties indices go in a direction opposite to that of the adult sample, with those in Catholic schools being a bit less tolerant on these measures but somewhat more tolerant in their racial attitudes. While the differences are small and not significant, and the different directions can be explained by the use of slightly different scales, we are still faced with determining why there is no indica-

Table 8.1 Per Cent of Adolescents[a] Scoring High on Indices of Religious Behavior and Social Attitudes, by School Attendance, and Gamma Associations

Indices	School Attendance				Gamma Associ- ation[b]
	All Catholic	Some Catholic	No Catholic	Protestant	
Sacramental index	80	47[c]	20[d]		+.44
Honesty index	71	54[c]	52[c]	65	+.20
Sexual mores index	52	39	28[c]	21[d]	+.31
Doctrinal orthodoxy index	75	57[c]	41[d]		+.38
Religious knowledge index	61	20[c]	2[d]		+.67
Anti-civil-liberties index	25	17	19		+.13
Religious extremism index	32	20	22		+.07
Anti-Semitism index	32	24	32	31	.00
Racism index	12	15	22	24	−.10
More than half of friends Catholic	80	37[c]	28[c]	52[e]	
N	147	192	211	183	

[a] All adolescents are in high school.
[b] Among Catholics.
[c] Significantly different from "All Catholic."
[d] Significantly different from "All Catholic" and "Some Catholic."
[e] More than half of friends Protestant.

tion of the more tolerant and "liberal" attitudes reported in previous chapters. Perhaps it is necessary for young people to get into college before their attitudes begin to change significantly.

There are two explanations for the very strong associations between Catholic education and religious behavior observed in our teen-age respondents in comparison with the more moderate associations of the adults. It could be that Catholic schools have become more effective in developing religious values in recent years, or it could be that, once he is out of the school environment, a young person's religious activity is considerably less likely to be influenced by the atmosphere of the school. If the latter explanation is correct, the associations in Table 8.1 are very temporary. If there has been a change in the effectiveness of religious training, it has been very recent, and if erosion does take place, it takes place very quickly, because no trace of these powerful relationships was found among respondents in their twenties in our adult sample.[4]

Finally, those in Catholic schools are very much more likely to report that more than one-half of their friends are Catholic than are the other groups of respondents. In Chapter 5 we noted this phenomenon in the previous generation, but the differences were not as great. Several explanations might be adduced. Adult Catholics may not remember their friendship patterns in adolescence accurately, and hence the differences among the three groups in the older generation may have been greater than they were reported to be. Second, the high proportion of Catholic friends for Catholics attending public schools a generation ago might have resulted from ethnic loyalties and from the concentration of Catholic ethnic groups in certain communities, making for public schools in which most of the students were Catholic. Third, non-Catholics may have become less reluctant to have Catholics as close friends, and vice versa. The important question is whether the present friendship patterns of those in Catholic schools will make them any less likely to have non-Catholic friends in adult life. If the experience of the previous generation is any indication, they will have as many non-Catholic friends as those who went to public schools will have, but the changes in

---

[4] See Table A–3.2 in Appendix 3.

American society in the last quarter of a century are such that we must await the test of time to be certain.

Are the very substantial associations in Table 8.1 the result of social-class difference or of religious differences in the families from which the teen-agers come?[5] Table 8.2 seems to indicate that SES has no effect whatever on the associations. The net partial gammas with a control for SES are almost exactly the same as the zero-order associations. The question of parental religiousness is more complex. The associations of religious education with three of the variables (sexual mores, doctrinal orthodoxy, and religious knowledge) are diminished by a control for parental religiousness, but as the partial associations in Table 8.3 reveal, a control for religiousness of parents seems to produce a phenomenon in the adolescent sample the opposite of that which it produced in the adult sample. Those who came from very religious families are *less* likely to be influenced by Catholic education than those who came from less religious families. Those with at least one parent who takes Communion weekly have (with the exception of the honesty index) lower gamma associations than the other three groups.

It might be that in more recent years Catholic high schools have found means of developing values in those from the less religious families which were previously unavailable. Or it may be that the impact of the Catholic school on the young persons

[5] The relationship between Catholic school attendance and sex was .02, so no control for sex was used in this analysis.

Table 8.2 Zero-Order and Net Partial Gamma Associations between Catholic School Attendance and Religious Behavior for Adolescents, with Parents' Religiousness and SES Controlled

Indices	Zero-Order	Net Partials—Control For:	
		Parents' Religiousness	Parents' SES
Sacramental index	.44	.41	.44
Honesty index	.20	.25	.21
Sexual mores index	.31	.21	.31
Doctrinal orthodoxy index	.38	.30	.40
Religious knowledge index	.67	.57	.65

The Education of Catholic Americans

from less religious backgrounds is transient and will erode shortly after they leave the school. Thus the difference in associations found in the adult sample from those found in the adolescent sample may result from the fact that adolescents from less religious families are superficially influenced by Catholic high schools, but this influence quickly wanes. Those from religious families are also influenced, but because of the reinforcement received in the family milieu, this influence persists. It is interesting that the association between Catholic education and sacramental practice for those with highly religious backgrounds is .34 in the adult sample and .35 in the adolescent sample.

It would therefore seem that religiously oriented schools may have notable effects on those from less religious family backgrounds but that these effects will not last in the long run; as a matter of fact, they apparently do not last into the twenties.

At the risk of introducing a scriptural allusion in the strangest of places (i.e., a sociological analysis), we might observe that the seed will grow only if it falls on good ground, while that which falls on rocky ground will spring up quickly but wither away under the summer heat. To put the matter less graphically, unless

Table 8.3   Zero-Order, Partial, and Net Partial Gamma Coefficients between Religious Education and Behavior for Adolescents, with Parental Religiousness Controlled

Indices	Zero-Order	Partials (Parental Religiousness Controlled)				Net Partial
		High	Higher Middle	Lower Middle	Low	
Sacramental index	.44	.35	.44	.48	.45	.41
Honesty index	.20	.27	.18	.23	.03	.25
Sexual mores index	.31	.12	.25	.48	.23	.21
Doctrinal orthodoxy index	.38	.19	.42	.12	.46	.30
Religious knowledge index	.67	.53	.53	.82	.78	.57
N, all Catholic		73	27	17	11	
N, some Catholic		50	42	30	38	
N, no Catholic		34	30	27	81	

the work of the school is reinforced by other institutions of socialization, its effectiveness is very likely to be minimal in the long run, no matter how spectacular it may be in the short run. Americans have a strong and pious faith in the power of education to work wonders. If there are, for example, many problems of highway safety, the solution to those problems is sought in courses in school. If there are people who are Catholics in name but not in practice, the solution is to educate them in Catholicism. If the Catholic schools are only reaching some of these people, then perhaps the schools ought to be closed so that the resources of the Church could be spread more widely in order that all might receive some religious instruction. Such a faith in the power of religious education may be edifying, but it is also naïve. Leaving aside the question whether there might be a substantial minority who do not want religious education, a more important question remains: whether there may not be a considerable number who are going to be quite unaffected in the long run by religious education, because there is nothing in their lives outside the school which reinforces what they learn in school. Presumably a careful reading of the Gospel stories would persuade Catholics that the founder of Christianity was not altogether successful in His educational efforts when there was no predisposition to listen to Him. Nevertheless, it seems that a fair number of both the critics and defenders of Catholic schools expect formal education to accomplish what the Master could not.

In other words, if religious schools can have a long-term impact on those who are predisposed to acquire religious values, then this in itself is quite an accomplishment. For the schools to change the lives of those who are not so predisposed would be little short of miraculous. It might be argued that the Church (or, for that matter, any educator) must therefore dedicate its efforts to creating predispositions. Such a contention is undeniable, but it should be clear that the inertia of family and ethnic group traditions, of folklore and myth, of indifference and fear, of greed and ignorance is not cleared away with ease or in a brief period of time. To put the matter more bluntly, there is little reason to think that anyone knows how to create predispositions for learning. Indeed, the strong association between social class and religious behavior leads one to the pessimistic (from the religious viewpoint) conclusion that the rise in per capita national income may well have much more to do with the increase in Church attendance than all the efforts of religious educators.

RELIGIOUS INSTRUCTION CLASSES

In addition to its school system, the Roman Catholic Church maintains, with varying degrees of interest and commitment, religious instruction classes for those not attending Catholic schools—usually under the auspices of the Confraternity of Christian Doctrine (CCD). In recent years considerable emphasis has been put on CCD programs in some localities, and certain writers have suggested that CCD classes may well be a functional alternative to Catholic schools which would produce the same level of religious behavior while avoiding what they consider the negative effects of a separate school system.

We asked our adolescent respondents who were not in Catholic schools whether they were presently attending any kind of religious instruction class. A little less than one-third of those not in Catholic schools were in such classes, but it does not appear (from Table 8.4) that the classes were having much impact on their religious attitudes and behavior. The young people in the

Table 8.4 Per Cent Scoring High on Religious and Behavioral Indices, for Adolescents in Catholic or Public Secondary Schools or in CCD Religious Instruction Classes, and Gamma Associations between Kinds of Instruction

Indices	Catholic Secondary Schooling	Public Secondary Schooling	CCD Classes	Gamma Associations	
				Catholic vs. Public	Catholic vs. CCD
Sacramental index	80	34	47	.77	.64
Honesty index	71	53	49	.37	.44
Sexual mores index	52	34	38	.36	.28
Doctrinal orthodoxy index	75	49	59	.51	.35
Religious knowledge index	61	11	17	.85	.77
N	153	403	175		

CCD programs are much more like those in public schools with no religious instruction than they are like those in Catholic schools. At their present level of success, not only are CCD classes not a functional alternative to Catholic schools, they do not seem to accomplish very much at all.

This finding should not be particularly shocking. At this point we have become fully aware of how difficult it is to modify religious attitudes even in a comprehensive system of formal education. It would be practically unthinkable that a one-night-a-week session of religious instruction could do nearly as well. The romance of certain liberal Catholic writers with CCD is probably more the result of their own ideological (and personal) objections to Catholic schools than any solid proof of accomplishment by the CCD programs. That CCD might have more effect if there were considerable reinforcement of its work at home is probably true. But as we have seen already, only one-fourth of the Catholics in the United States came from families that provided reinforcement forceful enough to make the consequences of a comprehensive religious education impressive.

Two points should be noted. We are, as in all sociological analysis, dealing with averages. There may very well be CCD programs in the country which are elaborate and very effective, but if so, they are apparently not extensive enough to show up in a national sample. Second, for a long time CCD programs were considered something of an unwelcome stepsister to Catholic schools; it may be that the recent revival of enthusiasm for religious instruction classes may produce an effect in years to come that is much more impressive than the one currently observed.

THE SCHOOL ENVIRONMENT

In Chapter 6 we discovered that Catholic education showed relatively small but persistent associations with educational and occupational achievement, but we were unable to explain whether this was a result of the school experience itself or the motivation which a student brought to the school from his family experiences. The adolescent sample gives us a chance to inquire whether any trace of greater scholastic endeavor can be found among teenagers in Catholic schools today. The answer provided by Table 8.5

The Education of Catholic Americans

is unequivocal—those in Catholic high schools are significantly more likely to plan to go to college, to spend two or more hours a day on homework, and (if they are males) to want to be remembered as "A" students. They are also significantly less likely to report that they are sometimes unprepared for class or that they cheat in their schoolwork. In some instances they are also significantly different from public school Protestants, and in all but one item (cheating) they score higher than public school Protestants on measures of academic effort.

Furthermore (Table 8.6), those in Catholic high schools are significantly more likely to spend five or more nights at home, significantly less likely than the "Some Catholic" group to date once a week or more, and significantly less likely than the "Some Catholic" and Protestant groups to be "going steady." Despite the contention of some authors that Catholicism promotes "famil-

Table 8.5 Scholastic Behavior and Attitudes of Adolescents, by School Attendance (Per Cent), and Gamma Associations

Scholastic Behavior and Attitudes	School Attendance				Gamma Association[a]
	All Catholic	Some Catholic	No Catholic	Protestant	
Plan to go to college	70	55[b]	60	61	+.11
Spend two or more hours a day on homework	57	29[b]	29[b]	29[b]	+.35
Boys who want to be remembered as "A" student	50	32[b]	37[b]	43	+.14
Girls who want to be remembered as "A" student	44	47	47	44	−.05
Report that they are often or sometimes unprepared for class	41	54[b]	53[b]	53[b]	−.14
Report that they have cheated "more than once or twice"	35	28	29	36	−.06

[a] Among Catholics.
[b] Significantly different from "All Catholic."

ial" values which interfere with achievement, Catholic schools seem to do the exact opposite.

Finally (Table 8.7), in their judgments of their schools' "atmosphere," the students in Catholic high schools give no indication that their schools are any more "repressive" or "authoritarian" than other schools. There are no significant differences in the proportions saying they are free to disagree in class, that all students are treated equally, or that they are free to talk to the teacher if they think they have been treated unfairly. Indeed, in two of the three instances, the slight associations that do exist suggest that Catholic schools may be somewhat *more* liberal in these matters. There is no confirmation of the hoary stereotype of Catholic schools as rigid, inflexible, and obedience-centered institutions.

Thus those who are in Catholic high schools seem to be considerably more interested in scholastic matters than adolescents in other high schools. But we know that there is an association between social class and attending Catholic high schools and that Catholic schools are, or at least were in many instances in the survey, college-preparatory schools. Thus we must ask whether the greater academic commitment of the young people in Catholic schools is a result of either their social class or their college

Table 8.6 Social Activities of Adolescents, by School Attendance (Per Cent), and Gamma Associations

Social Activities	School Attendance				Gamma Association[a]
	All Catholic	Some Catholic	No Catholic	Protestant	
Spend five or more nights at home	70	53[b]	57[b]	60	+.06
Spend an hour or more a day with members of the opposite sex	48	54	50	55	−.08
Date once a week or more	20	36[b]	23	36	−.07
Going steady	17	30[b]	24	30[b]	−.06

[a] Among Catholics.
[b] Significantly different from "All Catholic."

plans. In Table 8.8 we find virtually no confirmation for such a notion. Controls for SES, and for SES and college plans, produce net partial gamma associations which are almost exactly the same as the zero-order coefficients. The greater studiousness of those in Catholic high schools is not the result of their social class or their academic plans.

Table 8.7 Description of School, by School Attendance (Per Cent), and Gamma Associations

Description of School	School Attendance				Gamma Associ- ation[a]
	All Catholic	Some Catholic	No Catholic	Protestant	
Feel free to disagree in class	63	63	57	60	+.02
Say that all students are treated equally	29	22	23	18	+.09
Feel free to talk to teacher if treated unfairly	53	55	60	58	−.04

[a] Among Catholics.

Table 8.8 Zero-Order and Net Partial Gamma Associations between Catholic Education and Social and Scholastic Behavior and Attitudes

Social and Scholastic Behavior and Attitudes	Zero- Order	Net Partials	
		SES	SES and College Plans
Plan to go to college	+.11	+.08	−
Spend two or more hours a day on homework	+.35	+.30	+.32
Boys who want to be remembered as an "A" student	+.14	+.17	+.11
Girls who want to be remembered as an "A" student	−.05	−.05	−.06
Report that they are often or sometimes unprepared for class	−.13	−.13	−.14
Report that they have cheated "more than once or twice"	−.06	−.08	−.06
Spend five or more nights at home	+.06	+.06	+.06
Spend an hour or more a day with members of the opposite sex	−.05	−.06	−.08
Date once a week or more	−.01	−.03	−.07
Going steady	−.10	−.11	−.06

But what might the explanation be? Are Catholic high schools "better" than the public high schools to which Catholics go—and in some instances "better" than the ones to which Protestant adolescents go? Such a question is difficult to answer, since we are unable to define precisely what "better" means. Catholic schools are able to demand more academic effort from their students, but there might be many reasons for this. The adolescents in Catholic schools might be more strongly motivated (because of family-background factors that a control for SES does not filter out) to respond to heavier demands. Catholic schools may be able to maintain higher standards because their admission requirements are more rigorous and they are able to dismiss scholastically inept students. The faculties of Catholic schools may put more pressure on their students to achieve as a compensation for their minority-group status. The religious functionaries in Catholic schools, whose whole lives are dedicated to education, may be able to devote more of their time and energy to their students than are teachers in public high schools. The more "traditionalist" Catholic approach to education may have preserved an emphasis on "hard work" in Catholic schools, whereas "life adjustment" programs have in some instances made some public schools much "easier." At this point we are unable to resolve the problem with the data available to us. But whatever the input in ability or motivation in Catholic high schools, the output in scholastic diligence (and later in occupational achievement) is fairly impressive and deserves more careful study.

Finally we must ask whether the proportion of Catholic friends a person has in his adolescence reinforces his academic effort if he is in a Catholic school, as was suggested in Chapter 6. While the proof is very thin, the data presented in Table 8.9 give a faint suggestion that those in Catholic friendship cliques are more inclined to have higher scholastic values. In five of the six comparisons, the association between Catholic education and academic commitment is higher for those who reported that all or most of their friends were Catholic. The question raised by Morris Rosenberg about one's minority-group status in his youth and his subsequent performance in adult social situations obviously deserves more careful investigation.

Whatever the explanation may be, we can find no evidence of academic inferiority in Catholic high schools today. It might be argued that even though they study harder, get better marks, are more likely to go to college, and take school more seriously, the students in Catholic high schools are intellectually inferior—that what they are doing comes not from a high valuation of the intellectual life but rather from economic ambition. Catholics study hard, in other words, not because they value knowledge but because they value money; the last of the Protestants (in the Weberian sense) are the students in Catholic schools.

Presumably Catholics are somewhat more interested in economic success than are Protestants, if only because until very recently they have had less of it. The rough social and economic parity achieved by the Catholic population in very recent years certainly suggests that there has been a fair amount of striving, and there is no reason to think that the striving has come to an end. Thus it is not at all inconceivable that at the present state of the Catholic population's acculturation, there might well be a strong element of motivation for economic achievement in the superior academic performance of those in Catholic high schools.

Table 8.9 Partial Gamma Associations between Catholic Education and Scholastic Behavior and Attitudes, with Control for Proportion of Catholic Friends

Scholastic Behavior and Attitudes	Almost All or Most Friends Catholic	Half or Less than Half of Friends Catholic
Plan to go to college	+.22	+.05
Spend two or more hours a day on homework	+.38	+.29
Boys who want to be remembered as an "A" student	+.37	−.12
Girls who want to be remembered as an "A" student	−.07	−.09
Report that they are often or sometimes unprepared for class	−.11	−.07
Report that they have cheated "more than once or twice"	−.18	−.05
N, all Catholic	118	29
N, some Catholic	70	118
N, no Catholic	57	144

But it does not therefore follow that this academic superiority can be written off as anti-intellectual. The pure intellectual motivation for study with little or no concern for economic motives is, one would think, something of a rarity in American society, and there is no reason to think that intellectual concerns cannot coexist with economic ambition. It may just be possible that ambition will spur a person on to greater intellectual creativity.

In any event, even if we grant that Catholic school Catholics do have a considerable amount of economic motivation in their academic work, it seems to us quite probable that this is merely a stage in the acculturation process and that in another generation they will be no different from American Protestants in their Protestantism, again in the Weberian sense. Finally, while we make these concessions for the sake of discussion, we are frankly skeptical of this postulated anti-intellectualism in the academic performance of Catholic school Catholics. As sociologists we wonder how seriously we should take supposed personality characteristics whose linkage to actual behavior must remain in doubt.

CONCLUSION

At the conclusion of this chapter we would say to our visiting committee of policy-makers that nothing in our data indicates that Catholics need feel ashamed of the academic prowess of their schools—though they are not thereby excused from seeking greater excellence. We would further warn them that, from the religious point of view, the CCD programs do not seem to be a very attractive substitute for Catholic schools, at least at the present time. Finally we would caution them against putting too much confidence in the apparent impact of Catholic education on adolescents from less religious families; we fear that this impact is quite transitory. There does not yet seem to be any substitute for the predispositions created by the family milieu—at least short of the college level.

In this chapter we focused on the current state of Catholic education and discovered that there are much stronger associations between the religious behavior of adolescents and their education than were observed in the adult respondents. It appeared that the strength of these associations would be eroded with the passage of time, particularly for those respondents who came from relatively nonreligious families. However, there is the possibility that further education in Catholic colleges may sustain the influence of Catholic secondary schools. There was no evidence that the religious instruction classes conducted by the Confraternity of Christian Doctrine serve at present as a functional substitute for Catholic secondary education. Those in Catholic schools seemed much more academically oriented than Catholics in public schools and even more so than Protestants in public schools; these associations did not vanish under controls for social class and plans to attend college. Finally, the view of adolescents currently in Catholic schools indicated that there was no substantiation for the notion that Catholic schools were more likely to be "unfair" or "authoritarian."

9
The Future of Catholic Schools

We now come to the last substantive question which we proposed to investigate in the beginning of our study: What is the future of Catholic education? Our concern is primarily with whether the Catholic school system will survive and continue to expand. On the face of it, such a question may seem quite theoretical; established social institutions rarely commit suicide, especially after experiencing periods of dramatic expansion. On the other hand, if one viewed the existence of Catholic schools as essentially a defensive measure during an era when an immigrant Church was adjusting to a new society, he might suspect that, as the immigration experience waned, the popularity of Catholic schools might decline. It could be argued that as Catholics become more and more acculturated into American society and less and less dependent on their clergy to make their decisions for them, the propensity to send offspring to Catholic schools will grow weaker. We have already expressed doubt (in Chapter 1) about the "ghetto" explanation for the growth of Catholic schools in the last quarter-century. If it should develop that the relationship between social class and Catholic school attendance is not negative but positive, our doubts will grow even stronger.

Thus the essential question to be faced in this chapter is whether there is a relationship between social class and Catholic education. Three subquestions are in order.

1. What is the relationship between parents' social class and their children's attending Catholic schools today?

199

2. What are the attitudes of Catholics toward their schools, and how do these attitudes relate to social class?
3. What are the attitudes of a Catholic elite group (represented by the *Commonweal* sample) toward Catholic education?

In brief, our findings will be that, as social class increases, there is an increase both in attendance at Catholic schools and in criticism of the schools. The *Commonweal* sample merely confirms this trend and suggests that in years to come criticism and attendance will continue to increase.

WHO GOES TO CATHOLIC SCHOOLS?

In this section we will use data gathered in another study of the same sample frame we are using in our study. We will be considering, not families, but children from the sample families who are presently of school age (thus if a family has two children in school at the present time, it "votes" twice; if no children are attending school, the family does not "vote" at all). The entire article from which Table 9.1 is drawn can be found in Appendix 4.

As we noted in the introduction to this chapter, the crucial question is whether there is a relationship between social class and Catholic school attendance. If attendance at Catholic schools declines with social class, it would follow that there will be a decline in attendance of Catholic schools as the Catholic population improves its social position. If on the other hand Catholic school attendance increases with social class, then either involvement in the immigrant ghetto is reinforced by education and social improvement (which does not seem very likely) or some other correlate of social class is reinforcing loyalty to Catholic schools. (Our guess is that concern about the religious education of children is associated with social class.) In either event, a positive relationship between Catholic education and social class would indicate that the future of Catholic education may be much like the past—continued growth.

The data strongly indicate that growth is precisely what is going to happen. Using parental educational level as a measure of social class in Table 9.1, we observe the substantial positive association between social class and attendance at Catholic schools for school-age Catholics today. Persons whose parental head had gone to graduate school are more than three times as likely to be in Catholic elementary schools as are those whose parental head did not get beyond fourth grade. Furthermore the proportion of offspring in Catholic elementary schools increases with each increase in parental educational level. Even though the association is not so strong at the secondary level, those whose parents have gone beyond primary education are still more likely to be attending Catholic high schools. Thus, far from indicating a decline in Catholic school attendance, the relationship between Catholic education and social class seems to portend considerable expansion. As Catholics become more and more successful in American society, their loyalty to Catholic schools increases rather than decreases.

This should be surprising only to those who view the Catholic schools as still essentially a defensive system designed to protect the threatened faith and culture of an alien immigrant group. As we pointed out before, the tremendous growth of Catholic schools in the last two decades—precisely when American Catholics were achieving approximate social and economic parity with

Table 9.1 Per Cent of Children of Catholic Marriages Attending Catholic Schools, by Education of Head of Household

Education of Head of Household	Primary	Secondary
1–4 years	22 (41)	14 (28)
5–7 years	36 (111)	28 (71)
8 years	41 (203)	34 (125)
9–11 years	42 (341)	38 (195)
12 years	49 (480)	34 (184)
13–15 years	54 (207)	30 (93)
16 years	56 (79)	38 (29)
More than 16 years	70 (66)	35 (20)
N	2,273	
NA	31	
Total N	2,304	

Protestants—can hardly be attributed to greater insecurity and defensiveness. It is much more likely that economic improvement for Catholics has in fact made the financing of the school expansion possible. In contemporary society it must be taken for granted that the more middle class a person is, the more he will be concerned about both religion and education and hence, it seems safe to conclude, about religious education. Upward mobility has made Catholics more concerned about religious education and more able to finance a rapid growth in the system of religious education which they happen to have at hand. It may be hard for many observers to do so, but it is apparently time to put aside the notion that acculturation and greater loyalty to a separate school system are incompatible. One can obviously be thoroughly Americanized in his job, style of life, and general system of values and still not retreat from the peculiar tenets of his own religious system—including an emphasis on having his own schools. It seems very likely that Catholic schools will continue to exist and that Catholics will continue in general to be loyal to them. It might considerably improve the harmony of interreligious relations in American society if non-Catholics were able to accept these facts. We add that popular journalists who have frequently suggested that Catholic schools were about to vanish—in face of the overwhelming evidence to the contrary—have done little service to the cause of religious pluralism in our society. It seems to us that the hope that Catholics are going to abandon their separate school system is wishful thinking.

ATTITUDES TOWARD CATHOLIC SCHOOLS

In the last section we observed that the strong positive association between social class and Catholic school attendance which existed in the generation of our respondents persisted into the generation of the respondents' children. Thus we could find no trace of a defection of loyalty of contemporary Catholics to the Catholic school system. As a matter of fact it seemed probable that, with the increase in Catholics' social prestige, there would be an increased demand in the future for classroom space in Catholic schools. But while the present generation of adults is just as likely to send its children to Catholic schools, there remains the possibility that it would be much more sophisticated in its criticism of Catholic schools than generations gone by.

Unfortunately it is impossible to know with any degree of accuracy what previous generations thought of Catholic schools. However, we can determine from data in our study how strong are the criticisms which contemporary Catholic adults direct against Catholic schools.

Why Not?

About one-third of the total respondents said that all their children had received exclusively Catholic education. Another one-third reported that none of their children had attended Catholic schools, and yet another one-third reported a mixed situation (Table 9.2). In the mixed group, some three-quarters of the respondents had children who had attended public grammar schools, and four-fifths had children who had attended public high schools. Thus we might be able to assume that the mixed group, whose children had experience in both Catholic and public schools, would be in an especially strategic position to make judgments about the quality of Catholic education.

The most important reasons for not sending a child to Catholic elementary school seemed to be physical (Table 9.3). In 23 per cent of the cases there simply were no Catholic schools available, and in 29 per cent the schools were too far away. The next two most important reasons—both being mentioned by about one-fifth of the parents in the study—have to do with the cost of Catholic education and the overcrowding in Catholic schools.

Table 9.2 School Attendance of Respondents' Children (Per Cent)

All children went exclusively to Catholic schools	30
All children had some Catholic schooling, or some went exclusively to Catholic schools (mixed)[a]	36
No child went to Catholic schools	34
Total	100
N	1,481

[a] Level of public school attended by mixed group; elementary, 77 per cent; secondary, 80 per cent; higher, 20 per cent.

Other reasons for not attending received scant mention. Non-attendance of Catholic elementary school can thus be explained in most instances by the availability of the school, the cost of Catholic education, and the apparent overcrowding of Catholic schools. Only a small minority of respondents made negative judgments about the quality of education in Catholic schools or about the religious atmosphere of the schools. It would be very difficult to conclude from Table 9.3 that there is widespread dissatisfaction in the Catholic population with either the existence of a Catholic school system or the quality of education provided.

The reasons for not attending Catholic secondary schools or Catholic colleges are similar to the reasons for not attending elementary schools. At the secondary level, the influence of a friend on a child's wish to go to a public school seems to be stronger than it does at the primary level; at the higher educational level the choice of friends becomes of prime importance, while cost continues to be important and the specialized programs available in non-Catholic schools also are an important factor. Availability, distance, and overcrowding, as one might expect, are of less concern at the level of higher education.

There is a certain unspectacular quality about the findings

Table 9.3 Reasons Why Child or Children Did Not Attend Catholic Schools (Per Cent Naming Each Reason)

Reason	Educational Level		
	Elementary	Secondary	Higher
Not available	23	24	11
Distance	29	18	12
Cost	18	22	25
Discipline	3	2	1
Child wanted to be with friend	5	18	28
Public education better	5	3	2
Special courses	3	8	21
Too much religion	5	3	3
Catholic school too narrow	2	2	3
Too crowded	20	13	9
Total[a]	113	113	115
N	832	625	151

[a] Totals are greater than 100 per cent because of multiple answers.

reported in Table 9.3. Children do not go to Catholic schools because there are no Catholic schools available or because they cost too much or (beyond the elementary level) because they want to go to school with their friends or (at the college level) because Catholic colleges do not have certain specialized courses available. It might be much more exciting to report that non-attendance of Catholic schools represents some kind of turning-away from the influence of an immigrant religious organization as its members become acculturated into American society. There may be some of this rejection implicit in nonattendance of Catholic schools, but it certainly was not filtered out by the question why children of certain Catholic parents did not attend Catholic schools.

If there is any surprise over the lack of ideological objection to Catholic education, it may well be due to the fact that many observers have a somewhat naïve conception of the organizational discipline of Roman Catholicsm. Catholics do not simply do what their clergy tells them to do without thought or deliberation. If large numbers of American Catholics send their children to religious schools, they do so not merely because it is the rule of their Church but also because they have decided to go along with the rule. If others do not sent their children to such schools, the reason may be not so much a revolt against an oppressive ideology as an avoidance of physical inconvenience. In the ordinary course of events most American Catholics do not find their religion oppressive and are not disposed to revolt against it. This may be disappointing to some non-Catholics and to some Catholic critics who feel they ought to be in revolt, but the truth of the matter seems to be that ideological opposition to any religion presupposes a level of religious concern which the average American probably does not have.

At all three educational levels, cost was a factor of some importance in some children's nonattendance at Catholic schools. One might wonder what the cost of Catholic education is for a typical family each year. In Table 9.4 we see that the average yearly cost for our respondents does not seem excessively high; almost two-thirds of them said that the average annual cost was less than $100.

Advantages

Presumably Catholics send their children to Catholic schools because the Catholic Church has built these schools and requires, in some fashion or other, that Catholics attend them. It is possible, therefore, that American Catholics send their children to Catholic schools out of loyalty to the Church but with little faith or confidence in the quality of their education. In Table 9.5 we see the responses to the question concerning what advantages respondents could find in Catholic education. While it is not especially surprising that three-quarters of the respondents mentioned the religious instruction to be obtained in Catholic schools, it is somewhat surprising that almost one-third think that better education can be obtained in Catholic schools than in public schools and that only 6 per cent of the respondents could think of no advantage in Catholic education.

Table 9.4 Average Annual Tuition Costs of Catholic Education (Per Cent in Each Category)

None	22
Under $100	40
$100–$199	17
$200–$399	13
More than $400	7
Total	99
N	907

Table 9.5 Reported Advantages of Catholic Education (Per Cent Giving Each Response)

Religious instruction	73
Better education	31
Better discipline	38
Better (unspecified)	10
No advantage	6
Total[a]	158
N	2,038

[a] Total greater than 100 per cent because of multiple answers.

Whether those who think that Catholic schools are academically better than public schools are deceiving themselves or accurately judging the situation it is difficult to say. However, it is altogether possible, at least in certain urban centers, that Catholic schools really are somewhat better academically than public schools, since they do not face the social problems the public schools face. Even though they are constrained to support and use the Catholic school system, it appears that American Catholics are generally sympathetic to the schools and place a high value on the religious instruction to be obtained in them. It seems very doubtful, in fact, that the level of financial commitment to Catholic schools could be sustained in the absence of at least a fair amount of enthusiasm for these schools by their clients.

There can be no doubt that this finding is at variance with some of the recent popular journalistic evaluations of Catholic education. At times one has the impression that magazine editors are absolutely convinced that there must be "trouble in the Catholic schools" and that all that is required is undocumented assertions to prove it. But there is a more charitable explanation: the dissatisfaction recorded in popular articles may be very real but also very untypical, and dissatisfaction—especially among an articulate and liberal minority—is news while satisfaction is not.

Improvements
Even though a substantial segment of the Catholic population send their children to Catholic schools and place a fairly high evaluation on the academic worth of these schools, they are not necessarily unaware of deficiencies in the Catholic educational system. However, their criticisms, implied in the suggested improvements reported in Table 9.6 are of the same rather unspectacular nature as the reasons why some parents do not send their children to Catholic schools. A need for improvement in physical facilities was indicated by 14 per cent. A similar number (15 per cent) would like to see changes in the teacher situation in Catholic schools. This group is about evenly divided among those who want more lay teachers, those who want more nuns, and those

who want better teacher-education programs. Curricular improvement within the schools was felt to be needed by 11 per cent; that is to say, these parents would like to see a wider variety of courses offered. A rather surprising 6 per cent are interested in improving the athletic programs in Catholic schools. The same proportion would like to see a reduction of tuition costs, while 10 per cent of the respondents are in favor of modernizing the attitudes and disciplinary approach within the Catholic schools. As much as 15 per cent could think of no improvements to suggest, and only 1 per cent were interested in a greater parental share in the decision-making processes within the Catholic educational system.

The recent suggestions in popular journals that Catholics are restless and dissatisfied with situations within their schools get little support from the tables in this chapter. Almost one-half of the respondents suggested no improvement. Two-fifths spontaneously said that they thought Catholic schools were better than public schools. The improvements suggested seem to be of a very moderate—one might almost say minor—variety. Indeed, only 1 per cent of the respondents seemed particularly unhappy with their lack of share in decision-making and planning processes

Table 9.6 Opinions on Needed Improvements in Catholic Education (Per Cent Giving Each Opinion)

Better physical plant	14
Improvement in teaching	15
Wider curriculum	11
Better athletic program	6
Less crowding	10
Lower tuition	6
Modernization of approach (less homework, less discipline, less emphasis on religion, more tolerance for other religions)	10
More parental responsibility	1
Don't know	30
No improvement needed	15
Total[a]	118
N	2,038

[a] Total greater than 100 per cent because of multiple answers.

within the school. Parents are apparently much less worried about this than they are about the lack of adequate athletic programs for their school-age children. Combining the data reported in Tables 9.5 and 9.6 with information from the previous section about the association between social class and Catholic education, we can reasonably conclude that there is no major revolt astir among Catholic parents, or, if there is a revolt, it is not one that they want to talk about to survey research interviewers.

We must note of course that the level of complaint represented by Table 9.6 may represent a considerable increase in dissatisfaction over that which might have been observed a decade ago. Indeed it would be quite astonishing if the upward movement of the Catholic population and the reappraisal of institutions going on within the Roman Church did not lead to increased criticism of Catholic education—intensive criticism by a small minority and vague dissatisfaction among a somewhat larger group. While it would be a mistake for Catholic educators to panic over this criticism (as some apparently have), it would also be a mistake to consider it unimportant—especially when, as we shall see, it seems strongest in those groups most loyal to Catholic schools. But the findings thus far reported in this chapter do not indicate any massive unrest within the Catholic population. It is still possible that there is much more widespread dissatisfaction in certain groups than there is in the total population. We must ascertain, therefore, whether the fact of having children in Catholic schools changes attitudes toward the school and whether criticism might be related to social class. It is altogether possible that increased attendance in Catholic schools among well-to-do Catholics does not preclude an increase in criticism in the same groups; it is well known that the most articulate critics of education are precisely those who are the most educated.

First of all we ask whether the reasons for not going to Catholic schools might be affected either by social class or by whether parents had ever sent their children to these schools. It is clear from Table 9.7 that reasons for nonattendance which imply some sort of educational deficiency are somewhat more likely to be reported by those of higher social class, though there is no relationship between having had some experience with Catholic schools and citing a reason implying deficiency. Second (Table 9.8) a positive attitude toward Catholic schools (i.e., that they are "better" than public schools) is related neither to social class nor to whether one's children went to Catholic schools. Finally (Table 9.9), suggested improvements which imply criticism are much more common in the upper-class groups and slightly more common among those whose children had a mixed educational experience.

Thus attendance at Catholic schools and negative criticism are both related to social class. It is precisely those who are most likely to send their children to Catholic schools (and who are no less likely to have positive attitudes toward the schools) who are the most inclined to be critical. Should this phenomenon continue as Catholics improve their social station, Catholic education can expect both more pupils and more criticism.

Table 9.7 Per Cent of Respondents Giving Reasons for Not Attending Catholic Schools That Imply Educational Deficiency, by SES and Children's Education

| SES | Children's Education | |
	Mixed[a]	No Catholic
High (Duncan score 6–10)	42(150)	44(118)
Low (Duncan score 1–5)	34(306)	32(310)

[a] At least some children had Catholic education.

Table 9.8 Per Cent of Respondents Saying Catholic Education Is "Better," by SES and Children's Education

| SES | Children's Education | | |
	All Catholic	Mixed[a]	No Catholic
High (Duncan score 6–10)	50(134)	48(150)	46(118)
Low (Duncan score 1–5)	51(236)	42(306)	51(310)

[a] At least some children had Catholic education.

The Catholic Elite

The data reported in the previous chapter and thus far in this chapter do not suggest that Catholic adults show a widespread dissatisfaction with the Catholic school system. The more well-to-do Catholics are the ones who are more likely to send their children to Catholic schools. They send them principally because they want religious education and secondarily because they tend to believe that Catholic schools provide better discipline and better education. Catholics who do not send their children to Catholic schools generally fail to do so because the schools are not available, are too far away, or are too crowded. There seems to be general agreement on what needs to be improved in the schools but no dissatisfaction with the presumably minor role that parents play in the educational system.

There is, therefore, nothing in the data to suggest that the Catholic educational system will not continue into the foreseeable future. Most Catholic education correlates with social class, and Catholics are improving socially and economically. There will, in all likelihood, be an increased demand for desks in Catholic schools. There will also be an increase in the demand for physical and academic improvements within the school system. But at this point nonattendance of Catholic schools does not seem to be very strongly related to such demands. It is of course possible that in the future, if some of the demands are not met, there will be a decline in attendance, but there is nothing in the data now

Table 9.9   Per Cent of Respondents Whose Suggested Improvements Indicate Some Objection to Quality of Catholic Education, by SES and Children's Education

SES	Children's Education		
	All Catholic	Mixed[a]	No Catholic
High (Duncan score 6–10)	51 (134)	55 (150)	42 (118)
Low (Duncan score 1–5)	29 (236)	33 (306)	24 (310)

[a] At least some children had Catholic education.

available to us which indicates that a trend of this sort has begun.

The question of the Catholic elite remains. It is possible that, while the majority of the Catholics in the country are reasonably satisfied with the school system, there is a small but crucial minority which is strongly dissatisfied. To test this possibility we report here some data available from a random sample of the readership of *The Commonweal* magazine. *The Commonweal* is a favorite journal among liberal American Catholics and has in recent years tended to be critical of Catholic education. We can reasonably assume that if there are any strong feelings against Catholic education, these feelings will be found in the sample of the readers of *The Commonweal*.

Judging from the data in Table 9.10, the liberal elite as represented by the *Commonweal* reader is, if anything, more likely to send his children to Catholic schools than are Catholics of a comparable social class in the general population. The *Commonweal* readers, as we note below, may have somewhat more stringent criticisms, yet at this point they are also more likely to send their children to Catholic schools. But those *Commonweal* Catholics who do not send their children to Catholic schools are inclined to be much more critical in the reasons they give for nonattendance. While it is clear in Table 9.11 that this group is no less likely to mention availability or distance, it is considerably less likely to mention cost and much more likely to suggest that public schools are better and that Catholic schools are overcrowded. Thus even though *Commonweal* readers are apparently more will-

Table 9.10 School Attendance (Per Cent) of Children of Catholic Readers of *Commonweal* and Children of High-SES Parents in the General Population

School Attendance of Respondents' Children	Commonweal Readers	High-SES Parents (Duncan Score 7–10)
All Catholic	42	33
Some Catholic	37	40
No Catholic	21	27
Total	100	100
N	210	300

ing to send their children to Catholic schools, those who do not do so give reasons that are often heard in the criticisms of Catholic education by the contemporary liberal elite.

Furthermore, the *Commonweal* reader, while he is more inclined than anyone in the general sample to stress religious training in Catholic schools, is somewhat less concerned about disciplinary training in the Catholic schools (Table 9.12). There are also some dramatic differences between the *Commonweal* reader and the typical Catholic in their recommendations for improvements in Catholic schools (Table 9.13). The *Commonweal* reader is less concerned about improvements in physical facilities and much more concerned about modifications in teaching and about classroom size. While he is not particularly interested in broadening the academic curriculum, improving the athletic program, or curtailing the costs of the schools, he is somewhat more interested in the modernizing procedures within the school and somewhat less likely to think that there is no need for improvement. However, only 7 per cent of the *Commonweal* readers feel that parents should have more participation in the decision-making that goes on in the schools. This last item is rather surprising, since one would have thought that members of the lay elite who read *The Commonweal* would be particularly concerned with the layman's influence on Catholic school administration. But it appears that

Table 9.11   Reasons Given by Catholic Readers of *Commonweal* Why Children Did Not Go to Catholic Schools (Per Cent Giving Each Reason)

Not available	37
Distance	22
Cost	5
Discipline in Catholic schools	5
Friend in public school	1
Public schools better	24
Special courses in public schools	2
Too religious or too narrow	11
Overcrowded	44
Total	151
N	89

the *Commonweal* reader, while he feels very strongly about improvement in teaching, reduction of classroom size, and modernization of the schools' operations, does not feel that he could or should assume more personal responsibility for what goes on in the schools' administration.

If one cares to assume that the readership of *The Commonweal* is avant-garde in the strict sense of the word, and represents the feelings of the general Catholic population ten or fifteen years from now, then we would again say that both attending Catholic schools and criticizing them will increase. Those who do not send their children to Catholic schools will continue to avoid them in the future, but more on the grounds of academic and cultural inferiority than for reasons of cost or availability. Even those

Table 9.12 Advantages of Catholic Education as Seen by *Commonweal* Readers (Per Cent Indicating Each)

Religious instruction	93
Better education	29
Better discipline	24
Better (unspecified)	9
No advantage	7
Total	162
N	460

Table 9.13 Improvements Needed in Catholic Schools as Seen by *Commonweal* Readers (Per Cent Indicating Each)

Physical plant	8
Teaching	54
Curriculum	12
Less crowding	31
Athletic program	4
Tuition	10
Modernization	25
Parental participation	7
No improvement	14
Total	165
N	460

who do send their children to Catholic schools will be much more critical of what goes on in them and more likely to demand improvement in instruction and administration, though perhaps they will be less likely to demand new buildings or expansion of athletic programs. However, if *Commonweal* readers are indeed the wave of the future, there is not very much probability, within the next decade or two, of the Catholic laity's requesting more control in the administration of the schools. If the trend toward greater lay participation in Catholic education (both on the parochial and diocesan levels) does point to future growth, it may well be that the clergy will be in the position of pushing the laity into assuming greater responsibilities within Catholic education.

If we had asked the *Commonweal* readers (and indeed the rest of our respondents) outright whether they would like to see greater parental participation in the administration of Catholic schools, we can reasonably assume that they would have replied in the affirmative. But greater parental participation was not the first or second thing that came to their minds when they were asked what improvements they would like to see. Such a reaction should not be totally unexpected. Parents have more than enough things to keep them occupied and are not eager for new responsibilities. They would be much more concerned about the quality of education in their schools than about whether they had much to say about what goes on in them. It would be a mistake therefore to assume that more parental participation will necessarily appease the demand for higher quality.

THE LIMITS OF EXPANSION

In the last two years there has been a leveling-off of enrollment in Catholic primary schools, which has led to new alarm among some Catholic educators and new cries of triumph from certain critics. The fact that this leveling-off has been predicted for years on demographic grounds does not seem to restrain either side. Those parents who are most likely to be enrolling children in the early primary grades were born during the low-birth-rate years of the depression. Thus there are less children enrolling in first grade because the birth rate has been declining steadily for the last six years—at least in part because of the small size of the parental group in its most fertile years. In addition it is possible that there has been a pause in new school construction both because of financial reasons and because of the long absences of bishops attending the Ecumenical Council.

After the fantastic growth of the last two decades, a "breather" for re-evaluation might well be in order. But barring a revolution in attitudes in the months since our data were collected (a very unlikely event), we find it difficult to project anything but more expansion for Catholic education.

If our convenient committee of policy-makers should demand to know what sort of expansion they might expect on the basis of the present chapter, we would first caution them that our data are very indirect and second advise them to wait for the publication of the forthcoming Notre Dame University study, which considers this question with a vast amount of statistical data.

However, we could still be persuaded to make some observations. Judging by the information reported in our article reprinted in Appendix 4, the upper limit of demand for religious training seems to be about two-thirds of the Catholic population, with the proportion in Catholic schools and the proportion in religious instruction classes varying according to availability of schools and social class of parents. Furthermore, apparently some 70 per cent of our respondents for whom schools were available actually attended Catholic schools at least for some time during their education. We would therefore guess that if schools were available for every Catholic, and if all Catholics were in the white-collar social class, no more than 70 per cent of the Catholics of school age would attend Catholic schools. We would not want to exclude the possibility that under favorable circumstances the proportion of Catholics in Catholic schools could increase from the present 45 per cent to close to 60 per cent in the next quarter-century. This would in turn mean that, instead of 14 per cent of the school children in the country being in Catholic schools, the proportion might be closer to 20 per cent by 1990.

Granted the continued social mobility of the Catholic population and the leveling-off of the birth rate in recent years, such an expansion might require proportionately less financial sacrifice than did the tremendous growth of the last quarter-century. We wish to make it as clear as possible that we are not advocating such an expansion, but merely suggesting that our very incomplete data indicate that effective demand might make such an expansion feasible. Whether the demand will be vigorous enough to make it necessary is not evident to us.

The one obstacle to such growth would be the teacher situation. The economics of Catholic education have thus far assumed that a considerable proportion of the teachers would be nuns. However, the decline in "vocations" which apparently is taking place makes an even larger proportion of lay teachers necessary. If good teachers—or indeed any teachers—are to be recruited, it will be necessary for the salary scale of Catholic schools to be roughly competitive with urban and suburban public systems. Some observers argue that without drastic modernization of the religious orders the "vocation shortage" will increase and grow worse. If our mythical committee does decide to pursue a course of further expansion and is frightened by the prohibitive costs of an ever increasing proportion of lay teachers, it might be well advised to determine whether those observers who are calling for changes in the communities of teaching nuns may not have put their finger on *the* crucial problem of the future of Catholic education.

CONCLUSION

The data reported in this chapter are somewhat paradoxical. They confirm the impression of many Catholic educators that Catholic education has never been more popular. Truly the demand seems to be at an all-time high and is likely to increase with the increase in social class appearing among American Catholics. Furthermore, American Catholics seem to place a high value on their schools and especially on the religious training to be obtained in them. Despite the fact that Catholic schools are popular and evidently will remain popular with a large number of Catholics, it also seems that, at least among the upper class and especially among the liberal elite, criticisms are growing stronger. Criticisms have not thus far led to a decline in attendance of Catholic schools, and apparently they will not do so for some time to come. But as the Catholic population becomes better educated and more articulate, it will inevitably grow more concerned about what goes on in its schools, particularly about the qualifications of teachers and the overcrowding of classrooms.

It is a short jump beyond the data reported in these two chapters to suggest that there will be some critical years ahead for Catholic education if these concerns about teachers' competence and classroom size are disregarded.

10

Conclusion

MAJOR FINDINGS

In this final chapter we will summarize the major findings of the study and then select certain of them for more extensive commentary.

1. There is a moderate but significant association (usually between .2 and .3) between Catholic education and adult religious behavior, an association which survives under a wide variety of socio-economic, demographic, and religious controls.

2. Contrary to our expectations, the association is strongest among those who come from very religious family backgrounds (defined as those in which one parent went to Communion every week). For these respondents the relationship between religious education and adult behavior is between .3 and .4, while for other respondents the gamma coefficient declines to .1. The association is also strongest among those who married persons who are practicing Catholics.

3. The association between Catholic education and adult behavior is strongest for those who went to Catholic colleges (generally between .4 and .6). It is especially strong among men who went to Catholic colleges (as high as .8).

4. Family religiousness apparently does not strengthen the association between religious education and adult behavior for those who went to Catholic colleges.

5. There are very strong relationships between Catholic education and religious behavior for teen-agers currently in school (between .4 and .6).

6. The differences in the relationships between education and religious behavior found among adults and those found among adolescents are apparently due to the weaker long-run impact of Catholic education on those who do not come from very religious families or who do not marry religious persons.

7. No confirmation was found for the notion that Catholic schools are "divisive." There is divisiveness in American society, but it is apparently based more on religion than on religious education.

8. In the general population there were only very weak associations (less than .11) between religious education and enlightened social attitudes.

9. The relationship between religious education and enlightened social attitudes was slightly stronger for those who went to Catholic high schools.

10. Among those who were in their twenties, and among those who went to college, the relationship between religious education and social consciousness was stronger. When age and education were combined, even more powerful relationships emerged (at least one of them statistically significant).

11. The strongest associations between religious education and social attitudes were found among those who went to Catholic colleges (usually between .2 and .4); most of these associations were statistically significant. They were even stronger for men who went to Catholic colleges.

12. The impact of the Catholic high school and the Catholic college on religious behavior and social attitudes apparently is the result of a cumulation of Catholic educational experience and not the result of the particular educational level operating by itself.

13. There is a weak but persistent association between Catholic education and economic and social achievement (usually about .1).

14. The relationship with achievement is stronger among those from higher socio-economic status backgrounds.

15. This relationship apparently occurs specifically among those who belonged to Catholic friendship cliques in adolescence and even more specifically (.35) among those who had Catholic friends during adolescence and scored low on an anomie measure.

16. There are apparently two ways by which Catholics can succeed markedly: the path of alienation from the Catholic community and the path of integration into the Catholic subculture. The latter is somewhat more effective in leading to achievement,

much more desirable from the Church's viewpoint, and apparently not dysfunctional for the larger society.

17. Among adolescents today there is a moderately strong relationship between academic commitment and religious education (.3 for time spent on homework).

18. There is also an apparent persistence of the effect of friendship cliques on the academic performance of adolescents today.

19. There is a direct relationship between social class and sending one's children to Catholic schools, at least for marriages where both partners are Catholic.

20. The most frequent reasons for not sending children to Catholic schools have to do with their availability; the most common criticisms of the schools have to do with their physical facilities.

21. Both Catholic school attendance and criticism increase with social class, suggesting that the proportion of Catholics in Catholic schools and the criticism of the schools will increase in years to come.

22. Very little relationship could be found between religious behavior and attending CCD classes.

23. Religious education is a more important predictor of adult behavior than is an individual's sex, but it is less important than his educational level or the religiousness of his parents.

24. There is no evidence that Catholic schools have been necessary for the survival of American Catholicism.

DETAILED COMMENTARY ON FINDINGS

1. *There is a moderate but statistically significant relationship between Catholic education and adult religious behavior.*—For most of the present century, the Roman Catholic Church in the United States has been involved in an acculturation process. Only 10 per cent of our respondents were foreign-born, but almost one-half were immigrants or the children of immigrants. At the risk of oversimplifying a historical epoch, we could say that the Church's concern during the years when the respondents were in school was almost entirely focused on protecting the faith of its people. Certain elements of Catholic creed, code, and cult took on major importance as symbols of the faith which was to be preserved.

Regular church attendance was a manifestation of loyalty to the Church of one's ancestors; acceptance of Church authority distinguished one from other Americans who did not vest their church with very much authority. Strict sexual morality not only preserved the rigorous morals of the old world, it also marked Catholics as different from other Americans, whose sexual morality was taken to be undergoing a "revolution" with the increase in birth control and divorce. By emphasizing external devotion, authority, and chastity, the Church not only preserved its distinctiveness but also defended its members from what it took to be the most serious threats of New World culture—moral, doctrinal, and cultic indifferentism.

To achieve these goals of "pattern maintenance" was certainly one of the principal reasons for establishing a separate school system (though, as Robert D. Cross has shown, there were many other reasons too). No school can hope to inculcate all the values in its world view; some choice must be made, and the choice is very likely to be made in terms of those values which, for historical and social reasons, seem at a given time to be most important or most threatened.

Sunday Mass, monthly Communion, Confession several times a year, Catholic education of children, financial contribution to the Church, acceptance of the Church as an authoritative teacher, acknowledgment of papal and hierarchical authority, informality with the clergy, strict sexual morality, more detailed knowledge about one's religion—these are not only the apparent effects of Catholic education, they comprise as well a reasonable description of what the American Church has expected from its laity during the years when it was still concentrating on the preservation of the faith of the immigrant and his children and grandchildren. If these represented the goals of American Catholicism for the first half of this century, there does not seem to be much doubt that the schools have made a substantial, though not overwhelming, contribution to the achievement of these goals. In this perspective one could say that the Catholic experiment in value-oriented education has been a moderate (though expensive) success, and that therefore there is some reason to think that value-oriented education can affect human behavior and attitudes in matters that are invested with heavy symbolic importance.

2. *The association is strongest among those who come from very religious family backgrounds.*—Apparently the religiousness of the family of origin predisposes a child to influence by the religious education he receives in school. Only those having had at least one parent who went to Communion every Sunday seem to show notable signs of improving their religious behavior as a result of Catholic education. Weekly Communion by at least one parent is not only a "breaking point" for the effectiveness of Catholic education, it also indicates the presence of a "multiplier effect," since the quarter of the population coming from this kind of religious background are very much more likely to be influenced by religious education. It seems possible that taking weekly Communion may show the difference between a "devout" Catholic and a "practicing" Catholic and that Catholic education influences only the children of the "devout."

3, 4. *The association is strongest among those who went to Catholic colleges (especially the males).*—The effect on the males is to bring them up to the level of practice of the Catholic college-educated females, while the males who did not go to Catholic colleges are considerably lower than comparable females on measures of religious devotion and social tolerance. We know that educational level is a strong predictor of religious behavior (no matter what kind of school a respondent went to). The combination of college and a cumulation of years of religious education apparently produces another multiplier effect. So strong are these relationships that we were led to conclude that religious education will probably produce the effect its supporters seek for it only when it is "comprehensive" (from first grade to college degree). It seems also that family religiousness does not predispose those who went to Catholic colleges to greater influence by religious education; quite possibly this "predisposing effect" for the college level is accomplished by attending religious primary and secondary schools.

5. *There is a strong relationship between religious education and religious behavior for teen-agers now in high school.*—These relationships, by far the strongest in the study, either indicate

a notable increase in the effectiveness of Catholic education or suggest that some of the variance between Catholics educated in Catholic schools and those who are not erodes with time. If the latter is the case, the erosion must be rather rapid, since we could find few differences between respondents in their twenties and respondents in their fifties.

6. *The differences in the relationships between education and religious behavior found among adults and those found among the adolescents are apparently due to the weaker long-run impact of Catholic education on those who do not come from very religious families.*—Even though parental religiousness reinforced the impact of Catholic education on adult respondents, it did not do so among the youthful respondents. As a matter of fact, those from very religious families had the lowest gamma associations. However, these relationships were of approximately the same order as those among adults from similar religious backgrounds. Hence, we were led to conclude that there is little erosion of the impact of religious education among those who come from very religious families and considerable erosion among those from less religious families. Thus the reinforcing influence of family life on the effect of religious education is apparently a long-run rather than a short-run phenomenon. In the short run, those from less religious families are also affected by Catholic education.

7. *No confirmation was found for the notion that Catholic schools are "divisive."*—Community involvement, interaction with non-Catholics, concern about "worldly problems," and attitudes toward other groups were not affected by attendance at Catholic schools. The majority of Catholics reported that their three best friends were Catholic, but the difference was not appreciably great between those who had had Catholic education and those who had not. Americans apparently choose their friends from their own religious group no matter what kind of education they have.

8-11. *While there are very weak relationships between social consciousness and Catholic education at all levels, these relationships become relatively strong when Catholic high-school-educated respondents, college-educated respondents, and those in their twenties are under consideration. The strongest associations were among those educated in Catholic colleges.*—Apparently higher education in a Catholic school leads not only to improved religious behavior but also to more tolerant attitudes. It may be only at the college level that a young person sorts out those attitudes from his youth which he will keep and those which he will modify and revise as part of his permanent *Weltanschauung*. If this sorting-out process goes on at a Catholic college (after previous experience in Catholic grammar and high schools) the young person seems more likely to adopt the "liberal" social teachings of his Church. It is also possible that the college experience "plugs him in" more effectively to the Church's "communication network," so that he is able to detect changes in emphasis in Catholic teaching more quickly than others. In addition, he may be readier to accept the change both because of his greater loyalty to the Church and because he may have heard hints in school which have prepared him for the new emphases. Whatever the mechanisms at work, those who attended Catholic colleges are not only significantly more "liberal" than Catholics who did not, they are, on the measure of anti-Semitism, significantly more "liberal" than college-educated Protestants. Our findings about those who attended Catholic colleges suggest that some stereotypes about Catholicism and Catholic education might need rethinking.

12. *Catholic high school and college apparently affect religious behavior only when they have been preceded by exclusively Catholic schooling.*—Even though the data on which this assertion is based are rather thin, the assertion itself is in harmony with the general finding of the study about the cumulation of predictors of religious behavior.

13–18. *Associations between Catholic education and achievement are generally weak but persistent, but stronger among those with high-SES backgrounds (especially those in adolescent Catholic friendship cliques with low anomie scores); Catholics succeed either by alienation from or integration into the Catholic subcommunity; adolescents today show a fairly strong relation between academic commitment and religious education and between friendship cliques and academic performance.*—The findings reported in these propositions are probably the most surprising in the study. Not only do Catholic schools accelerate the upward mobility of Catholics, but they apparently do so through some kind of complicated operation of friendship patterns among young Catholics. Whether Catholic high schools are academically better than the public high schools to which Catholics go is difficult to judge, because it is hard to say precisely what "academically better" means. Surely the young people in Catholic schools do more homework (especially if their close friends are Catholic), but whether this is because the schools demand more or because the students are better motivated to begin with cannot be judged. At the present time, however, the greater scholastic diligence of Catholic high-school students is not a function of their being more likely to plan on going to college. Nor do controls for parents' social status notably change the greater achievement of the adults who went to Catholic schools or the greater industriousness of the present generation of adolescents in Catholic schools.

Thus four explanations, probably in combination, can be advanced for the greater achievement of those who went to (or are going to) Catholic schools.

a) A parent's choosing of a private school indicates his greater educational concern and hence more disposition to study on the part of the child—even with social class held constant.

b) Catholic schools are able to be more selective in choosing whom to admit and to demand more study from their students— even within social-class groups.

c) The emotional security and well-being provided by friendship cliques from one's own religious group makes achievement somewhat easier.

d) Faculties of Catholic schools have accelerated the social and economic acculturation of Catholics precisely because they felt that this was the best way to adjust to a new society.

19–21. *There is a direct relationship between social class and sending one's children to Catholic schools; nonavailability most often is the reason given for not doing so; physical facilities, the most common criticism; the proportion of Catholics in Catholic schools will probably increase.*—The phenomenon of greater interest in private education and greater concern about and criticism of education is a correlate of a change in social-class level for most population groups. Contrary to some recent articles, there does not seem to be any loss of support for the idea of Catholic education, not even among the liberal elite who read *The Commonweal*. It appears that the major problems the schools face are increasing the number of facilities available and at the same time improving quality of instruction—quality which, at its present level, does not seem to be harming those who have attended Catholic schools and may indeed be no worse than that in public schools.

22. *Very little relationship could be found between religious behavior and attending CCD classes.*—While no attempt was made to distinguish between poor CCD programs and good ones, we could not find that, on the national average, the present CCD program has much effect; it would certainly have to be improved considerably to be realistically considered a functional substitute for Catholic schools.

23. *Religious education is a more important predictor of adult behavior than is an individual's sex, but it is less important than his educational level or the religiousness of his parents.*—Religious education is therefore not the most important predictor of adult religious behavior; indeed, a respondent who went all the way through public schools and attended a non-Catholic college will be as likely to have the same score on the sacramental index as someone who went to Catholic grammar schools and public high school but did not go to college. Thus, the amount of education is more important in predicting adult behavior than whether the education was religious. Of course, if the level of education is high and all of it is religious, the combination of the two predictor variables produces a very strong "exponential" improvement in religious behavior.

It is not especially surprising that family religious background and social class—both of which are twenty-four-hour-a-day factors of immense power and importance—should have more influence on religious behavior than religious education, which is necessarily limited to a small proportion of the day and the life of a young person.

24. *There is no evidence that Catholic schools have been necessary for the survival of American Catholicism.*—While there is some indication that the impact of Catholic education is increased by

the Catholic education of one's parents, it does not appear that two generations of public school education lead to a notable decline in the minimal religious observance of Catholics. Thus three-fifths of those who went to public schools and whose parents went to public schools go to Mass every Sunday. It is perfectly true that, while Catholic schools apparently make the "elite" more elite, the absence of a Catholic education does not seem to lead to a notable decline in minimal allegiance. Rather than causing the comparatively high level of minimal allegiance to be found in American Catholics, the schools may be a result of it.

DISCUSSION AND CONCLUSIONS

Our work started out with both a theoretical and a practical concern. It is now time to attempt to answer the questions raised in the first chapter.

The first theoretical question was whether the values of a religious group can be effectively taught in a religiously oriented educational system. Our answer to this question is that, to some extent, they can. The students who attend such schools can be expected in adult life to do even better those things which most members of their religious group do reasonably well. Value-oriented education can affect behavior in adult life in precisely those areas in which adults can be expected to adhere to the norms of their religious group even without education. Those who have the education will simply be even more likely to exhibit the desired behavior.

But intervening variables can affect the amount of difference in religious behavior between those who went to value-oriented schools and those from the same religion who did not. Social class, level of education, religiousness of parents, cumulation of years in a value-oriented system—all increase the strength of the association between religious education and adult religious behavior; but these variables tend to combine to produce a multiplier effect after certain breaking points. While the dynamics of these combinations are not yet clear, there can be no question that those who have had a "comprehensive" education in a religious system will be notably different both in religious behavior and social attitudes from those who did not have such schooling—

with the breaking point apparently being between high school and college.

The second theoretical question was whether such separate systems of education were "divisive." We could find no evidence that the products of such a system were less involved in community activities, less likely to have friends from other religious groups, more intolerant in their attitudes, or less likely to achieve occupationally or academically. On the contrary, we found that they were slightly more successful in the world of study and work and—after the breaking point of college—much more tolerant. The achievement, and perhaps even the tolerance, seems to be related to the degree to which a young person was integrated into his religious subculture during adolescence.

The collapse of the expectations about "divisiveness," as well as the greater "liberalism" of those who went to Catholic colleges, even led us to suggest that a fair number of assumptions about the attitudes and values of American Catholicism need to be seriously re-examined.

The practical question with which we were concerned is whether Catholic schools have achieved that which they set out to do— whether they have been worth the tremendous effort in time and money which has gone into them. Such a question is much more difficult to answer. Have Catholic schools succeeded in making most of their graduates model Christians? Have they been able to undo the work of other cultural institutions which shape the values of a young person as he grows up? The answers to these questions are clearly that they have not. But it would not have taken a quarter of a million dollars and two years of study to come to that answer; any expectations that formal education will accomplish miracles of conversion or personality change are naïve and hardly relevant.

Have the schools been responsible for the health and survival of the American Church? Apparently they have not. Although there is little doubt that some individuals have been notably influenced by them, on the average Catholics who did not go to Catholic schools are, by most standards of Catholic practice in the world, quite good Catholics.

But have the Catholic schools accomplished anything? Here the answer is that they have; in some instances at least, the average differences between Catholics who went to Catholic schools and those who did not are quite impressive and would lead most social scientists to say that the relationship was very powerful. We will stick our necks out to the extent of observing that we were surprised by the strength of the associations of Catholic college attendance with adult religious behavior and social attitudes; we did not expect differences as great as those we discovered.

Has it been worth all the time, money, and effort? Such a question is beyond the scope of sociological analysis, but we suggest that a more relevant question is whether there exists at the present time an alternative institution which would accomplish the same goals with less expenditure. Our data suggest that CCD programs will need major improvement before they can be seriously considered a functional alternative. The various shared-time programs are still too recent to pass judgment on them.

Is the Catholic school the kind of institution which will produce the Catholic needed in an age of modernization within the Church and ecumenical dialogue beyond the Church? Again we are in no position to render an answer, though our data suggest that those who went to these schools are more aware of, and more interested in, the most recent developments. One would want to know how suggested alternatives function before attempting an answer.

Is there still immense room for improvement in Catholic schools? There can be no doubt that the answer to this is in the affirmative. While the schools have some religious impact and are more than adequate academically, the changing emphases in Catholic doctrine and the changing social status of the Catholic population indicate that much improvement is essential. In particular, while the Catholic school Catholic is no less involved in community activities, one could argue that he ought to be more involved if he takes the new ecumenical emphases seriously. Further, no one would claim that the associations between Catholic education and attitudes of tolerance are as strong as they ought to be.

Finally, should Catholic schools continue? Are Catholic schools "the answer"? The "should" must be judged by the policy-makers—hierarchical, clerical, and lay—within the Church.

We have no doubt, however, that they will continue. There is nothing in our data to indicate that the expansion of the last quarter-century will be reversed, and there is in our data at least some reason to think that it will continue. Our opinion, for what it is worth, is that discussion by Catholics and non-Catholics alike concerning whether there will be Catholic schools is quite irrelevant. A system which involves one out of every seven school children in our republic does not go out of business, either all at once or gradually. It seems to us, rather, that the relevant question is how the distinctive system of Catholic schools can make the strongest possible contribution to the health of American society. In the fierce exchanges between those who are "pro" and those who are "con" this question is often overlooked. Yet, being for or against a school system with over five million students is like being for or against the Rocky Mountains: it is great fun but it does not notably alter the reality.

Yet we two authors, with our diverse ambivalences and prejudices, must confess that at the conclusion of this report we find ourselves in a somewhat awkward position. The problem is not that we fear that our findings will be taken out of context to back either side of a controversial position—of course they will, but this is an occupational hazard for the social researcher. Nor are we embarrassed because some of the more popular notions about the disadvantages of Catholic education have not been supported by the data; putting myths to rest is one of the joys of sociology. We are rather made uneasy by the thought that both Catholic educators and their critics may be so eager to seize upon our findings that they will overlook what we take to be the major theme behind all the findings: like other American schools, Catholic schools are neither as bad as their most severe critics would portray them nor as good as they might be. There has apparently been considerable improvement in Catholic schools in recent years, at least some of it no doubt because of the strong criticisms that have been leveled at Catholic education. There is nothing in our data which indicates that Catholic schools are a threat to American society, nor are they academically or religiously so poor they ought to be "phased out" if it were at all possible. But neither is there any indication that the schools are so good that all criticism should cease and that the search for "excellence" can be called off. The controversy about Catholic schools ought to go on—and it seems safe to say that it will, aided, we trust, by a little more light because of our study. But if in the midst of the controversy our data are used to obscure the fact that the essential question is how to make education in Catholic schools—in both its sacred and its profane aspects (should such a distinction be admitted in an age of theological change)—as good as possible, then we will regretfully conclude that our effort in the sociology of education has been a failure.

Appendix 1

Sampling and Fieldwork: A Methodological Note

The original listing for this sample was conducted in 1962 for the NORC study dealing with adult education.[1] At that time 12,000 households were asked a series of screening questions, of which religion was one and age another. The sample for this study was selected from those adults in the proper age group whose religion was Catholic. The major advantage of this method was in the reduction of the cost of finding Catholics for interviewing. The problems in using the method centered around the fact that the listing was more than a year old and that some respondents had moved. How this was handled will be discussed later.

The sample of Protestants is not a random sample of American Protestants but was selected to be comparable to the Catholics in age and geographic distribution. Thus, the number of Protestants selected from a primary sampling unit depended not on the number of Protestants in that area but on the number of Catholics. The Protestant sample was always one-fourth of the Catholic sample in each primary sampling unit (PSU). The same age limits of twenty-three to fifty-seven were used for the Protestant sample, which was also drawn from the 1962 listing.

THE SAMPLE DESIGN

The universe sampled in these studies is the total noninstitutional Catholic population of the United States, twenty-three to

[1] This has been published as *Volunteers for Learning* (Johnstone and Rivera, 1965). A more detailed description of the overall NORC sample is given there.

fifty-seven years of age, and a comparable group of Protestants. The sample is a standard multistage area probability sample.

SELECTION OF PSU'S

The primary sampling units (PSU's) employed were taken from NORC's 1953 master sample. The primary sampling units in the master sample had been selected with probabilities proportionate to their estimated 1953 populations. Population shifts in the past decade have rendered that set of PSU's a less efficient primary stage than it was when initially selected. Nevertheless, since a well-trained and experienced field force was available in that set of PSU's, it was obviously desirable to update the sample by some procedure which minimized the number of sampling units which needed to be changed. A procedure suggested by Keyfitz (1951) was employed. It involved comparing the desired 1960 probabilities of selection for PSU's to their original 1950 probabilities. If the originally selected PSU had a lower original probability than was warranted by its 1960 population, it was retained in the new sample and assigned the desired probability. If the originally selected PSU had a higher probability than was now warranted, it was subjected to the possibility of being dropped. The probability of retention for such a PSU was the ratio of its desired probability to its original probability. Replacements for dropped PSU's were made from among those PSU's which had not fallen into the 1953 sample and for which the 1953 probability was lower than that desired in 1960, the probability of 1960 selection being a function of the amount of growth the unit had undergone.

Basically, this method preserves the stratification based on the 1950 classifications by geographic region, size of largest town median family income, economic characteristics, and, in the South, by race. Counties which the Census Bureau classified as non-metropolitan in 1950 but as metropolitan in 1960 were, however, shifted to metropolitan strata. This restratification complicated the computing of selection probabilities but, in all likelihood, served to increase the efficiency of the sample somewhat.

The current set of PSU's is to be used until the 1970 census is available. For this reason, the 1960 census figures were extrapolated to 1967, the midpoint between the availability of the 1960 and 1970 census reports. For each PSU, the extrapolation was based on its population change between 1950 and 1960.

SELECTION OF SAMPLE WITHIN PSU'S

Within each selected PSU, localities were ordered according to cities with block statistics, other urban places, urbanized minor civil divisions, and nonurbanized MCD's, with the places ordered by 1960 population within each of these categories. Localities were selected from this list using a random start and applying a designated skip interval to the cumulative 1960 population. This provided stratification according to size and urban type of locality, and at the same time selection with probability proportional to size.

When available, 1960 census block statistics were used. Blocks were selected with probabilities proportional to the population in the block. In places without block statistics, census enumeration districts were selected with probabilities proportional to the number of households. The selected districts were then divided into segments, and estimates of the number of households within each segment were obtained by field counts. The selection of segments was then made with probability proportional to the number of households.

LOCATION OF HOUSEHOLDS WHICH MOVED

Vigorous efforts were made to locate selected sample households which had moved. The initial effort involved the use of a third-class mailing to all households, with a request for change-of-address information from the post office if the household had moved. This service from the post office succeeded in locating many moves, but for the other cases, interviewers checked with neighbors to determine the new address. All respondents who had moved to PSU's in which interviewers were available were included in the final sample.

The losses from the original list included the following types of respondents: moved to a PSU where no interviewer was available; moved—nonlocatable; died; or originally misclassified. As a result of these losses, the initial list of respondents shrank from 4,073 to 3,406, or 83.6 per cent.

SAMPLE EXECUTION

The overall cooperation rate on this study was 77 per cent, while the refusal rate was 18 per cent and other losses were 5 per cent. This rate is about 5 percentage points lower than the normal cooperation rates achieved by NORC on national studies, although every effort was made to obtain maximum cooperation. Two major demographic factors are responsible for the below-average cooperation. First, the Catholic and Protestant respondents in this study are concentrated in the largest metropolitan areas of this country, where it has always been most difficult to obtain cooperation on surveys. Second, older people with more spare time, who are generally more willing to cooperate on surveys, were excluded from the current survey. Thus, while this is a national sample of the universe it is intended to represent, this universe is substantially more difficult to survey than a sample of all adults or households.

When respondents were not at home, at least six call-backs were made. In almost all cases of refusal, a second interviewer attempted to obtain cooperation. The high refusal rate is not due to lack of effort, but it is to some extent due to the follow-up efforts which reduced the noncontacted households. It should be pointed out, however, that some of this high refusal rate may be due to interviewers who anticipated problems because of the nature of the questionnaire. Only three respondents refused to complete the survey after they started answering questions.

Appendix 2

Supplementary Tables on Indices

All tabular data in the appendix are percentage distributions. Percentage totals less than, or greater than, 100 per cent are the result of rounding.

Table A–2.1 Sacramental Index: Score Scale

Scale	All Catholic	Some Catholic	No Catholic	Convert	Protestant
1 (highly religious)	37	24	14	25	–
2	20	17	17	21	–
3	28	31	32	24	–
4	8	12	17	14	–
5 (not very religious)	6	15	19	15	–
Total	99	99	99	99	
N	340	691	784	228	
Exclusions	5	8	12	3	

Table A–2.2 Response Pattern for Individual Components of the Sacramental Index

	How Often Do You Go to Mass?				
Response	All Catholic	Some Catholic	No Catholic	Convert	Protestant
Every day	3	2	2	3	–
Several times a week	10	6	6	6	–
Every week	73	65	56	63	–
Several times a month	5	7	9	9	–
About once a month	2	4	6	3	–
Several times a year	4	6	10	8	–
About once a year	2	4	5	4	–

(Table A–2.2 continued)

Table A-2.2 Continued

Response	All Catholic	Some Catholic	No Catholic	Convert	Protestant
Practically never or not at all	2	7	7	5	–
Total	101	101	101	101	
N	343	697	792	231	
Exclusions	1	2	4	1	
About How Often Do You Receive Holy Communion?					
Every day	2	1	1	2	–
Several times a week	3	2	1	1	–
Every week	16	12	6	12	–
Several times a month	17	10	8	12	–
About once a month	26	20	20	26	–
Several times a year	23	26	28	24	–
About once a year	6	12	12	9	–
Practically never or not at all	7	18	24	15	–
Total	100	101	100	101	
N	343	694	788	231	
Exclusions	1	2	4	1	
How Often Do You Go to Confession?					
Every day	–	–	–	–	–
Several times a week	0	–	–	–	–
Every week	1	1	1	1	–
Several times a month	8	8	6	8	–
About once a month	42	29	25	33	–
Several times a year	35	35	32	32	–
About once a year	7	11	13	10	–
Practically never or not at all	7	17	24	17	–
Total	100	101	101	101	
N	339	691	786	229	
Exclusions	5	8	10	3	

Table A-2.3 Church-as-Teacher Index: Score Scale

Scale[a]	All Catholic	Some Catholic	No Catholic	Convert	Protestant
0 (low limit)	3	6	9	7	28
1	10	15	17	12	24
2	20	21	21	21	22
3	22	24	22	26	15
4	21	15	14	19	7
5	12	10	9	7	2
6	8	6	4	5	1
7 (high limit)	5	4	4	2	1
Total	101	101	100	99	100
N	345	699	796	231	530

[a] A high score indicates total agreement with the Church's right to teach on the topics listed.

Table A–2.4 Response Pattern for Individual Components of the
Church-as-Teacher Index

	Government Regulation of Business and Labor				
Response	All Catholic	Some Catholic	No Catholic	Convert	Protestant
Yes	16	11	10	7	4
No	2	2	3	2	2
Don't know	82	87	87	91	94
Total	100	100	100	100	100
N	343	696	788	231	528
Exclusions	1	3	8	1	2
	Racial Integration				
Yes	58	48	46	50	34
No	2	2	4	1	2
Don't know	40	50	50	49	64
Total	100	100	100	100	100
N	343	695	785	231	527
Exclusions	1	4	11	1	3
	U.S. Recognition of Red China				
Yes	19	15	15	15	8
No	5	6	9	3	4
Don't know	77	79	76	81	88
Total	101	100	100	99	100
N	342	693	787	229	526
Exclusions	2	6	9	2	4
	What Are Immoral Books or Movies?				
Yes	91	87	82	85	56
No	1	1	1	1	1
Don't know	8	12	17	13	43
Total	100	100	100	99	100
N	343	693	787	230	528
Exclusions	1	6	9	2	2
	Proper Means for Family Limitation				
Yes	66	56	46	57	18
No	4	4	5	4	1
Don't know	30	40	49	39	81
Total	100	100	100	100	100
N	343	692	784	230	528
Exclusions	1	7	12	2	2

(Table A–2.4   continued)

Table A–2.4 Continued

	Federal Aid to Education				
Response	All Catholic	Some Catholic	No Catholic	Convert	Protestant
Yes	50	44	42	37	16
No	3	4	6	4	2
Don't know	47	53	53	59	83
Total	100	101	101	100	101
N	343	694	786	231	527
Exclusions	1	5	10	1	3
	Communist Infiltration into Government				
Yes	43	42	40	43	27
No	5	4	7	5	2
Don't know	52	54	52	52	71
Total	100	100	99	100	100
N	343	693	783	229	527
Exclusions	1	6	13	3	3

Table A–2.5 Doctrinal Orthodoxy Index: Score Scale

Scale	All Catholic	Some Catholic	No Catholic	Convert	Protestant
0 (high agreement)	6	7	11	8	15
1	10	15	20	17	25
2	22	27	26	21	20
3	29	28	26	29	18
4	24	18	12	18	14
5 (low agreement)	9	6	5	7	8
Total	100	101	100	100	100
N	345	699	796	231	530

Table A–2.6 Response Pattern for Individual Components of the Doctrinal Orthodoxy Index

	There Is No Definite Proof That God Exists				
Response	All Catholic	Some Catholic	No Catholic	Convert	Protestant
Certainly true	10	11	13	12	14
Probably true	7	8	11	9	17
Uncertain	0	1	2	1	2
Probably false	3	7	9	7	12
Certainly false	80	74	65	72	55
Total	100	101	101	101	100
N	342	697	791	232	529
Exclusions	2	2	5	–	1

(Table A–2.6 continued)

Table A–2.6 Continued

God Doesn't Really Care How He Is Worshiped, So Long as He Is Worshiped					
Response	All Catholic	Some Catholic	No Catholic	Convert	Protestant
Certainly true	38	48	49	41	42
Probably true	30	26	25	25	26
Uncertain	2	2	2	2	2
Probably false	8	7	8	9	9
Certainly false	23	18	16	24	22
Total	101	101	100	100	101
N	342	698	789	232	529
Exclusions	2	1	7	–	1

God Will Punish the Evil for All Eternity					
Certainly true	62	52	49	42	34
Probably true	17	22	23	19	21
Uncertain	4	4	5	5	7
Probably false	8	12	14	19	21
Certainly false	8	10	9	15	17
Total	100	100	100	100	100
N	341	697	787	232	529
Exclusions	3	2	9	–	1

Science Proves That Christ's Resurrection Was Impossible					
Certainly true	5	3	5	1	4
Probably true	5	8	9	6	9
Uncertain	4	6	7	5	8
Probably false	14	18	20	21	28
Certainly false	73	66	60	68	51
Total	101	101	101	101	100
N	343	697	782	231	528
Exclusions	1	2	14	1	2

A Good Man Can Earn Heaven by His Own Efforts Alone					
Certainly true	34	40	43	35	30
Probably true	28	23	26	24	23
Uncertain	2	2	4	3	2
Probably false	13	15	14	17	16
Certainly false	24	20	14	22	30
Total	101	100	101	101	101
N	343	698	787	232	529
Exclusions	1	1	9	–	1

Table A–2.7 Ethical Orthodoxy Index: Score Scale

Scale	All Catholic	Some Catholic	No Catholic	Convert	Protestant
R (low—0 answers)	1	1	1	0	1
X (highest value)	2	1	0	0	0
0 (10 correct answers)	5	5	2	7	0
1 (1 correct answer)	1	1	1	0	1
2	2	4	4	2	4
3	5	8	9	6	9
4	9	12	14	12	16
5	13	14	16	14	20
6	20	16	19	18	21
7	15	16	14	15	15
8	19	14	12	15	9
9 (9 correct answers)	9	8	8	11	3
Total	101	100	100	100	99
N	345	699	796	231	530

Table A–2.8 Response Pattern for Individual Components of the Ethical Orthodoxy Index

It Is All Right To Ask an Insurance Company for More Money than You Deserve after an Auto Accident if You Think They Might Cut Your Claim

Response	All Catholic	Some Catholic	No Catholic	Convert	Protestant
Agree strongly	10	13	13	3	4
Agree somewhat	20	24	24	19	21
Disagree somewhat	26	24	27	27	26
Disagree strongly	43	37	33	49	47
Don't know	2	2	4	2	1
Total	101	100	101	100	99
N	343	696	792	231	529
Exclusions	1	3	4	1	1

Even Though You Find Some People Unpleasant, It Is Wrong To Try To Avoid Them

Agree strongly	17	23	24	21	22
Agree somewhat	38	36	35	34	37
Disagree somewhat	30	28	25	32	25
Disagree strongly	15	13	14	13	16
Don't know	0	0	1	1	1
Total	100	100	99	100	101
N	343	696	793	231	527
Exclusions	1	3	3	1	3

(Table A–2.8   continued)

Table A–2.8 Continued

A Married Couple Who Feel They Have as Many Children as They
Want Are Really Not Doing Anything Wrong when They Use
Artificial Means To Prevent Conception

Response	All Catholic	Some Catholic	No Catholic	Convert	Protestant
Agree strongly	14	24	28	26	72
Agree somewhat	16	22	23	18	19
Disagree somewhat	14	12	14	18	4
Disagree strongly	54	40	30	35	4
Don't know	2	3	5	4	2
Total	100	101	100	100	100
N	341	694	788	231	526
Exclusions	3	5	8	1	4

A Salesman Has the Right To Exaggerate How Good His Product
Is when a Customer Is Too Suspicious

Agree strongly	5	8	9	4	7
Agree somewhat	18	19	17	12	15
Disagree somewhat	19	20	21	24	19
Disagree strongly	57	52	52	56	57
Don't know	2	2	2	3	1
Total	101	101	101	99	99
N	343	696	794	231	528
Exclusions	1	3	2	1	2

Two People Who Are in Love Do Not Do Anything Wrong when They
Marry, Even Though One of Them Has Been Divorced

Agree strongly	18	26	30	22	58
Agree somewhat	20	28	26	32	29
Disagree somewhat	20	16	15	20	6
Disagree strongly	40	28	26	25	6
Don't know	3	2	3	2	1
Total	101	100	100	101	100
N	341	691	791	231	529
Exclusions	3	8	5	1	1

There Is an Obligation To Work for the End of Racial Segregation

Agree strongly	47	47	43	51	45
Agree somewhat	33	30	35	37	33
Disagree somewhat	11	11	10	8	12
Disagree strongly	6	8	8	3	6
Don't know	3	4	5	2	4
Total	100	100	101	101	100
N	343	696	791	231	527
Exclusions	1	3	5	1	3

(Table A–2.8   continued)

Table A–2.8   Continued

It Is All Right To Refuse To Talk to Some Member of the Family after a Disagreement, Especially if the Argument Was the Fault of the Other					
Response	All Catholic	Some Catholic	No Catholic	Convert	Protestant
Agree strongly	9	10	11	8	7
Agree somewhat	16	18	16	15	18
Disagree somewhat	22	21	23	22	21
Disagree strongly	52	50	49	55	52
Don't know	1	1	1	9	2
Total	100	100	100	99	100
N	343	696	793	230	528
Exclusions	1	3	3	2	2

If the Government Wastes Tax Money, People Don't Have To Be Too Exact on Their Income Tax Returns					
Agree strongly	3	6	6	4	4
Agree somewhat	9	8	9	6	6
Disagree somewhat	23	19	20	18	18
Disagree strongly	64	67	62	70	70
Don't know	2	1	3	1	2
Total	101	101	100	99	100
N	343	695	791	231	529
Exclusions	1	4	5	1	1

It Would Be Wrong To Take Considerable Time Off While Working for a Large Company, Even Though the Company Would Not Be Hurt by It at All					
Agree strongly	32	37	36	37	39
Agree somewhat	17	13	14	13	16
Disagree somewhat	16	16	16	16	14
Disagree strongly	34	32	31	32	30
Don't know	1	2	2	2	1
Total	100	100	99	100	100
N	343	696	789	231	527
Exclusions	1	3	7	1	3

It Is Not Really Wrong for an Engaged Couple To Have Some Sexual Relations before They Are Married					
Agree strongly	2	3	6	3	5
Agree somewhat	6	8	9	5	13
Disagree somewhat	9	12	12	12	16
Disagree strongly	81	74	71	77	63
Don't know	2	2	3	3	3
Total	100	99	101	100	100
N	342	695	790	231	524
Exclusions	2	4	6	1	6

(Table A–2.8   continued)

Table A–2.8 Continued

Even Though a Person Has a Hard Time Making Ends Meet, He Should Still Try To Give Some of His Money to the Help of the Poor					
Response	All Catholic	Some Catholic	No Catholic	Convert	Protestant
Agree strongly	44	41	41	47	37
Agree somewhat	38	41	39	37	39
Disagree somewhat	12	10	13	11	15
Disagree strongly	6	8	7	5	8
Don't know	0	0	1	0	1
Total	100	100	101	100	100
N	343	696	791	231	529
Exclusions	1	3	5	1	1

Table A–2.9 Sexual Mores Index: Score Scale

Scale	All Catholic	Some Catholic	No Catholic	Convert	Protestant
0	7	15	16	9	32
1	19	27	33	33	54
2	28	26	25	28	12
3 (high on holding to rigid sex norms)	46	32	25	29	1
Total	100	100	99	99	99
N	319	649	723	216	499
Exclusions	26	50	73	15	31

Table A–2.10 Honesty Index: Score Scale

Scale	All Catholic	Some Catholic	No Catholic	Convert	Protestant
0	8	10	11	6	7
1	22	26	26	18	19
2	38	35	35	37	38
3 (high)	31	29	28	39	36
Total	99	100	100	100	100
N	333	670	740	217	508
Exclusions	12	29	56	14	22

Table A–2.11 Religious Knowledge Index: Score Scale

Scale	All Catholic	Some Catholic	No Catholic	Convert	Protestant
R (low—0 answers)	13	26	36	35	–
1	25	31	34	30	–
2	26	21	17	19	–
3	14	11	9	6	–
4	9	6	2	2	–
5	9	3	1	6	–
6 (high)	4	1	1	1	–
Total	100	99	100	99	
N	345	699	796	231	

Table A–2.12 Response Pattern for Individual Components of the Religious Knowledge Index

The Word We Use To Describe the Fact That the Second Person of the Trinity Became Man Is . . .					
Response	All Catholic	Some Catholic	No Catholic	Convert	Protestant
Transfiguration	27	31	31	30	–
Incarnation	48	38	35	31	–
Transubstantiation	10	9	7	8	–
Immaculate Conception	15	22	28	31	–
Total	100	100	101	100	
N	319	632	637	201	
Exclusions	25	67	159	31	
Supernatural Life Is . . .					
The life we receive from our parents	4	4	9	2	–
Sanctifying grace in our souls	46	34	27	33	–
Our life after death	42	53	44	48	–
The power to work miracles	7	9	19	16	–
Total	99	100	99	99	
N	323	656	705	213	
Exclusions	21	43	91	19	
The "Mystical Body" Is . . .					
Christ's body in heaven	12	9	14	14	–

(Table A–2.12   continued)

Table A–2.12 Continued

Response	All Catholic	Some Catholic	No Catholic	Convert	Protestant
Christ in Holy Communion	59	69	66	67	–
Christ united with His followers	23	15	9	14	–
None of the above	6	7	10	5	–
Total	100	100	99	100	
N	327	650	687	218	
Exclusions	17	49	109	14	
Uncharitable Talk Is Forbidden By . . .					
The 2nd commandment	22	20	20	19	–
The 4th commandment	13	21	23	30	–
The 8th commandment	55	47	44	42	–
The 10th commandment	10	12	13	8	–
Total	100	100	100	99	
N	308	599	615	191	
Exclusions	36	100	181	41	
A Man Is Judged Immediately after He Dies. This Judgment Is Called . . .					
General judgment	19	18	15	18	–
Natural judgment	4	7	10	13	–
Particular judgment	37	22	14	20	–
Final judgment	40	53	61	49	–
Total	100	100	100	100	
N	329	659	709	212	
Exclusions	15	40	87	20	
The Encyclicals *Rerum novarum* of Leo XIII and *Quadragesimo anno* of Pius XI Both Deal With . . .					
Christian marriage	15	18	15	12	–
Christian education	19	26	34	25	–
The condition of labor	34	17	10	16	–
Papal infallibility	32	38	41	47	–
Total	100	99	100	100	
N	252	504	529	161	
Exclusions	92	195	267	71	

Table A–2.13 Community Involvement Index[a]: Response Pattern for Individual Components

Response	All Catholic	Some Catholic	No Catholic	Convert	Protestant
How Many Organizations Do You Belong to Besides Religious Ones— Such as Unions, Professional Organizations, Clubs, Neighborhood Organizations, Etc.?					
None	57	45	49	41	40
One	21	26	29	34	26
Two	11	16	12	15	14
Three or four	7	10	9	7	14
Five or more	4	3	2	3	7
Total	100	100	101	100	101
N	344	697	790	230	529
Exclusions	0	2	6	1	1
In General, Would You Say You Are Very Active in These Organizations, Fairly Active, or Inactive?					
Very active	21	19	22	24	20
Fairly active	49	55	47	44	58
Inactive	30	26	31	31	22
Total	100	100	100	99	100
N	146	381	406	135	318
Exclusions	198	318	390	96	212
Do You Read Any Nonreligious Magazines Regularly?					
Yes	71	72	66	77	79
No	29	28	34	23	21
Total	100	100	100	100	100
N	344	697	789	230	530
Exclusions	0	2	7	1	0
How Interested Are You in What Goes On in the World Today? For Instance, Do You Follow the International News Very Closely, Fairly Closely, or Not Too Closely?					
Very closely	31	30	26	30	27
Fairly closely	52	50	55	51	59
Not too closely	17	20	19	19	15
Total	100	100	100	100	101
N	344	698	791	230	530
Exclusions	0	1	5	1	0

[a] A scale score of 7 is high on involvement. The index refers to outer community and activity and not to restricted horizons.

(Table A–2.13   continued)

Table A–2.13 Continued

What about Local News—the Things That Happen Here in Your
(Town) (Area)? Do You Follow Local News Very Closely,
Fairly Closely, or Not Too Closely?

Response	All Catholic	Some Catholic	No Catholic	Convert	Protestant
Very closely	42	46	43	44	44
Fairly closely	48	45	43	45	48
Not too closely	10	9	14	11	8
Total	100	100	100	100	100
N	344	697	790	230	530
Exclusions	0	2	6	1	0

Do You Ever Get as Worked Up by Something That Happens in the News
as You Do by Something That Happens in Your Personal Life?

	All Catholic	Some Catholic	No Catholic	Convert	Protestant
Yes	63	58	59	60	52
No	37	42	41	40	48
Total	100	100	100	100	100
N	343	694	787	228	530
Exclusions	1	5	9	3	0

Table A–2.14 General Knowledge Index: Score Scale

Scale	All Catholic	Some Catholic	No Catholic	Convert	Protestant
0	5	2	5	1	1
1	9	8	10	4	4
2	13	13	15	14	12
3	16	18	21	15	20
4	16	19	18	26	17
5	14	15	16	14	18
6	14	15	10	14	15
7 (high)	13	9	6	11	13
Total	100	99	101	99	100
N	337	683	777	227	522
Exclusions	7	16	19	5	8

Table A–2.15 Response Pattern for Individual Components of the
General Knowledge Index

What Ocean Would One Cross in Going from the United States to England?

Response	All Catholic	Some Catholic	No Catholic	Convert	Protestant
Don't know	9	5	9	5	5
Right	84	90	84	88	91

(Table A–2.15 continued)

Table A–2.15 Continued

Response	All Catholic	Some Catholic	No Catholic	Convert	Protestant
Wrong	8	6	7	7	4
Total	101	101	100	100	100
N	343	694	788	230	527
Exclusions	1	5	8	2	3

Could You Tell Me Who Billy Graham Is?					
Don't know	9	6	9	3	2
Right	87	89	84	93	96
Wrong	5	6	7	4	2
Total	101	101	100	100	100
N	342	691	787	231	527
Exclusions	2	8	9	1	3

What Mineral or Metal Is Important in the Making of the Atomic Bomb?					
Don't know	41	37	42	37	33
Right	42	45	42	47	49
Wrong	18	18	17	16	17
Total	101	100	101	100	99
N	343	689	785	230	527
Exclusions	1	10	11	2	3

Will You Tell Me Who Plato Was?					
Don't know	40	35	47	33	32
Right	41	39	26	45	41
Wrong	19	27	28	23	27
Total	100	101	101	101	100
N	342	693	786	230	528
Exclusions	2	6	10	2	2

Will You Tell Me Who Robert McNamara Is?					
Don't know	29	24	33	28	23
Right	50	46	39	40	47
Wrong	22	31	29	31	30
Total	101	101	100	99	100
N	342	692	787	230	529
Exclusions	2	7	9	2	1

How about Charles Lindbergh—Can You Tell Me What He Was Famous For?					
Don't know	6	4	8	3	4
Right	69	72	67	73	78
Wrong	26	25	26	24	18
Total	101	101	101	100	100
N	343	695	788	231	529
Exclusions	1	4	8	1	1

(Table A–2.15   continued)

Table A–2.15   Continued

	Who Wrote *War and Peace*?				
Don't know	68	69	79	65	65
Right	24	20	12	25	24
Wrong	8	12	10	10	11
Total	100	101	101	100	100
N	340	689	782	230	527
Exclusions	4	10	14	2	3
	What Is the Name of the Pope?				
Don't know	7	10	13	10	26
Right	82	74	71	76	50
Wrong	12	16	17	14	24
Total	101	100	101	100	100
N	344	695	788	230	528
Exclusions	–	4	8	2	2

Table A–2.16   Anti-Semitism Index: Score Scale

Scale	All Catholic	Some Catholic	No Catholic	Convert	Protestant
0	30	29	26	30	27
1	26	26	28	34	27
2 (high anti-Semitism)	44	44	47	36	45
Total	101	99	101	100	99
N	336	668	731	221	506
Exclusions	9	31	65	10	24

Table A–2.17   Response Pattern for Individual Components of the Anti-Semitism Index

Response	All Catholic	Some Catholic	No Catholic	Convert	Protestant
	Jews Have Too Much Power in the United States				
Agree strongly	6.2	6.0	6.1	4.4	5.7
Agree somewhat	13.5	11.2	15.4	9.7	13.3
Disagree somewhat	34.0	39.1	35.5	36.1	37.0
Disagree strongly	44.9	41.8	37.2	48.4	41.5
Don't know	1.5	1.9	5.7	1.3	2.5
Total	100.1	100.0	99.9	99.9	100.0
N	341	685	785	227	525
Exclusions	3	14	11	4	5

(Table A–2.17   continued)

Table A–2.17 Continued

Jewish Businessmen Are About as Honest as Other Businessmen					
Response	All Catholic	Some Catholic	No Catholic	Convert	Protestant
Agree strongly	40.5	41.2	37.6	43.8	38.4
Agree somewhat	38.5	41.6	39.0	37.2	41.8
Disagree somewhat	14.9	13.0	14.3	14.4	13.9
Disagree strongly	5.5	3.5	5.2	2.6	4.6
Don't know	.6	.7	3.9	1.8	1.3
Total	100.0	100.0	100.0	99.9	100.0
N	343	690	785	228	525
Exclusions	3	14	11	4	5

Table A–2.18 Racism Index: Score Scale

Scale	All Catholic	Some Catholic	No Catholic	Convert	Protestant
0	13	12	9	16	12
1	14	16	18	20	16
2	23	22	22	21	20
3	22	20	22	21	22
4	21	20	18	13	17
5 (high anti-Negro)	8	9	10	9	12
Total	101	99	99	100	99
N	320	638	707	213	489
Exclusions	25	61	89	18	41

Table A.2.19 Response Pattern for the Individual Components of the Racism Index

Negroes Shouldn't Push Themselves Where They Are Not Wanted					
Response	All Catholic	Some Catholic	No Catholic	Convert	Protestant
Agree strongly	23.7	26.3	26.8	19.3	26.3
Agree somewhat	38.3	35.3	32.5	39.9	36.4
Disagree somewhat	23.7	22.4	23.5	23.2	22.5
Disagree strongly	13.5	15.4	15.1	16.6	13.1
Don't know	.9	.6	2.0	.9	1.7
Total	100.1	100.0	100.0	99.9	100.0
N	342	688	790	228	525
Exclusions	2	11	6	3	5

(Table A–2.19   continued)

Table A–2.19 Continued

Response	All Catholic	Some Catholic	No Catholic	Convert	Protestant
White People Have a Right To Live in an All-White Neighborhood if They Want To, and Negroes Should Respect That Right					
Agree strongly	43	43	43	35	46
Agree somewhat	32	30	29	36	29
Disagree somewhat	14	18	18	17	16
Disagree strongly	10	8	8	9	8
Don't know	1	1	2	2	1
Total	100	100	100	99	100
N	343	691	788	227	526
Exclusions	1	8	8	4	4
I Would Strongly Disapprove If a Negro Family Moved Next Door to Me					
Agree strongly	14	17	17	15	21
Agree somewhat	25	22	18	21	19
Disagree somewhat	34	38	40	43	35
Disagree strongly	24	22	22	19	23
Don't know	3	1	3	2	2
Total	100	100	100	100	100
N	341	691	785	228	526
Exclusions	3	8	11	3	4
Negroes Would Be Satisfied if It Were Not for a Few People Who Stir Up Trouble					
Agree strongly	21	18	19	12	15
Agree somewhat	31	35	34	31	36
Disagree somewhat	26	25	33	33	24
Disagree strongly	21	21	18	23	24
Don't know	1	1	3	1	1
Total	100	100	100	100	100
N	343	688	786	228	524
Exclusions	1	11	10	3	6
There Is an Obligation To Work toward the End of Racial Segregation					
Agree strongly	47	47	43	50	45
Agree somewhat	33	30	35	37	33
Disagree somewhat	11	11	10	8	12
Disagree strongly	6	8	8	3	6
Don't know	3	4	5	2	4
Total	100	100	100	100	100
N	343	696	791	229	527
Exclusions	1	3	5	1	3

Table A–2.20 Anti-Protestant Index: Score Scale

Scale	All Catholic	Some Catholic	No Catholic	Convert	Protestant[a]
0	57	60	54	48	44
1	29	31	32	36	32
2 (high anti-Protestant feelings)	14	9	14	16	23
Total	100	100	100	100	99
N	330	672	733	220	490
Exclusions	15	27	63	11	40

[a] Anti-Catholic feelings measured.

Table A–2.21 Response Pattern for Individual Components of the Anti-Protestant Index

Most Protestants Are Inclined to Discriminate against Catholics					
Response	All Catholic	Some Catholic	No Catholic	Convert	Protestant
Agree strongly	7	6	8	9	–
Agree somewhat	21	20	23	29	–
Disagree somewhat	42	43	39	39	–
Disagree strongly	28	30	28	21	–
Don't know	2	1	3	2	–
Total	100	100	101	100	
N	341	687	778	228	
Exclusions	3	12	18	3	
Protestants Don't Really Take Their Religion Seriously Compared to Catholics					
Agree strongly	7	8	8	8	–
Agree somewhat	21	15	20	20	–
Disagree somewhat	36	37	35	30	–
Disagree strongly	34	38	33	40	–
Don't know	2	2	4	2	–
Total	100	100	100	100	
N	344	699	796	227	
Exclusions	0	0	0	4	

Table A–2.22   "Manichaean" Index: Score Scale

Scale	All Catholic	Some Catholic	No Catholic	Convert	Protestant
0	26	27	22	28	28
1	34	30	31	32	29
2	21	27	28	28	27
3 ("Manichaean")	19	16	19	11	15
Total	100	100	100	99	99
N	325	665	733	212	515
Exclusions	20	34	63	19	15

Table A–2.23   Response Pattern for Individual Components of the "Manichaean" Index

Although Christ Saved the Spiritual World by His Death and Resurrection, the Material World Is under the Control of the Devil

Response	All Catholic	Some Catholic	No Catholic	Convert	Protestant
Agree strongly	10	7	7	7	7
Agree somewhat	13	14	18	12	18
Disagree somewhat	21	23	24	24	24
Disagree strongly	54	54	48	53	51
Don't know	3	1	4	4	0
Total	100	99	101	100	100
N	342	687	778	229	524
Exclusions	2	12	18	2	6

The World Is Basically a Dangerous Place where There Is Much Evil and Sin

Agree strongly	21	19	21	16	17
Agree somewhat	28	30	29	33	32
Disagree somewhat	26	26	25	22	23
Disagree strongly	23	24	23	26	28
Don't know	2	1	2	3	0
Total	100	100	100	100	100
N	339	687	777	228	524
Exclusions	5	12	19	3	6

The Catholic Church Teaches That a Good Christian Ought To Think about the Next Life and Not Worry about Fighting against Poverty and Injustice in This Life

Agree strongly	18	15	15	11	11
Agree somewhat	19	23	26	18	20
Disagree somewhat	25	28	24	29	29
Disagree strongly	35	33	32	40	40
Don't know	3	1	3	2	1
Total	100	100	100	100	101
N	341	686	777	229	526
Exclusions	3	13	19	2	4

Table A–2.24 Anti-Civil-Liberties Index: Score Scale

Scale	All Catholic	Some Catholic	No Catholic	Convert	Protestant
0	10	12	9	13	28
1	22	24	18	22	32
2	33	30	29	25	29
3	23	24	28	16	10
4 (high)	12	11	16	13	–
Total	100	101	100	99	99
N	315	639	706	214	518
Exclusions	30	60	90	17	12

Table A–2.25 Response Pattern for Individual Components of the Anti-Civil-Liberties Index

People Who Don't Believe in God Have as Much Right to Freedom of Speech as Anyone Else					
Response	All Catholic	Some Catholic	No Catholic	Convert	Protestant
Agree strongly	59	62	52	57	55
Agree somewhat	26	27	31	30	30
Disagree somewhat	9	8	10	6	7
Disagree strongly	5	3	6	6	6
Don't know	1	0	2	1	1
Total	100	100	101	100	99
N	344	699	796	227	527
Exclusions	0	0	0	4	3
Books Written by Communists Should Not Be Permitted in Public Libraries					
Agree strongly	41	36	45	32	28
Agree somewhat	16	17	15	20	17
Disagree somewhat	23	26	22	28	29
Disagree strongly	19	20	16	19	26
Don't know	1	1	1	1	1
Total	100	100	99	100	100
N	343	691	787	228	526
Exclusions	1	8	9	3	4
Only People Who Believe in God Can Be Good American Citizens					
Agree strongly	19	21	23	25	15
Agree somewhat	14	16	17	19	18
Disagree somewhat	25	26	24	23	28
Disagree strongly	40	37	35	32	38
Don't know	1	0	1	1	0
Total	99	100	100	100	99
N	340	686	778	227	526
Exclusions	4	13	18	4	4

(Table A–2.25   continued)

Table A–2.25 Continued

Response	All Catholic	Some Catholic	No Catholic	Convert	Protestant
Protestant Ministers Should Not Be Permitted To Teach Things Publicly Which Are Opposed to Catholic Doctrine					
Agree strongly	16	17	18	13	–
Agree somewhat	18	15	18	20	–
Disagree somewhat	31	32	34	29	–
Disagree strongly	32	34	26	36	–
Don't know	2	2	4	2	–
Total	99	100	100	100	
N	340	687	777	228	
Exclusions	4	12	19	3	

Table A–2.26 Religious Extremism Index: Score Scale

Response	All Catholic	Some Catholic	No Catholic	Convert	Protestant
0	7	10	7	12	–
1	18	22	18	26	–
2	21	22	22	26	–
3	24	23	27	18	–
4	22	17	19	16	–
5 (extremist)	7	6	7	3	–
Total	99	100	100	101	
N	312	650	712	212	
Exclusions	33	49	84	19	

Table A–2.27 Response Pattern for Individual Components of the Religious Extremism Index

Response	All Catholic	Some Catholic	No Catholic	Convert	Protestant
A Family Should Have as Many Children as Possible and God Will Provide for Them					
Agree strongly	26	18	17	12	4
Agree somewhat	28	23	23	15	8
Disagree somewhat	31	36	32	43	26
Disagree strongly	13	22	27	29	61
Don't know	1	1	1	1	1
Total	100	100	100	100	100
N	341	690	787	228	527
Exclusions	3	9	9	3	3

(Table A–2.27 continued)

Table A–2.27 Continued

Scale	All Catholic	Some Catholic	No Catholic	Convert	Protestant
Love of Neighbor Is More Important than Avoiding Meat on Friday					
Agree strongly	32	38	35	40	–
Agree somewhat	21	26	26	26	–
Disagree somewhat	18	17	17	16	–
Disagree strongly	26	19	20	16	–
Don't know	3	1	2	2	–
Total	100	101	100	100	
N	339	684	781	229	
Exclusions	5	15	15	2	
The Catholic Church Teaches That Large Families Are More Christian than Small Families					
Agree strongly	14	11	12	9	–
Agree somewhat	14	19	18	15	–
Disagree somewhat	26	24	29	28	–
Disagree strongly	45	45	39	46	–
Don't know	2	1	2	2	–
Total	101	100	101	100	
N	342	686	777	227	
Exclusions	2	13	19	4	
The Catholic Church Teaches That If There Is Ever a Majority of Catholics in This Country, Catholicism Must Become the Official Religion of the United States					
Agree strongly	7	3	6	3	–
Agree somewhat	8	8	11	7	–
Disagree somewhat	19	23	26	22	–
Disagree strongly	64	65	55	66	–
Don't know	2	1	2	2	–
Total	100	100	100	100	
N	341	689	776	229	
Exclusions	3	10	20	2	
Protestant Ministers Should Not Be Permitted To Teach Things Publicly Which Are Opposed to Catholic Doctrine					
Agree strongly	16	17	18	13	–
Agree somewhat	19	15	18	20	–
Disagree somewhat	31	32	34	29	–
Disagree strongly	32	34	26	36	–
Don't know	2	2	4	2	–
Total	100	100	100	100	
N	340	687	777	228	
Exclusions	4	12	19	3	

Table A–2.28 Permissiveness Index: Score Scale

Scale	All Catholic	Some Catholic	No Catholic	Convert	Protestant
0	18	15	17	11	13
1	35	39	37	38	28
2	36	37	38	39	44
3 (highly permissive)	11	9	9	13	14
Total	100	100	101	101	99
N	339	679	760	224	515
Exclusions	6	20	36	7	15

Table A–2.29 Response Pattern for Individual Components of the Permissiveness Index

When Parents Are Wrong They Should Be Willing To Admit It to Their Children

Response	All Catholic	Some Catholic	No Catholic	Convert	Protestant
Agree strongly	49	49	52	54	59
Agree somewhat	31	32	32	31	28
Disagree somewhat	15	14	11	13	10
Disagree strongly	4	4	4	2	2
Don't know	1	1	2	0	1
Total	100	100	101	100	100
N	343	692	790	229	527
Exclusions	1	7	6	2	3

It Is as Important for a Child To Think for Himself as To Be Obedient to His Parents

	All Catholic	Some Catholic	No Catholic	Convert	Protestant
Agree strongly	54	57	53	55	60
Agree somewhat	25	31	32	27	28
Disagree somewhat	14	8	9	11	10
Disagree strongly	6	4	4	6	2
Don't know	1	0	2	1	1
Total	100	100	100	100	101
N	342	691	787	229	527
Exclusions	2	6	9	2	3

Rules Should Never Be Relaxed, Because Children Will Take Advantage of It

	All Catholic	Some Catholic	No Catholic	Convert	Protestant
Agree strongly	33	32	37	25	25
Agree somewhat	30	34	30	31	36
Disagree somewhat	28	26	23	32	27
Disagree strongly	9	8	8	11	12
Don't know	1	1	1	1	0
Total	101	101	99	100	100
N	343	692	786	228	525
Exclusions	1	7	10	3	5

Appendix 3

Further Supplementary Tables

Table A–3.1   Sex and Religious Behavior

| | Per Cent High on Index | | | | | | Partial Gammas | | |
| | Male | | | Female | | | | | Net |
Index	All Cath- olic	Some Cath- olic	No Cath- olic	All Cath- olic	Some Cath- olic	No Cath- olic	Male	Female	Partial Gammas
Sacramental index	29	17	10	41	30	18	.30	.22	.26
Church-as-teacher index	47	34	30	45	35	33	.17	.13	.15
Religious knowledge index	35	20	11	35	22	15	.32	.30	.31
Doctrinal orthodoxy index	34	23	15	31	23	18	.22	.17	.19
Ethical orthodoxy index	30	22	17	37	32	27	.12	.12	.12
Sexual mores index	41	26	21	49	36	29	.18	.19	.19
N	129	324	365	216	324	431			

Table A–3.2 Age and Religious Behavior

Index	Per Cent High on Index (by Age)												Partial Gammas (by Age)				Net Partial Gammas
	20–29			30–39			40–49			50–59			20–29	30–39	40–49	50–59	
	All Cath-olic	Some Cath-olic	No Cath-olic	All Cath-olic	Some Cath-olic	No Cath-olic	All Cath-olic	Some Cath-olic	No Cath-olic	All Cath-olic	Some Cath-olic	No Cath-olic					
Sacramental index	33	21	14	38	24	16	32	23	11	44	28	18	.27	.24	.26	.33	.27
Church-as-teacher index	39	27	24	50	37	31	48	37	33	45	35	33	.18	.20	.11	.14	.16
Religious knowledge index	42	20	11	35	22	12	34	21	13	32	23	16	.48	.29	.29	.25	.32
Doctrinal orthodoxy index	40	24	14	36	23	16	36	23	19	19	26	16	.30	.21	.15	.17	.20
Ethical orthodoxy index	35	29	19	37	27	24	32	29	25	31	28	18	.17	.14	.07	.15	.12
Sexual mores index	41	26	23	55	36	23	45	30	27	36	34	29	.18	.27	.13	.19	.19
N	60	133	116	118	208	253	95	243	277	65	105	146					

Table A–3.3 Size of Place Respondent Was Reared and Religious Behavior

Index	Per Cent High on Index (by City Size)												Partial Gammas				Net Partial Gammas
	Farm or Open			Small Town			Small City			Large City			Farm or Open	Small Town	Small City	Large City	
	All Cath-olic	Some Cath-olic	No Cath-olic	All Cath-olic	Some Cath-olic	No Cath-olic	All Cath-olic	Some Cath-olic	No Cath-olic	All Cath-olic	Some Cath-olic	No Cath-olic					
Sacramental index	50	38	22	35	20	15	29	26	8	39	22	11	.28	.13	.32	.34	.27
Church-as-teacher index	34	33	34	48	30	29	40	37	32	52	37	32	.04	.16	.15	.19	.15
Religious knowledge index	41	16	14	35	21	13	27	23	13	40	22	12	.26	.29	.25	.36	.30
Doctrinal orthodoxy index	31	26	20	30	24	15	34	26	17	32	20	25	.25	.10	.24	.23	.20
Ethical orthodoxy index	19	33	26	33	28	34	48	33	20	35.	22	20	.08	.08	.17	.18	.14
Sexual mores index	46	46	30	45	32	29	49	32	15	43	27	26	.33	.09	.29	.19	.20
N	32	80	160	54	152	265	119	187	168	137	276	194					

Table A–3.4 Generation Index and Religious Behavior (Per Cent)

Index	Generation Index (by Order of Generation)															Partial Gammas					Net Partial Gammas
	1st			2nd			3rd			4th			5th			1st	2nd	3rd	4th	5th	
	All Cath-olic	Some Cath-olic	No Cath-olic	All Cath-olic	Some Cath-olic	No Cath-olic	All Cath-olic	Some Cath-olic	No Cath-olic	All Cath-olic	Some Cath-olic	No Cath-olic	All Cath-olic	Some Cath-olic	No Cath-olic						
Sacramental index	25	18	17	31	21	11	35	27	20	52	30	15	46	26	21	.23	.26	.17	.37	.17	.24
Church-as-teacher index	39	33	30	42	35	28	46	35	28	52	40	37	50	28	38	.09	.16	.09	.10	.18	.14
Religious knowledge index	33	8	8	27	20	10	46	25	18	41	26	16	45	24	16	.46	.26	.31	.25	.36	.30
Doctrinal orthodoxy index	19	15	7	27	19	17	37	33	17	39	21	22	48	27	19	.20	.10	.28	.16	.27	.17
Ethical orthodoxy index	28	23	16	33	23	20	3.	27	20	41	33	32	38	34	29	.16	.10	.15	.14	.05	.11
Sexual mores index	45	22	22	43	25	18	43	35	31	59	40	36	53	35	44	.18	.22	.12	.17	.10	.18
N	36	39	108	118	253	379	52	112	88	46	117	78	54	113	79						

Table A–3.5 Respondent's Father's Main National Background and Religious Behavior

Respondent's Father's Main National Background (Per Cent)

Index	(1) English, Scotch, Australian, New Zealand, etc.			(2) Irish			(3) German, Austrian, Swiss			(4) Italian			(5) French, French-Canadian, Belgian			(6) Polish		
	All Cath-olic	Some Cath-olic	No Cath-olic	All Cath-olic	Some Cath-olic	No Cath-olic	All Cath-olic	Some Cath-olic	No Cath-olic	All Cath-olic	Some Cath-olic	No Cath-olic	All Cath-olic	Some Cath-olic	No Cath-olic	All Cath-olic	Some Cath-olic	No Cath-olic
Sacramental index	33	17	17	45	31	21	51	33	21	24	20	8	32	20	14	24	15	16
Church-as-teacher index	38	23	38	55	43	35	43	33	34	31	37	26	37	28	36	49	31	44
Religious knowledge index	29	20	21	48	29	25	41	30	18	31	18	10	30	17	19	22	20	6
Doctrinal orthodoxy index	33	34	38	40	24	15	32	27	25	21	20	13	33	24	8	19	23	20
Ethical orthodoxy index	24	25	31	39	37	30	35	36	32	20	15	16	43	25	17	29	23	34
Sexual mores index	26	27	38	51	37	42	60	45	39	37	21	15	45	26	39	39	25	29
N	21	35	42	92	141	71	63	126	71	29	85	249	60	75	36	41	92	50

Respondent's Father's Main National Background (Per Cent)

Index	(7) Russian and Other Eastern European			(8) Spanish, Portuguese, Latin American, Puerto Rican			(9) Scandinavian and Lithuanian			Partial Gammas									Net Partial Gammas
	All Cath-olic	Some Cath-olic	No Cath-olic	All Cath-olic	Some Cath-olic	No Cath-olic	All Cath-olic	Some Cath-olic	No Cath-olic	1	2	3	4	5	6	7	8	9	
Sacramental index	25	12	19	17	8	11	27	24	12	.03	.25	.33	.16	.24	.25	.05	.13	.01	.19
Church-as-teacher index	50	31	28	84	32	31	45	34	27	.06	.20	.08	.15	.12	.03	.16	.19	.13	.13
Religious knowledge index	25	12	9	33	0	5	18	15	19	.16	.31	.35	.20	.30	.16	.38	.33	.00	.26
Doctrinal orthodoxy index	63	26	17	0	20	12	9	15	12	.04	.25	.13	.16	.23	.08	.26	.02	.04	.15
Ethical orthodoxy index	25	32	25	17	16	13	36	29	28	.09	.04	.08	.09	.24	.01	.06	.02	.04	.08
Sexual mores index	56	25	21	0	4	16	40	27	25	.01	.12	.13	.18	.25	.08	.22	.13	.05	.14
N	16	51	64	6	25	105	11	41	51										

Table A–3.6 PSU Size and Religious Behavior

Index	PSU Size (Per Cent)												Partial Gammas				Net Partial Gammas
	Big City			Small City			Big County			Small County			Big City	Small City	Big County	Small County	
	All Cath-olic	Some Cath-olic	No Cath-olic	All Cath-olic	Some Cath-olic	No Cath-olic	All Cath-olic	Some Cath-olic	No Cath-olic	All Cath-olic	Some Cath-olic	No Cath-olic					
Sacramental index	39	22	9	33	20	13	39	43	24	40	18	23	.33	.29	.23	.08	.28
Church-as-teacher index	51	40	30	43	34	30	45	30	43	40	22	30	.17	.18	.03	.03	.14
Religious knowledge index	41	21	11	32	19	14	29	27	24	33	20	8	.38	.26	.13	.40	.30
Doctrinal orthodoxy index	30	12	12	44	24	16	32	30	29	53	18	21	.25	.22	.01	.16	.20
Ethical orthodoxy index	40	23	21	34	31	19	21	30	28	27	24	31	.20	.15	.02	.16	.15
Sexual mores index	48	31	22	44	29	24	39	46	35	57	25	31	.26	.20	.03	.05	.19
N	128	237	274	164	320	318	38	97	79	15	45	125					

Table A–3.7 Father's Occupation (Duncan Score) and Religious Behavior

Index	Father's Occupation (Duncan Score) (Per Cent)												Partial Gammas				Net Partial Gammas
	0			1			2–4			5 or More			0	1	2–4	5 or More	
	All Cath-olic	Some Cath-olic	No Cath-olic	All Cath-olic	Some Cath-olic	No Cath-olic	All Cath-olic	Some Cath-olic	No Cath-olic	All Cath-olic	Some Cath-olic	No Cath-olic					
Sacramental index	27	16	9	36	27	17	36	25	15	52	27	11	.30	.22	.19	.40	.26
Church-as-teacher index	44	35	30	42	31	33	45	35	35	54	37	21	.19	.07	.10	.29	.14
Religious knowledge index	30	15	10	33	19	13	33	25	15	45	22	15	.33	.25	.26	.40	.30
Doctrinal orthodoxy index	23	29	17	34	26	16	34	21	16	43	32	19	.12	.21	.19	.28	.20
Ethical orthodoxy index	28	21	15	34	26	24	38	25	25	26	32	23	.09	.08	.15	.16	.12
Sexual mores index	38	27	19	47	29	27	48	33	30	51	36	23	.22	.19	.12	.24	.27
N	70	124	147	86	194	287	111	227	207	65	132	128					

Table A–3.8 Respondent's Father's Educational Level and Religious Behavior

| | Respondent's Father's Educational Level (Per Cent) | | | | | | | | | | | | Partial Gammas | | | | Net Partial Gammas |
| | 6th Grade or Less | | | 7th or 8th Grade | | | Attended High School | | | Attended College | | | | | | | |
Index	All Cath-olic	Some Cath-olic	No Cath-olic	All Cath-olic	Some Cath-olic	No Cath-olic	All Cath-olic	Some Cath-olic	No Cath-olic	All Cath-olic	Some Cath-olic	No Cath-olic	6th	7th or 8th	High School	Col-lege	
Sacramental index	24	22	13	44	27	20	50	25	17	50	32	22	.21	.25	.35	.17	.25
Church-as-teacher index	37	37	35	55	36	35	59	35	34	41	36	14	.07	.16	.18	.27	.14
Religious knowledge index	32	16	12	38	28	17	42	26	13	44	23	13	.27	.30	.22	.39	.28
Doctrinal orthodoxy index	26	19	19	41	26	19	41	25	17	34	36	14	.12	.26	.24	.14	.25
Ethical orthodoxy index	34	25	20	39	30	26	38	29	22	31	31	23	.13	.12	.12	.01	.12
Sexual mores index	41	25	24	55	36	33	51	34	30	40	43	22	.15	.18	.16	.14	.16
N	104	186	319	80	205	155	66	130	102	32	47	37					

Table A–3.9 Respondent's Mother's Educational Level and Religious Behavior

| | Respondent's Mother's Educational Level (Per Cent) | | | | | | | | | | | | Partial Gammas | | | | Net Partial Gammas |
| | 6th Grade or Less | | | 7th or 8th Grade | | | Attended High School | | | Attended College | | | | | | | |
Index	All Cath-olic	Some Cath-olic	No Cath-olic	All Cath-olic	Some Cath-olic	No Cath-olic	All Cath-olic	Some Cath-olic	No Cath-olic	All Cath-olic	Some Cath-olic	No Cath-olic	6th	7th or 8th	High School	Col-lege	
Sacramental index	24	18	14	47	28	17	38	29	15	73	32	22	.19	.30	.26	.18	.24
Church-as-teacher index	37	32	33	55	37	32	47	36	32	55	23	40	.09	.18	.14	.05	.13
Religious knowledge index	27	19	12	40	24	17	45	25	16	55	26	33	.28	.31	.28	.33	.29
Doctrinal orthodoxy index	23	22	18	40	24	20	37	27	18	45	23	47	.10	.17	.26	.08	.16
Ethical orthodoxy index	32	23	21	36	17	26	38	37	20	55	29	47	.10	.11	.18	.18	.13
Sexual mores index	44	23	24	52	34	30	46	40	24	45	29	47	.13	.17	.22	.12	.17
N	88	164	300	96	222	182	99	162	138	11	31	33					

Table A–3.10 Respondent's SES (Duncan Score) and Religious Behavior

| | Respondent's SES (Duncan Score) (Per Cent) | | | | | | | | | | | Partial Gamma | | | | Net Partial Gammas |
| | 0, 1 | | | 2, 3 | | | 4–6 | | | 7–9 | | | 0, 1 | 2, 3 | 4–6 | 7–9 | |
Index	All Cath-olic	Some Cath-olic	No Cath-olic	All Cath-olic	Some Cath-olic	No Cath-olic	All Cath-olic	Some Cath-olic	No Cath-olic	All Cath-olic	Some Cath-olic	No Cath-olic					
Sacramental index	20	21	9	38	23	12	38	22	15	49	35	30	.19	.32	.20	.25	.23
Church-as-teacher index	38	27	29	51	33	30	47	39	33	51	41	31	.09	.21	.14	.17	.15
Religious knowledge index	19	14	9	37	15	8	36	27	18	52	31	24	.25	.32	.24	.38	.28
Doctrinal orthodoxy index	22	21	13	21	21	15	37	24	23	41	31	19	.12	.22	.15	.24	.17
Ethical orthodoxy index	19	21	16	37	22	16	45	21	31	35	30	29	.04	.12	.06	.07	.07
Sexual mores index	39	24	19	40	21	23	52	37	29	50	45	36	.00	.00	.00	.00	.00
N	86	170	259	71	165	185	110	239	233	71	111	89					

Table A–3.11 Respondent's Educational Level and Religious Behavior

| | Respondent's Educational Level (Per Cent) | | | | | | | | | | | | Partial Gammas | | | | Net Partial Gammas |
| | 8th Grade or Less | | | Some High School | | | High School Graduate | | | Attended College | | | 8th Grade or Less | Some High School | High School Grad-uate | At-tended Col-lege | |
Index	All Cath-olic	Some Cath-olic	No Cath-olic	All Cath-olic	Some Cath-olic	No Cath-olic	All Cath-olic	Some Cath-olic	No Cath-olic	All Cath-olic	Some Cath-olic	No Cath-olic					
Sacramental index	25	22	12	24	15	10	45	27	15	51	31	21	.28	.16	.26	.28	.24
Church-as-teacher index	35	15	31	42	31	25	51	40	31	54	40	40	.12	.18	.20	.07	.15
Religious knowledge index	19	8	8	26	12	13	32	23	12	61	37	22	.25	.14	.35	.41	.29
Doctrinal orthodoxy index	16	14	11	27	16	11	32	27	19	51	33	27	.15	.16	.17	.25	.18
Ethical orthodoxy index	19	12	14	40	22	14	40	30	29	42	37	32	.15	.15	.07	.10	.10
Sexual mores index	35	20	21	44	17	17	51	40	30	52	41	34	.24	.18	.19	.11	.18
N	102	85	194	38	196	192	114	266	268	91	151	142					

Table A–3.12 Spouse's Church Attendance and Religious Behavior

| Index | Spouse's Church Attendance (Per Cent) | | | | | | | | | | | | Partial Gammas | | | | Net Partial Gammas |
| | Several Times Weekly | | | Every Week | | | Several Times Yearly | | | Once a Year | | | Several Times Weekly | Every Week | Several Times Yearly | Once a Year | |
	All Cath-olic	Some Cath-olic	No Cath-olic	All Cath-olic	Some Cath-olic	No Cath-olic	All Cath-olic	Some Cath-olic	No Cath-olic	All Cath-olic	Some Cath-olic	No Cath-olic					
Sacramental index	58	56	42	38	30	16	10	5	7	24	9	7	.22	.28	.10	.20	.23
Church-as-teacher index	50	45	44	48	40	33	34	31	25	39	22	24	.10	.13	.20	.10	.14
Religious knowledge index	42	37	24	37	24	13	17	12	11	21	8	13	.28	.33	.13	.15	.26
Doctrinal orthodoxy index	29	35	26	33	27	19	21	21	13	39	10	9	.11	.16	.14	.26	.17
Ethical orthodoxy index	64	50	36	36	32	27	28	19	15	21	18	11	.21	.11	.02	.08	.10
Sexual mores index	78	59	55	50	39	30	29	15	13	23	17	10	.25	.20	.09	.13	.17
N	24	48	50	209	353	361	29	107	157	33	109	127					

Table A–3.13 Parental Score on Parental Religiousness Index and Religious Behavior

| Index | Parental Score on Religiousness Index (Per Cent) | | | | | | | | | | | | Partial Gammas | | | | Net Partial Gammas |
| | 0 | | | 1 | | | 2 | | | 3 | | | 0 | 1 | 2 | 3 | |
	All Cath-olic	Some Cath-olic	No Cath-olic	All Cath-olic	Some Cath-olic	No Cath-olic	All Cath-olic	Some Cath-olic	No Cath-olic	All Cath-olic	Some Cath-olic	No Cath-olic					
Sacramental index	24	14	10	20	21	9	28	28	23	55	34	21	.10	.09	.11	.34	.14
Church-as-teacher index	38	35	27	44	33	30	40	32	37	53	40	33	.12	.16	.03	.22	.11
Religious knowledge index	22	20	10	28	18	14	33	23	16	42	23	19	.22	.20	.26	.40	.26
Doctrinal orthodoxy index	38	21	12	31	15	14	33	26	25	31	33	21	.24	.06	.08	.23	.15
Ethical orthodoxy index	24	24	19	28	26	20	36	29	29	38	33	25	.01	.07	.05	.20	.07
Sexual mores index	35	22	16	26	25	19	43	32	16	50	40	33	.11	.09	.08	.21	.11
N	37	161	269	39	122	186	130	269	215	118	113	75					

Appendix 4

Correlates of Catholic School Attendance

INTRODUCTION

The future of Catholic education depends not so much on who went to Catholic schools in the past as on whether the past trends have continued into the present and can reasonably be expected to continue in years to come. We deal here with these questions.

Data reported in Chapter 2 indicated that the more well-to-do the respondent's parent was, the more likely the respondent was to have attended a Catholic school; thus in the previous generation economic and social success of the Catholic immigrant groups did not weaken their predilection for Catholic education but, on the contrary, reinforced it. If this trend were to continue, and if the Catholic population continues to move up the status ladder (as our study would indicate), then the proportion of Catholics in Catholic schools will certainly not decline and may actually increase in years to come.

While the respondents in our study were asked whether their children had attended Catholic schools, we did not attempt to find out whether their children were in Catholic schools at the present time. There were two reasons for this decision. First, such a question would have involved fairly complicated interviewing techniques, which would have prolonged an interview that was already too lengthy, forcing elimination of more impor-

Reprinted from *The School Review,* **72,** No. 1 (Spring, 1964), 52–73, by permission of the University of Chicago Press. Copyright 1964 by the University of Chicago.

The research reported herein was done originally on a grant from The Study of Catholic Education of the University of Notre Dame.

tant items. Second, information was already available about current Catholic school attendance of our respondents' children from another survey of the same sample frame.

Some 12,000 households, drawn in a national probability sample, were visited by members of the NORC interviewing staff in May of 1962. Approximately 3,000 of these households had Catholics as their heads. In these households and those where the parent who was not head was Catholic, there were 2,708 Catholic children who were in primary or secondary schools. Since our analysis is concerned with children rather than with households, the characteristics of the household and its members are herein considered as attributes of the children. Thus one family with two children of school age will in effect be "voting" twice in our tabulations.[1]

Only one serious problem was encountered in the mechanics of analysis. Even though we knew the religion of both parents of the children studied, we did not know the religion of the child. If both parents are Catholic, it is reasonably fair to presume that the child is a Catholic too. However, no such presumption can be made of the children of mixed marriages. We did not know how many of the children of mixed marriages were baptized Catholics or were reared as Catholics; hence, we do not know how many of the 404 children of mixed marriages in our sample would properly fit in the denominator of a proportion of Catholics attending Catholic schools. Our strategy, therefore, has been to treat these offspring of mixed marriages as belonging to a separate category.

Table A–4.1, in addition to presenting data on the proportion

[1] All children of school age but not in school were excluded from the analysis.

Table A–4.1   Catholic School Attendance of Children of Catholic Parents, by Marital Status of Parents

Marriage	Per Cent	N
Endogamous marriage	42.0	2,304
Exogamous marriage	20.5	404
All marriages	38.8	2,708

of American Catholics of school age in Catholic schools, also indicates the dimensions of the analytical problem concerning the children of mixed marriages. While 42 per cent of the children of Catholic marriages are in Catholic schools, less than half that proportion (20 per cent) of the children of mixed marriages are in Catholic schools. Clearly this twenty-two percentage-point margin represents some children who were not baptized Catholics and others who are not Catholics now in any practical sense of the word. However, when the two groups are lumped together, the proportion of the total going to Catholic schools falls only in the vicinity of 39 per cent. Thus, despite the obscurity of the mixed-marriage situation, we can say with confidence that somewhere between 40 and 42 per cent of American Catholics of school age are in Catholic grammar or high schools.

This proportion is not greatly different from that estimated by certain Catholic experts in recent years; however, it does obscure the differences which might be presumed to exist between primary and secondary school attendance. Table A–4.2 shows that there is indeed a substantial difference, with 46 per cent of the children of Catholic marriages attending Catholic grammar schools and only one-third in Catholic high schools.[2] The decline in the percentage attending Catholic schools is somewhat less sharp for the children of mixed marriages. However, the important conclusion from Tables A–4.1 and A–4.2 has to do not so much with the differences between mixed marriages and Catholic marriages, or with the differences between primary and secondary schools, but rather with the blunt fact that less than one-half of the Catholic

[2] Unfortunately, we do not know from the available data how many of the children between seven and sixteen years old are in grammar schools and how many in high schools, even though we do have this information for six-year-olds and for those seventeen and over. Thus we were forced to put arbitrarily all those fourteen and over in high school and those thirteen and under in grammar school. Since the survey was taken in May, it is very likely that there were some fourteen year-olds still in grammar school. Thus, the number of high-school students is somewhat overestimated in this study. It was felt that there would be less distortion in this procedure than in putting the fourteen-year-old group in grammar school. This procedure also rests on the assumption that the Catholic school system operates generally on a basis of eight elementary and four secondary years rather than six elementary and six secondary years.

children in the country are in Catholic schools. Despite the tremendous efforts put into the Catholic school system, it is still reaching less than 50 per cent of its potential students.

DEMOGRAPHY

In Table A–4.3 we begin to examine the specific correlates of Catholic school attendance for the children of Catholic marriages. The table shows that Catholic boys are somewhat less likely than Catholic girls to be in Catholic grammar schools (though there are no differences at the high-school level). Perhaps this difference can be attributed to the fact that the Catholic schools are in a position to dismiss children who are more serious disciplinary problems, and boys traditionally have been more likely to be disciplinary problems. It could be further argued that the sisters of these boys, even though they would not be expelled from the schools, probably would not go to Catholic high schools, and hence there is no difference at the secondary level.

Table A–4.4 shows that there is a strong relationship between some kind of family disorganization and nonattendance at Catholic schools (at both levels). There is a decline of thirteen per-

Table A–4.2   Per Cent of Children of Catholic Parents Attending Catholic Schools, by Marital Status of Parents

Marriage	Primary	Secondary
Endogamous marriage	46.1 (1,551)	33.7 (753)
Exogamous marriage	23.3 (274)	14.6 (130)
All marriages	42.7 (1,825)	30.8 (883)

Table A–4.3   Per Cent of Children of All Catholic Marriages Attending Catholic Schools, by Sex

Educational Level of Child	Male	Female
Primary[a]	44 (798)	48 (753)
Secondary	33 (375)	34 (378)

[a] Age thirteen and under.

centage points in grammar school and fifteen percentage points in high school among those families where the child is not living with both his parents.

Even though family disorganization has an effect which might be expected, family size has an effect which is contrary to expectations—as is demonstrated by Table A–4.5.[3] It would have been assumed that, as the size of the family increases, Catholic school attendance will decline because of the increased expense of providing tuition for a large family. However, the tendency seems to be in the opposite direction, especially at the grammar-

---

[3] It must be remembered that childless families are not counted, nor are families which are small and do not have anyone of school age. Thus the average number of children per family will seem higher than for the total population.

Table A–4.4   Per Cent of Children of All Catholic Marriages Attending Catholic Schools, by Relation to Head of Household

Educational Level of Child	Child with Both Parents in Household	Other
Primary	$47_{(1,411)}$	$34_{(140)}$
Secondary	$35_{(667)}$	$20_{(86)}$

Table A–4.5   Per Cent of Children of All Catholic Marriages Attending Catholic Schools, by Number of Persons under Twenty-one for Whom Head of Household Is Responsible

Number under Twenty-one	Primary	Secondary
One	$33_{(130)}$	$33_{(139)}$
Two	$39_{(278)}$	$38_{(184)}$
Three	$51_{(377)}$	$33_{(180)}$
Four	$45_{(269)}$	$35_{(93)}$
Five	$47_{(182)}$	$24_{(61)}$
Six	$53_{(149)}$	$23_{(40)}$
Seven	$51_{(93)}$	$30_{(23)}$
Eight	$58_{(24)}$	$83_{(6)}$
Nine	$44_{(49)}$	$59_{(27)}$

school level, the smallest proportion in attendance at Catholic schools being from families where there is only one child and the largest from families with eight children. The same trend is observable at the secondary level, though it is more erratic here, perhaps because of the small number of cases in some categories. Nevertheless, it is clear even at the high-school level that large family size is not an insurmountable obstacle to Catholic school attendance.

An explanation for this phenomenon might be found in the fact that, while those who have large families are indeed under heavier financial pressure, they also are more inclined to be in sympathy with Catholic education, since both a larger family and Catholic education result from value premises which are taken to be part of the Catholic system of beliefs. "Good Catholics" have bigger families and send their children to Catholic schools in greater proportion precisely because they are "good Catholics" and despite the financial problems involved.[4] It should also be noted that many Catholic schools have tuition systems that charge for families and not for individual children. Thus, the "extra" children attend free.

GEOGRAPHY AND ECOLOGY

In Tables A–4.6 and A–4.7 we turn to the geographic and ecological correlates of Catholic school attendance. It has been assumed for some time that Catholic school attendance would be high in those parts of the country where the majority of the Catholic population is concentrated. While Table A–4.6 supports such an assumption, it does not do so in as dramatic a fashion as might be expected. Attendance is higher in the eortheastern and north central regions than in the West, but with the exception of the 51 per cent attending Catholic grammar schools in the east north central region, more than one-half of the students in the north central and northeastern states are not in Catholic elementa-

---

[4] The direct relationship between family size and Catholic school attendance s a white-collar phenomenon. Some 39 per cent of the children of blue-collar amilies are in Catholic schools, with size of family having practically no effect)n such attendance. However, in white-collar families those with five or more 'hildren have 62 per cent in Catholic schools, and those with one to four children ıave 46 per cent in Catholic schools.

ry schools. The "problem" of nonattendance is more serious in the West, but it is nonetheless a national "problem." The three southern subregions have a much higher attendance rate than would have been expected from the South. However, the twenty-eight respondents in the south central cells are hardly an adequate case base, and the southeastern cell shows the influence of the school system of the oldest Catholic diocese in the country—Baltimore. Hence, the figures we report for the South must not be taken to represent the deep South, where there are so very few Catholics.

In Table A–4.7 we observe that Catholics from areas where there are more than ten thousand people in the central cities are more likely to go to Catholic schools (on both levels) than are those from more rural counties. Interestingly enough, however,

Table A–4.6   Per Cent of Children of Catholic Marriages Attending Catholic Schools, by Region of Country

Region	Primary	Secondary
New England	44(162)	31 (80)
Middle Atlantic	48(537)	35(256)
East north central	51(351)	35(155)
West north central	47(139)	39 (80)
Southeast	57 (75)	50 (29)
East south central	56 (9)	40 (5)
West south central	74 (19)	56 (9)
Mountain	32 (38)	7 (14)
Pacific	30(221)	26(125)

Table A–4.7   Per Cent of Children of Catholic Marriages Attending Catholic Schools, by Ecological Situation

Ecological Situation	Primary	Secondary
SMSA over two million	49(514)	39(262)
SMSA under two million	47(679)	32(315)
Counties with central city over 10,000	54(199)	38 (92)
Counties with central city under 10,000	23(159)	17 (84)

the rate for SMSA's (Standard Metropolitan Statistical Area) under two million is somewhat less than for counties with central cities over ten thousand. Once again we should note that while nonattendance is higher in rural areas, it is also extant in urban areas outside the inner city, where less than one-half of the children of Catholic marriages are in Catholic grammar schools and less than two-fifths are in Catholic high schools.

It is within the cities themselves that Catholic school attendance is the highest, as can be seen in Table A–4.8. Indeed with one exception, the farther away is the central city in a given sampling unit, the lower becomes the rate of Catholic school attendance. Thus we observe that living in an area near a fairly large city increases Catholic school attendance, and living within the city increases it even more. In Table A–4.9 we combine our geographic and ecological information to see how city size, location of dwelling, and region combine to influence going to Catholic schools. It is clear that city size and location of dwelling have a more important effect in the western and north central regions than they do in the East. Thus the difference between the central city and areas outside an SMSA is only six percentage points in the East but twenty-three percentage points in the Midwest and thirty-two percentage points in the Far West. The spread in the Midwest is not the result of the lower rates in the non-central-city groups

Table A–4.8 Per Cent of Children of Catholic Marriages Attending Catholic Schools, by Location of Dwelling Units

Location	Primary	Secondary
Inside city[a]	55 (693)	40 (370)
In suburbs	44 (429)	32 (171)
In outskirts	34 (341)	22 (167)
In open country	36 (72)	27 (44)
N	2,287	
NA	17	
Total N	2,304	

[a] The central city of the sampling unit, no matter how small the city is.

(which have about the same rates as their confreres in the Northeast) but of the very high rate of central-city dwellers from this
region; in this group we encounter the first proportion with a
large case base which is substantially over one-half. It appears
that the powerful and well-organized Catholic school systems of
the midwestern cities have both the capacity and the drawing
power for large numbers of students. If nonattendance at Catholic schools is to be defined as a "problem," then the problem
is least serious in the central cities of the Midwest—although,
and this is an important qualification, such a performance does
not appear to be maintained in the suburbs and hinterlands of
this region.

It seems to be reasonable to assume that the association between ecological site and Catholic school attendance might be
related to the size of the Catholic community in a given area.
A certain density of Catholic population must be assumed before
finances are available to support a school system; it also seems
likely that as the density of the Catholic population increases
there is more possibility for mobilizing support for the norms
requiring support of Catholic schools and attendance at them.
However, such an explanation must not be permitted to obscure
the real, but as yet only dimly understood, differences in Catholicism in different regions of the country. For historical reasons
that are still obscure, middle-western Catholics have traditionally
been stronger supporters of Catholic schools than eastern Catho-

Table A–4.9 Per Cent Attending Catholic Schools, by Region
and Ecological Site

Ecological Site	Region			
	Northeast	Central	South	West
City (in SMSA)	$48_{(417)}$	$61_{(235)}$	$55_{(54)}$	$45_{(144)}$
Suburb (in SMSA)	$44_{(383)}$	$43_{(230)}$	$71_{(64)}$	$22_{(190)}$
Not in SMSA	$42_{(235)}$	$38_{(257)}$	$44_{(23)}$	$13_{(49)}$
N		2,287		
NA		17		
Total N		2,304		

lics. This phenomenon seems to be true despite the apparent inclination of middle-western Catholics to be somewhat less "defensive" than their coreligionists in the eastern states.

SOCIAL CLASS

It would be surprising indeed if Catholics of whatever socioeconomic attainment had the same rate of attendance at Catholic schools. All we know about differences among the several socioeconomic levels leads us to expect that social class is one of the major differentiating factors in Catholic school attendance. It might at first be doubtful which way the influence operates. An argument could be made in theory for the case that as Catholics leave behind the immigration experience and move upward socially and economically, they would tend to adjust to the educational practices of other Americans and to become more independent of the demands of their church for religious education. However, recent studies of religious practice and participation

Table A–4.10 Per Cent of Children of Catholic Marriages Attending Catholic Schools, by Income

Income	Primary	Secondary
Under $1,000	17 (24)	27 (11)
$ 1,000–$ 1,999	22 (32)	22 (18)
$ 2,000–$ 2,999	30 (60)	37 (30)
$ 3,000–$ 3,999	38 (128)	22 (58)
$ 4,000–$ 4,999	47 (196)	39 (92)
$ 5,000–$ 5,999	42 (256)	35 (128)
$ 6,000–$ 6,999	49 (198)	30 (101)
$ 7,000–$ 7,999	48 (182)	34 (83)
$ 8,000–$ 9,999	57 (193)	36 (104)
$10,000–$14,999	52 (173)	35 (86)
$15,000 and over	69 (49)	50 (28)
N primary	1,491	
N secondary	73	
Total N	2,304	

suggest that religiousness increases with social class. Hence we would be justified in suspecting that Catholic school attendance is considered a mark of religious participation and has a direct relationship with social class. Tables A–4.10, A–4.11, and A–4.12 confirm this suspicion.

With only two relatively minor exceptions, grammar-school attendance increases as income increases, so that only 17 per cent of Catholics with income under $1,000 and almost 70 per cent of those with income over $15,000 attend Catholic grammar schools. The high-school rates do not vary consistently (perhaps because of the small case bases in some cells), but the proportions for the lower-income groups tend to be lower than those for the upper-income groups. However, there is only a difference of thirteen percentage points between the lowest rate (for those in the $1,000–$2,000 bracket) and the second highest rate ($10,000–$15,000).

Occupation has an effect (shown in Table A–4.11) similar to that of income; it differentiates strongly at the grammar-school level and somewhat less consistently at the high-school level.

Table A–4.11   Per Cent of Children of Catholic Marriages Attending Catholic Schools, by Occupation of Head of Household

Occupation	Primary	Secondary
Professional	61 (136)	43 (61)
Managerial	53 (225)	40 (104)
Clerical	59 (74)	44 (43)
Sales	64 (102)	27 (41)
Crafts	41 (363)	30 (156)
Operative	41 (227)	30 (160)
Service	42 (113)	39 (65)
Labor	44 (82)	36 (36)
Farm	40 (48)	40 (27)
N	2,113	
NA	191	
Total N	2,304	

Indeed at the primary level the break between white-collar workers and blue-collar workers is quite sharp, with a difference of nine percentage points between the lowest rate among the white-collar families (53 per cent for the children of managers) and the highest of the blue-collar groups (44 per cent for laborers).

Finally, Table A–4.12 presents the same pattern as the two preceding tables. The better educated the head of the household of a grammar school child is, the more likely the child is to be in a Catholic school—with a spread of forty-eight percentage points separating the lowest group from the highest. The pattern once again is less consistent among high-school students, but even here, those with less-educated parents tend to have somewhat lower scores than those with better-educated parents.

It is clear, therefore, that Catholic school attendance is more likely to occur on the grammar-school level among those with better education, more money, and more prestigious occupations. But it is not altogether clear why this phenomenon is not so pronounced at the high-school level. Table A–4.13 attempts to explain this phenomenon. It should be noted that the major differences between the social classes exist outside of the central

Table A–4.12 Per Cent of Children of Catholic Marriages Attending Catholic Schools, by Education of Head of Household

Education of Head of Household	Primary	Secondary
1–4 years	22 (41)	14 (28)
5–7 years	36 (111)	28 (71)
8 years	41 (203)	34 (125)
9–11 years	42 (341)	38 (195)
12 years	49 (480)	34 (184)
13–15 years	54 (207)	30 (93)
16 years	56 (79)	38 (29)
More than 16 years	70 (66)	35 (20)
N	2,273	
NA	31	
Total N	2,304	

cities and that the improved attendance rates for the upper-class group at the secondary level is entirely a noncity phenomenon. This is to say that whatever advantage class confers on attendance at a Catholic high school operates only outside of the central city. (Even at the grammar-school level, class seems to operate much more strongly for those outside central cities.) An explanation for this is not hard to fashion: inside the cities the Catholic school system is fairly well established, and relatively little "extra" effort is required to send children to Catholic schools. But outside the cities more effort, and perhaps greater sacrifices in terms of time and energy, are required, and the members of the more well-to-do class have values which are more likely to incline them to such effort. There are serious implications in this explanation for the future of Catholic schools. As the Catholic population spreads beyond the central city, there is a danger that the Catholic school system will become more and more a white-collar system— to a degree even greater than the degree to which the Catholic population will become a white-collar population. A more general explanation for the relationship between social class and that form of religious participation which encourages sending one's children to Catholic schools has yet to be evolved. It seems to be

Table A–4.13   Per Cent of Children of Catholic Marriages Attending Catholic Schools, by City Size, Educational Level, and Income

City Size and Educational Level	Under $6,000	Over $6,000
Central city:[a]		
Primary	$57_{(420)}$	$64_{(243)}$
Secondary	$40_{(228)}$	$41_{(139)}$
Non-central city:		
Primary	$34_{(474)}$	$52_{(354)}$
Secondary	$25_{(210)}$	$32_{(152)}$
N	2,230	
NA	74	
Total N	2,304	

[a] In SMSA.

reasonably clear that in most western countries the middle class is more active in its religious participation than the working class. Whether this is merely because the middle class participates more in all activities than the working class, or whether there is something in middle-class culture that predisposes it to religious "respectability," is not certain. A careful study of the "use" of religion by different classes has yet to be made. Whatever the explanation, the data reported in this paper suggest that as American Catholicism becomes more and more a middle-class religion, the demand for desks in Catholic schools will increase—as will the money available to pay for these desks.

SOCIAL CLASS AND ECOLOGY

We have discovered thus far that both the social class of the family and the location of the family home contribute to whether a child goes to Catholic schools. In Table A–4.14, region, class, and location of home are combined to give an overview of the joint influence of these three variables on Catholic school attendance.

The children of Catholic families in the sample have been

Table A–4.14   Per Cent of Children of Catholic Marriages Attending Catholic Schools, by Region, Ecological Situation, and Social Class

Ecology and Social Class	Region			
	Northeast	North Central	South	West
Central city:[a]				
White-collar	57 (125)	78 (92)	56 (17)	80 (41)
Blue-collar	43 (270)	53 (129)	55 (29)	31 (75)
Non-central city:				
White-collar	49 (218)	43 (222)	65 (54)	35 (74)
Blue-collar	42 (341)	41 (224)	59 (37)	14 (165)

N	2,113
NA on occupation	191
Total N	2,304

[a] In SMSA.

divided into sixteen groups, according to the section of the country they are from, whether they live in a central city of an SMSA, and whether their parental occupation is white-collar or blue-collar. While there are some great differences among the cells in the table (four-fifths of the children of white-collar workers in central cities in the central region are in Catholic schools, as opposed to one-seventh of the children of blue-collar workers outside of central cities in the far West), note that most of the cells with large bases fall within 10 per cent of the national average for Catholic school attendance. In fact, if the South, whose small original numbers may be leading to distortion, is excluded, there are only three groups which score more than ten percentage points above the national average (white-collar, central-city dwellers from the other three regions), and two which are more than ten percentage points below the national average. Thus there are only a few groups which are dramatically overrepresented and a few which are dramatically underrepresented (Table A–4.15).[5]

From the material analyzed we do not know the reasons for nonattendance at Catholic schools. Clearly there is a relationship between attendance at Catholic schools and various demographic, ecological, and sociological factors. But even in the groups most likely to go to Catholic schools there is still a substantial minority of children who are not in such schools. In many instances it is fair to assume that the schools are simply not available, and in other instances the explanation is that parents have made a deliberate decision not to send their children to Catholic schools.

---

[5] Table A–4.15 presents the same data in a somewhat different fashion. Association coefficients have been computed for the Catholic school attendance of each group versus all the other students in the sample. The Q-coefficient gives a rough idea of how much better are the chances of going to a Catholic school for a child in a given group than are the chances of other children. If one somewhat arbitrarily decides that a Q of ± .25 or more represents a substantial advantage or disadvantage, there are five advantaged groups (four of them white-collar and three from cities) and three disadvantaged groups (all of them from the West). Thus to be a white-collar worker may have considerable advantages in sending one's children to Catholic schools (especially if one lives in the central city), and to be from the West gives one substantial disadvantages (especially if one is not a white-collar city dweller). Within the other socio-ecological groups, differences tend to be relatively minor.

Very little is known about the motivation behind such decisions, much less about the differences in motivation which might be found in different classes. White-collar suburban nonattendance may be largely the result of the nonavailability of schools, although there is certainly a minority who have chosen public schools because they believe their children will receive better education in public schools. On the other hand, blue-collar urban nonattendance may be the result of the costs of Catholic schools and the inclination of Italian Catholics (as well as some, though not all, eastern European groups) to view Catholic education with some skepticism. Thus a total explanation of the correlates of Catholic school attendance will have to go beyond social class and demography and investigate not only social psychological factors but also the transitions going on within the various Catholic ethnic groups (which transitions may vary from region to region).

MIXED MARRIAGE

Thus far the concern of this appendix has been with those children who were presumably Catholic beyond any reasonable

Table A–4.15 Q-Coefficients for Socio-ecological Groups for Attendance at Catholic Schools

Region	Urban Status	Social Status	Q
West	City	White-collar	+.68
North central	City	White-collar	+.63
South	Not city	White-collar	+.39
South	Not city	Blue-collar	+.31
Northeast	City	White-collar	+.29
South	City	White-collar	+.28
South	City	Blue-collar	+.20
North central	City	Blue-collar	+.16
Northeast	Not city	White-collar	+.09
North central	Not city	White-collar	−.03
Northeast	City	Blue-collar	−.04
Northeast	Not city	Blue-collar	−.08
North central	Not city	Blue-collar	−.09
West	Not city	White-collar	−.27
West	City	Blue-collar	−.29
West	Not city	Blue-collar	−.70

doubt—those who have Catholic parents. However, there were still 404 children in the sample who came from mixed marriages and who may or may not be Catholics. It may well be asked whether the correlates of Catholic school attendance for this group are the same as those for the children of Catholic marriages. Table A–4.16 shows that the regional and central-city associations continue, though the latter association is somewhat weaker than for Catholic marriages. However, the social-class association shifts from positive to slightly negative, with the children of mixed marriages from blue-collar families more likely to be in Catholic schools than those from white-collar families. It is possible that the Catholic spouse is more readily able to insist on a Catholic school education in the blue-collar segment of the population, in which the partner is not so likely to have strong convictions on the subject, than in the white-collar segment.

RELIGIOUS INSTRUCTION

An almost inevitable question at this point concerns how many of the Catholics in non-Catholic schools received some kind of religious instruction. While we cannot answer this question with any degree of confidence, there is some information available in the data being analyzed which offers what might be a tentative answer. The parents interviewed were asked the following ques-

Table A–4.16 Per Cent of Children of Mixed Marriages Attending Catholic Schools, by Region, Occupation, and Ecology

Variable	Per Cent	N
Region:		
Northeast	28	170
North central	20	132
South	10	39
West	7	93
Occupation:		
White-collar	18	180
Blue-collar	23	224
Ecology:		
City[a]	23	115
Not city	19	289

[a] Central city in SMSA.

tion about their children: "During the past twelve months . . . has [name] taken lessons or received instruction in any subject not connected with regular school work, including things like music lessons, religious classes, swimming lessons, summer-school classes, or anything like this?" Parents of 44 per cent of the Catholic children not in Catholic grammar schools and 24 per cent of the high-school group reported their children to have had some religious instruction. Whether this is a high or low percentage depends to a considerable extent on one's point of view. It is certainly low by the standards of the Catholic goal of religious instruction for every Catholic child, since slightly more than one-third of the Catholic children of school age are neither in Catholic schools nor receiving religious instruction. However, the fact that almost two-thirds are receiving such instruction or are in Catholic schools certainly compares favorably with the religious educational achievements by other American religious groups or of Catholics in other industrialized countries (Table A–4.17).

In Table A–4.18 we examine whether the correlates for Catholic school attendance are also correlates for attendance of religious instruction and discover that, by and large, they are not. In both the northeastern and the western states, children of blue-collar workers are as likely or more likely than the children of white-collar workers to attend religious instruction classes if they are not in Catholic schools. In all regions but the south central states, city dwellers are less likely to send their children to instruction classes (except for white-collar workers in the Northeast). Finally, non-city dwellers from the West do as well or better than the same groups from the Northeast. What these phenomena suggest is that, with some exceptions, religious instruction has

Table A–4.17 Per Cent of Catholic Children Not in Catholic
Schools Attending Religion Classes

Primary students	43.6 (732)
Secondary students	23.7 (493)

The Education of Catholic Americans

a special importance precisely in those groups in which Catholic education is low—for one reason or another. It is possible, therefore, that if one combines those in Catholic schools and those receiving religious instruction, the differences among the various socio-ecological groups will decline.

Table A–4.19 confirms this hypothesis. With the exception of white-collar workers from the central city and those who are not central-city white-collar workers in the West, there is very little difference in the proportion receiving some kind of religious instruction in the various socio-ecological groups. It is possible that there is a relatively inflexible demand for religious education in the Catholic population and that this demand will be met in either Catholic schools or instruction classes, depending on the local situation. Hence it might be argued that for most of the groups in question, an increase in available Catholic school desks would lead to an increase in the Catholic school population but would not notably affect the proportion of Catholics receiving some kind of religious education. It is at least possible that, with the exception of white-collar workers in the central city, it

Table A–4.18 Per Cent of Children of Catholic Marriages Either Going to Catholic Schools or Receiving Religious Instruction, by Region, Ecological Situation, and Social Class

Ecological Situation	Region			
	Northeast	North Central	South	West
Central city:[a]				
White-collar	$73_{(125)}$	$88_{(92)}$	$75_{(17)}$	$85_{(41)}$
Blue-collar	$64_{(270)}$	$63_{(129)}$	$65_{(29)}$	$37_{(75)}$
Non-central city:				
White-collar	$63_{(218)}$	$72_{(222)}$	$65_{(54)}$	$53_{(74)}$
Blue-collar	$64_{(341)}$	$58_{(224)}$	$68_{(37)}$	$54_{(165)}$

N	2,113
NA on occupation	191
Total N	2,304

[a] In SMSA.

will always be difficult to get this religious education level above 66 per cent.

CONCLUSIONS

The major findings of this appendix may be stated as follows: Catholic school attendance correlates with social class, geographic area, and ecological situation. Children who come from higher-income, white-collar, and better-educated families are more likely to be in Catholic schools than are their opposites. So are children who live in central metropolitan cities, when compared to those outside of central cities. On the other hand, children from the West are less likely to be in Catholic schools than their coreligionists from other parts of the country. However, when these predictor variables are combined, there are only a few groups which are dramatically underprivileged or overprivileged. The differences among the various groups decline even more when we include the children of Catholic marriages who are not in Catholic schools but who are receiving religious instruction. Some 63 per cent of the Catholic children in the country are involved in some form of religious instruction, a proportion which remains rela-

Table A–4.19   Per Cent of Children of Catholic Marriages Not in Catholic Schools but Attending Religion Classes, by Region, Ecological Situation, and Social Class

Ecological Situation	Region			
	Northeast	North Central	South	West
Central city:[a]				
White-collar	38 (56)	45 (23)	43 (8)	25 (8)
Blue-collar	36 (160)	22 (63)	23 (13)	23 (53)
Non-central city:				
White-collar	27 (115)	53 (129)	0 (21)	27 (49)
Blue-collar	38 (201)	32 (136)	27 (17)	47 (153)

N	1,205
NA on occupation	130
In Catholic schools	969
Total N	2,304

[a] In SMSA.

tively constant for most of the socio-ecological groups that have been considered.

Two points need to be emphasized. There is evidence that the shift away from central cities may be leading to a decline in Catholic school attendance, especially for those in the lower socio-economic brackets. Thus there is some possibility that the association between social class and Catholic education will increase in years to come. Second, in only a few socio-ecological groups (white-collar workers in central cities and blue-collar workers in central cities in the central region) are more than half the Catholic children in Catholic schools. When this fact is considered in combination with the apparent lack of religious instruction for more than one-third of all Catholics of school age, it becomes clear that despite the tremendous amounts of money and work put into the Catholic educational system, it is not meeting the religious educational needs of the majority of Catholic children.

There seems to be very little change in the patterns of association of Catholic school attendance described in this appendix and the patterns reported in the text proper, Urbanites, females, residents of the northeastern and north central regions, and members of the upper social classes are the most likely to attend Catholic schools. Whether the proportions in Catholic schools have increased or decreased through the generations is more difficult to ascertain. In our study, 36 per cent of the fathers and 38 per cent of the mothers of respondents had attended Catholic grammar schools; 50 per cent of the respondents had had some Catholic grammar-school education; and 46 per cent of the children of respondents are currently in Catholic grammar schools. However, there is a difference in the variable measured, since we are unable to determine how many of the respondents' children currently in public schools had some of their education in Catholic schools. However, 46 per cent represents the bare minimum of those having had some Catholic grammar-school education; hence, it is very likely that those in public schools who had attended Catholic schools at one time would push the proportion of those who had been in Catholic schools well over 50 per cent. While we are thus unable to say with absolute certainty that there has been an increase in the proportion of Catholic children in Catholic elementary schools, we have no evidence of a decrease. At the high-school level the picture is somewhat clearer. One-fourth of the fathers and 28 per cent of the mothers of respondents went to Catholic high schools—if they went to high school at all. Of the respondents, 24 per cent attended Catholic high school, and 31 per cent of the high-school-age children of Catholics are in Catholic high schools today. Thus there has been a small increase in the proportion of Catholics in Catholic high schools. However, the expansion of the Catholic high-school system is much greater than these figures indicate, since the majority of the parental generation did not go to high school and neither did a good many of the respondents. Using as a base not merely those who went to high school but the whole generation, some 10 per cent of the fathers and 14 per cent of the mothers attended Catholic schools, as did 20 per cent of the respondents. Thus the slight increase in the proportion of today's adolescents in Catholic high schools indicates that the demand for Catholic secondary education has been able to keep pace with the expanding high-school population and at the same time somewhat increase the proportion of high-school-age Catholics who are in Catholic schools.

However, since demand for Catholic high-school desks apparently correlates with social class, it could very well be that the expansion of Catholic high schools has *not* kept pace with the increased demand: as we saw in Chapter 9 of the text, two-fifths of those who did not send their children to Catholic schools indicate that the reason was connected with the schools' being too far or altogether nonexistent.

It is clear, therefore, that the demand for Catholic schools has more than held its own in the face of the tremendous expansion of the school-age population and the simultaneous expansion of the proportion of school-age children who in fact go to school. If anything, the assimilation of Catholics into the main stream of American culture, as marked by improved social status, has increased their loyalties to Catholic schools. It is safe to conclude that the major problem such schools face at present is creating more facilities for those who seek admittance. But whether this demand will continue depends on attitudes toward the schools.

Appendix 5
The Questionnaires

THE ADULT QUESTIONNAIRE

NORC 476 CA
11/63

TIME INTER-VIEW BEGAN	:

NATIONAL OPINION RESEARCH CENTER
University of Chicago

_____(1-4)

Segment	
Case Number		(5-9)

Mr.
Mrs. _____   _____
Miss (first name)   (last name)

_____
(street address)

_____
(city and state)

Hello, I'm _____ from the National
Opinion Research Center. We're making a study
which deals mostly with the kinds of schools
people have attended, and also with other topics
of current interest. I believe you received a
letter a few weeks ago telling you I would be
stopping by.

HOUSEHOLD ENUMERATION

First, I have to ask for a little information about the members of your household.

How many people are living in this household? (BE SURE TO INCLUDE ALL CHILDREN LIVING IN THE HOUSEHOLD, PEOPLE TEMPORARILY AWAY, ROOMERS, ETC.)

_____
number

Let's go from the oldest person in the household to the youngest.

    A. What is the name of the oldest person? The next oldest person? (ENTER NAME IN COLUMN <u>A</u> OF THE ENUMERATION TABLE.)

    B. How old was (he) (she) at (his) (her) last birthday? (ENTER AGE IN COLUMN <u>B</u> BELOW.)

    C. What is (his) (her) relation to the head of the household? (ENTER RELATION IN COLUMN <u>C</u> BELOW.)

    D. (ENTER <u>M</u> FOR MALE AND <u>F</u> FOR FEMALE IN COLUMN <u>D</u>.)

    E. What is (his) (her) marital status? (ENTER IN COLUMN <u>E</u> BELOW.)

	<u>A</u> Name	<u>B</u> Age	<u>C</u> Relation to Household Head	<u>D</u> Sex	<u>E</u> Marital Status	<u>F</u> Indicate Respondent by √
1						
2						
3						
4						
5						
6						
7						
8						
9						
10						

BEGIN DECK 1

1. Taken altogether, how would you say things are these days--would you say that you are very happy, pretty happy, or not too happy?

Very happy . . . 7 <u>15</u>/6

Pretty happy . . 8

Not too happy . . 9

2. Has anyone talked to you about his personal problems in the last few months?

Yes . (ASK A AND B). X*<u>16</u>/y

No . (SKIP TO Q. 3) 0

*IF YES:

A. Who was that?

<u>17</u>/
NAP- 1
NAN- 2

B. What was the problem?

<u>18</u>/
NAP- 1
NAN- 2

3. Have you spent any time in the past few months helping someone who needed help?

Yes . (ASK A AND B). X*<u>19</u>/y

No . (SKIP TO Q. 4) 0

*IF YES:

A. Did you do that by yourself, or did others join in giving this help?

By myself . . . . . . 3 <u>20</u>/

With others . . . . . 4 NAP- 1
NAN- 2

B. What did you do? Could you tell me a bit about it?

<u>21</u>/
NAP- 1
NAN- 2

4. We are interested in how Americans judge certain actions. Here is a card with some answers on it. Which answer comes closest to telling whether you agree or disagree with each statement?

(HAND RESPONDENT CARD A.)	Agree Strongly	Agree Somewhat	Disagree Somewhat	Disagree Strongly	Don't Know	
A. It is alright to ask an insurance company for more money than you deserve after an auto accident if you think they might cut your claim.	X	0	2	3	1	22/y
B. Even though you find some people unpleasant, it is wrong to try to avoid them.	5	6	8	9	7	23/4
C. A married couple who feel they have as many children as they want are really not doing anything wrong when they use artificial means to prevent conception.	X	0	2	3	1	24/y
D. A salesman has the right to exaggerate how good his product is when a customer is too suspicious.	5	6	8	9	7	25/4
E. Two people who are in love do not do anything wrong when they marry, even though one of them has been divorced.	X	0	2	3	1	26/y
F. There is an obligation to work for the end of racial segregation.	5	6	8	9	7	27/4
G. It is alright to refuse to talk to some member of the family after a disagreement, especially if the argument was the fault of the other.	X	0	2	3	1	28/y
H. If the government wastes tax money, people don't have to be too exact on their income tax returns.	5	6	8	9	7	29/4
I. It would be wrong to take considerable time off while working for a large company, even though the company would not be hurt by it at all.	X	0	2	3	1	30/y
J. It is not really wrong for an engaged couple to have some sexual relations before they are married.	5	6	8	9	7	31/4
K. Even though a person has a hard time making ends meet, he should still try to give some of his money to help the poor.	X	0	2	3	1	32/y

Now I would like to ask about your background.

5. First of all, where were you born? (STATE OR COUNTRY)

_____ *

33-34/
yy

*IF OUTSIDE U.S.:

A. How old were you when you came to the U.S.?

35-36/
NAP- yy
NAN- XX

6. Were you brought up <u>mostly on a farm</u>, in <u>open country</u> but not on a farm, <u>in a small town</u>, <u>in a small city</u>, or <u>in a large city or its suburbs</u>?

Farm	X <u>37/</u>y
Open country (not farm)	0
Small town - 10,000	1
Small city - 10,000-500,000	2
Large city or suburb - 500,000+ . . .	3

7. Where were your father and mother born?

A. First your father? _____
(STATE OR COUNTRY)

38-39/
NAP- yy
NAN- XX
DK - 99

B. And your mother? _____
(STATE OR COUNTRY)

40-41/
NAP- yy
NAN- XX
DK - 99

(ASK ONLY IF BOTH PARENTS WERE BORN IN THIS COUNTRY.)

8. How many of your grandparents were born in this country?

None	0 <u>42/</u>
One	1 NAP- y NAN- X
Two	2
Three . . .	3
Four	4
Don't know .	5

9. A. What is your main national background--on your father's side? On your
mother's side?

IF CURRENTLY MARRIED, ASK B:

B. What is your (husband's, wife's) main national background? First on
(his) (her) father's side? On (his) (her) mother's side?

	A. Respondent's		B. Spouse's	
	Father	Mother	Father	Mother
English, Scotch, Welsh, English Canadian, Australian, New Zealand	00	00	00	00
Irish	01	01	01	01
German, Austrian, Swiss	02	02	02	02
Scandinavian	03	03	03	03
Italian	04	04	04	04
French, French Canadian, Belgian	05	05	05	05
Polish	06	06	06	06
Russian or other Eastern European	07	07	07	07
Lithuanian	08	08	08	08
Spanish, Portuguese, Latin American, including Puerto Rican	09	09	09	
Other (SPECIFY)_____	0X	0X	0X	
Don't know	3y	3y	3y	3y
Not currently married	___	___	1y	1y
	43-44/ 2y	45-46/ 2y	47-48/ 2y	49-50/ 2y

10. Did you always live together with both of your <u>real</u> parents up to the time
you were 16 years old?

Yes . . . . X 51/y

No . (ASK A AND B) . 0*

*IF NO:

A. What happened?

52/
NAP- y
NAN- X

B. How old were you when it happened?

_____
Age

53-54
NAP- yy
NAN- XX

11. We are also interested in what Americans think about religious matters. I am going to read you a number of statements. Please tell me the statement that comes closest to your own personal opinion about each of the statements.

(HAND RESPONDENT CARD B.) First... (READ)	Certainly True	Probably True	I am uncertain whether this is true or false	Probably False	Certainly False	
A. There is no definite proof that God exists.	X	0	1	2	3	55/y
B. God doesn't really care how He is worshipped, so long as He is worshipped.	5	6	7	8	9	56/4
C. God will punish the evil for all eternity.	X	0	1	2	3	57/y
D. Science proves that Christ's Resurrection was impossible.	5	6	7	8	9	58/4
E. Jesus directly handed over the leadership of His Church to Peter and the Popes.	X	0	1	2	3	59/y
F. A good man can earn heaven by his own efforts alone.	5	6	7	8	9	60/4

BEGIN DECK 2

12. Here is a sheet with a number of statements about which different people have different opinions. Please circle the letter of the answer which is closest to your own feeling. (HAND RESPONDENT GREEN SHEET.)

For example, if you agree strongly, you would circle "A"; if you disagree strongly, you would circle "D." You can choose any of the four answers on the sheet.

		Agree Strongly	Agree Somewhat	Disagree Somewhat	Disagree Strongly	Don't Know	
A.	In the long-run, war with the Communists is almost certain.	X	0	2	3	1	8/y
B.	I would try to stop the planned parenthood association from having a meeting in my community.	5	6	8	9	7	9/4
C.	Usually parents are just too busy to explain the reasons behind the orders they give their children.	X	0	2	3	1	10/y
D.	The Federal government should give religious schools money to help pay teachers' salaries and build new buildings.	5	6	8	9	7	11/4
E.	Negroes shouldn't push themselves where they are not wanted.	X	0	2	3	1	12/y
F.	A student should be free to make up his own mind on what he learns in school.	5	6	8	9	7	13/4
G.	Laws should change with the times.	X	0	2	3	1	14/y
H.	White people have a right to live in an all white neighborhood if they want to, and Negroes should respect that right.	5	6	8	9	7	15/4
I.	The United States should do more to help the poorer nations by building hospitals, schools, and homes in those places.	X	0	2	3	1	16/y
J.	Each country should be willing to give up some of its power so that the United Nations could do a better job.	5	6	8	9	7	17/4
K.	A family should have as many children as possible and God will provide for them.	X	0	2	3	1	18/y
L.	I would strongly disapprove if a Negro family moved next door to me.	5	6	8	9	7	19/4
M.	Working men have the right and duty to join unions.	X	0	2	3	1	20/y
N.	The government is responsible for preventing wide-spread unemployment.	5	6	8	9	7	21/4
O.	The Federal government ought to provide aid for the local public schools.	X	0	2	3	1	22/y
P.	Jews have too much power in the United States.	5	6	8	9	7	23/4
Q.	When parents are wrong they should always be willing to admit it to their children.	X	0	2	3	1	24/y

Q. 12 continued on facing page.

12. Continued

		Agree Strongly	Agree Somewhat	Disagree Somewhat	Disagree Strongly	Don't Know	
R.	It is as important for a child to think for himself as to be obedient to his parents.	5	6	8	9	7	25/4
S.	Rules should never be relaxed, because children will take advantage of it.	X	0	2	3	1	26/y
T.	Negroes would be satisfied, if it were not for a few people who stir up trouble.	5	6	8	9	7	27/4
U.	Jewish businessmen are about as honest as other businessmen.	X	0	2	3	1	28/y
V.	People who don't believe in God have as much right to freedom of speech as anyone else.	5	6	8	9	7	29/4
W.	Complete abstention from liquor is the best thing.	X	0	2	3	1	30/y
X.	Books written by Communists should not be permitted in public libraries.	5	6	8	9	7	31/4

13. What was the highest grade in school your father completed?

```
                         No schooling . . . . . . (SKIP TO Q. 14) 3     34/1
                         6th grade or less . . . . . . . . (ASK C) 4+
                         7th or 8th grade . . . . . . . (ASK C) 5+
                         Some high school . . . . . . (ASK B & C) 6#+
                         High school graduate . . . . (ASK B & C) 7*#+
                         Some college . . . . . . (ASK A, B, & C) 8*#+
                         College graduate or more . (ASK A, B, & C) 9*#+
                         Don't know . . . . . . . (SKIP TO Q. 14) 2
```

*IF FATHER ATTENDED COLLEGE:
   A. What kind of college did he go to--Catholic, non-Catholic, or both?
      (CIRCLE CODE UNDER A BELOW)

#IF FATHER ATTENDED HIGH SCHOOL:
   B. What kind of high school did he go to--Catholic, public, or both?
      (CIRCLE CODE UNDER B BELOW)

+IF FATHER ATTENDED ELEMENTARY SCHOOL:
   C. What kind of elementary school did he go to--Catholic, public, or both?
      (CIRCLE CODE UNDER C BELOW)

*A. IF FATHER ATTENDED COLLEGE:	#B. IF FATHER ATTENDED HIGH SCHOOL:	+C. IF FATHER ATTENDED ELEMENTARY SCHOOL:
Catholic . . . 0 35/ Non-Catholic . 1 NAP- y Both . . . . . 2 NAN- X Don't know . . 3	Catholic . . . 6 36/ Public . . . . 7 NAP- 4 Both . . . . . 8 NAN- 5 Don't know . . 9	Catholic . . . 0 37/ Public . . . . 1 NAP- y Both . . . . . 2 NAN- X Don't know . . 3

14. What was the highest grade in school your mother completed?

No schooling	(SKIP TO Q. 15)	3	38/1
6th grade or less	(ASK C)	4+	
7th or 8th grade	(ASK C)	5+	
Some high school	(ASK B & C)	6#+	
High school graduate	(ASK B & C)	7#+	
Some college	(ASK A, B, & C)	8*#+	
College graduate or more	(ASK A, B, & C)	9*#+	
Don't know	(SKIP TO Q. 15)	2	

*IF MOTHER ATTENDED COLLEGE:

A. What kind of college did she go to--Catholic, non-Catholic, or both?
   (CIRCLE CODE UNDER A BELOW)

#IF MOTHER ATTENDED HIGH SCHOOL:

B. What kind of high school did she go to--Catholic, public, or both?
   (CIRCLE CODE UNDER B BELOW)

+IF MOTHER ATTENDED ELEMENTARY SCHOOL:

C. What kind of elementary school did she go to--Catholic, public, or
   both? (CIRCLE CODE UNDER C BELOW)

*A. IF MOTHER ATTENDED COLLEGE:	#B. IF MOTHER ATTENDED HIGH SCHOOL:	+C. IF MOTHER ATTENDED ELEMENTARY SCHOOL:
Catholic . . 0 39/	Catholic . . 6 40/	Catholic . . 0 41/
Non-Catholic. 1 NAP- y	Public . . . 7 NAP- 4	Public . . . 1 NAP- y
Both . . . . 2 NAN- X	Both . . . . 8 NAN- 5	Both . . . . 2 NAN- X
Don't know . 3	Don't know . 9	Don't know . 3

---

15. What was your father's (or stepfather's) main occupation during the time you
    were growing up?   42-43/
    Occupation: _____ Industry:_____   NAP- yy
                                                                       NAN- XX

---

16. On the whole, how happy would you say your childhood was--<u>extremely happy</u>,
    <u>happier than average</u>, <u>average</u>, or <u>not too happy</u>?

Extremely happy . . .	5	44/4
Happier than average .	6	
Average	7	
Not too happy	8	
Other (SPECIFY)_____		
_____	9	

17. Everything considered, how happy would you say your parents' marriage was while you were growing up? Would you say <u>extremely happy</u>, <u>happier than average</u>, <u>average</u>, or <u>not too happy</u>?

Extremely happy . . .	0	<u>45</u>/
Happier than average .	1	NAP- y
		NAN- X
Average	2	
Not too happy	3	
Other (SPECIFY) _____		
_____	4	

18. A. When you were growing up, what was your <u>father's</u> (stepfather's) religious preference? (CIRCLE CODE UNDER <u>A</u> BELOW.)

    B. When you were growing up, what was your mother's (stepmother's) religious preference? (CIRCLE CODE UNDER <u>B</u> BELOW.)

A. Father's (stepfather's) religious preference	B. Mother's (stepmother's) religious preference
Protestant . . . . 0 <u>46</u>/	Protestant . . . . 0 <u>47</u>/
Catholic . . . . 1 NAP- y	Catholic . . . . 1 NAP- y
NAN- X	NAN- X
Jewish 2	Jewish 2
Other (SPECIFY) _____	Other (SPECIFY) _____
_____ 3	_____ 3
None 4	None 4

19. A. What is your religious preference?

Protestant . (ASK B, THEN DISCONTINUE INTERVIEW)	5*<u>48</u>/4
Catholic . . . . (ASK B)	6*
Jewish . . . (ASK B, THEN DISCONTINUE INTERVIEW)	7*
Other . . . (ASK B, THEN DISCONTINUE INTERVIEW)	8*
None . . . . (DISCONTINUE INTERVIEW)	9

<u>*UNLESS "NONE"</u>:

B. Were you raised a (Catholic) (Protestant) (Jew)?

Yes	2	<u>49</u>/
No . . . [ASK (1)]	3#	NAP- 0
		NAN- 1

<u>#IF "NO" TO B AND RESPONDENT IS CATHOLIC</u>:

(1) How old were you when you became a Catholic?

_____
age

<u>50-51</u>/
NAP- yy
NAN- XX

20. A. How religious would you say your father was while you were growing up--
     very, somewhat, not too, or not religious at all?

     B. How religious was your mother?

	A. Father	B. Mother
Very religious	6	1
Somewhat religious	7	2
Not too religious	8	3
Not at all religious	9	4
Don't know	5	0
No (father) (mother) present	3	y
	52/4	53/X

21. When you were growing up--
     (HAND RESPONDENT CARD C.)
     ASK A AND B UNLESS NO FATHER PRESENT:

	More Than Weekly	Weekly	1-3 Times a Month	Couple Times a Year	Almost Never	Don't Know	
A. About how often did your father attend (Mass) (Church)?	5	6	7	8	9	4	54/ NAP-2 NAN-3
B. About how often did your father receive Communion?	5	6	7	8	9	4	55/ NAP-2 NAN-3

     ASK C AND D UNLESS NO MOTHER PRESENT:

	More Than Weekly	Weekly	1-3 Times a Month	Couple Times a Year	Almost Never	Don't Know	
C. About how often did your mother attend (Mass) (Church)?	5	6	7	8	9	4	56/ NAP-2 NAN-3
D. About how often did your mother receive Communion?	5	6	7	8	9	4	57/ NAP-2 NAN-3

22. A. How religious would you say you are at the present time?
     IF CURRENTLY MARRIED:
     B. How religious would you say your (wife)(husband) is at the present time?

	A. Respondent	B. Spouse
Very religious	X	6
Somewhat religious . .	0	7
Not too religious . .	1	8
Not at all religious .	2	9
Not currently married.	-	4
	58/y	59/5

IF CURRENTLY MARRIED:
23. What is your (husband's) (wife's) religious preference?

Protestant 1 60/X
Catholic 2
Jewish 3
Other (SPECIFY)_____
_____ 4
None 0
Not currently married y

24. A. How many brothers do you have? (Includes any no longer living.)

_____
number

| | | 61-62/
NAN-yy

  B. How many sisters do you have? (Includes any no longer living.)

_____
number

| | | 63-64/
NAN-yy

IF NO BROTHERS OR SISTERS, SKIP TO Q. 26.

25. How many brothers and sisters were raised Catholics?

_____ *
number

| | | 65-66/
No Sib-yy
No Ans-XX

IF NONE, SKIP TO Q. 26.

*IF ANY, ASK A AND B:

A. (Of those raised as Catholics:) How many are not practicing Catholics today?

_____
number

| | | 67-68/
No Sib-yy
No Cth-XX
No Ans-99

B. (Of those raised as Catholics:) How many married Catholics?

_____
number

| | | 69-70/
No Sib-yy
No Cth-XX
No Ans-99

26. Think of the neighborhood in which you grew up. How many of your neighbors were Catholics--more than half, about half, less than half, or none?

(HAND RESPONDENT CARD D.)

BEGIN DECK 3

_____

More than half . 1   8/0
About half . . . 2
Less than half . 3
None 4

27. Here are some statements about the way in which families regard their religion. Tell me whether each statement was true or not true about your family when you were growing up.

	True	Not True	DK	
A. We were religious but not very devout.	X	1	0	9/y
B. There was a close relative who was a priest or a nun.	3	5	4	10/2
C. Priests visited the house.	7	9	8	11/6
D. We were Catholics, but we couldn't take some of the rules too seriously.	X	1	0	12/y
E. We always had masses said for dead relatives.	3	5	4	13/2
F. Mother was an active member of parish organizations.	7	9	8	14/6
G. Father was an active member of parish organizations.	X	1	0	15/y
H. Someone in the family attended novena services regularly.	3	5	4	16/2
I. Catholic magazines and newspapers came into the house regularly.	7	9	8	17/6
J. Someone in our family did charitable work for the church (like visiting hospitals and help-ing the poor).	X	1	0	18/y

28. Here are some experiences that people sometimes have when they are growing up. Was each of these true for you? First.... (CIRCLE CODE FOR EACH ACTIVITY WHICH WAS TRUE FOR RESPONDENT.)

I wanted to be a priest or nun 0	19/y
I made my Confirmation 1	
I stopped going to church as soon as I grew old enough to be able to make my own decisions 2	
I belonged to a parish club or played on an athletic team 3	
I dated a non-Catholic 4	
I went steady with a non-Catholic 5	
I played in the parish yard 6	
I was known by name by a priest 7	
I had a religious experience in which I really felt close to God and the Saints 8	
FOR MEN ONLY: I served as an altar boy 9	
None of the above X	

29. Thinking about the friends you had when you were about 13 or 14, how many would you say were Catholic--more than half, about half, less than half, or none?

More than half X	20/y
About half 0	
Less than half 1	
None 2	
Don't know--don't remember. 3	

30. What about when you were 17 or so--how many of your friends were Catholic-- more than half, about half, less than half, or none?

More than half 5	21/4
About half 6	
Less than half 7	
None 8	
Don't know--don't remember. 9	

31. A. How far did you go in school?

   ASK IF CURRENTLY MARRIED:
   B. How far did your spouse go in school?

	A. Self	B. Spouse
No schooling.	1	1
6th grade or less.	2	2
7th or 8th grade.	3	3
Some high school.	4	4
High school graduate.	5	5
Some college.	6	6
College graduate or more.	7	7
Don't know.	8	8
Not currently married.	-	9
	22/0	23/0

IF ATTENDED ELEMENTARY SCHOOL (Q. 31 A.):

32. When you were going to elementary school, about how many of the Catholic children in your neighborhood attended Catholic schools? Would you say more than
half, about half, less than half, a few, or none?

OFFICE USE

More than half 0   24/
About half . . 1   No Sch-y
Less than half 2   No Ans-X
A few 3
None 4

E
L
E
M 33. Thinking of the elementary schools you attended--did you go only to Catholic
E   schools, only to public schools, or did you go to both kinds of elementary
N   schools?
T   Catholic only (SKIP TO Q. 34) 7   25/
A   Public only . . . . (ASK A) 8*   No Sch-5
R   Both kinds . . . . . (ASK A) 9*   No Ans-6
Y

*IF ATTENDED ANY PUBLIC SCHOOLS:

A. While you were in public elementary school, was there ever a Catholic
school your parents could have sent you to? As you recall, was there
one most of the time, some of the time, or none of the time you were
in public elementary school?

Most of the time . [ASK (1)] 1+   26/
Some of the time . [ASK (1)] 2+   No Sch-y
None of the time . [ASK (2)] 3#   No Pub-X
                                     No Ans-0

+IF CATHOLIC SCHOOL AVAILABLE:

(1) Why do you think your parents sent you to public school(s)?

27/   28/
y- No Sch- y
X- No Pub- X
0- No Cth- 0
1- No Ans- 1

#IF CATHOLIC SCHOOL NOT AVAILABLE:

(2) Do you think your parents would have sent you to a Catholic elementary school if there had been one you could have attended?

Yes 8   29/
No   (ASK a) 9** No Sch-4
                     No Pub-5
                     Cth Av-6
                     No Ans-7

**IF NO:

a. Why would'nt your parents have sent you to a   30/
Catholic school, do you think?   No Sch-y
                                                   No Pub-X
                                                   Cth Av-0
                                                   If Yes-1
                                                   No Ans-2

IF ATTENDED HIGH SCHOOL (SEE Q. 31 A.):
34. Now think back to your high school years. When you were going to high school, about how many of the Catholic students in your neighborhood attended a Catholic high school? Would you say <u>more than half</u>, <u>about half</u>, <u>less than half</u>, <u>a few</u>, or <u>none</u>?

OFFICE USE ONLY

More than half . 0   <u>31</u>/
About half . . . 1   No Sch-y
Less than half . 2   No Ans-X
A few 3
None 4

---

35. Of the high schools you attended, did you go <u>only to Catholic schools</u>, <u>only to public schools</u>, or did you <u>go to both kinds</u> of high schools?

Only to Catholic schools. .(SKIP TO Q. 36 . 7   <u>32</u>/
Only to public schools . . . . . (ASK A). 8*   No Sch-5
Both kinds . . . . (ASK A). 9*   No Ans-6

*IF ATTENDED ANY PUBLIC HIGH SCHOOLS:

A. While you were in public high school, was there <u>ever a Catholic high school your parents could have sent you to</u>? As you recall, was there one <u>most</u> of the time, <u>some</u> of the time, or <u>none</u> of the time you were in public high school?

Most of the time   [ASK (1)]. 1+   <u>33</u>/
Some of the time   [ASK (1)]. 2+   No Sch-y
None of the time   [ASK (2)]. 3#   No Pub-X
                                   No Ans-0

+IF CATHOLIC HIGH SCHOOL AVAILABLE:

(1) Why did you go to public high school?

<u>34</u>/   <u>35</u>/
y- No Sch- y
X- No Pub- X
0- No Cth- 0
1- No Ans- 1

#IF CATHOLIC HIGH SCHOOL NOT AVAILABLE:

(2) Do you think your parents would have sent you to a Catholic high school if there had been one you could have attended?

Yes 8   <u>36</u>/
No . . (ASK a) 9** No Sch-4
                    No Pub-5
                    Cth Av-6
                    No Ans-7

**IF NO:

a. Why <u>wouldn't</u> you go to a Catholic high school?

<u>37</u>/
No Sch-y
No Pub-X
Cth Av-0
If Yes-1
No Ans-2

ASK IF RESPONDENT ATTENDED ANY COLLEGE (SEE Q. 31 A.):

36. Did you attend <u>only Catholic</u> colleges, <u>only non-Catholic</u> colleges, or did you attend <u>both kinds</u>?

Only Catholic . . . 7	<u>38</u>/	
Only non-Catholic . 8	NAP- 5	
Both kinds 9	NAN- 6	

---

37. ASK IF RESPONDENT ATTENDED ANY PUBLIC ELEMENTARY SCHOOL:

A. When you were attending public elementary school, did you receive religious instruction regularly from your church?

Yes 2	<u>39</u>/
No 3	NAP- 0
	NAN- 1

ASK IF RESPONDENT ATTENDED ANY PUBLIC HIGH SCHOOL:

B. When you were attending public high school, did you receive religious instruction regularly from your church or were you a member of a Catholic club?

Instruction only . 6	<u>40</u>/
Club only 7	NAP- 4
Both 8	NAN- 5
Neither 9	

IF RESPONDENT IS SINGLE (NEVER MARRIED) SKIP TO Q. 49.

38. How many children have you and your (husband) (wife) had? _____*
               number

	41-42/
	NR MAR-yy
	No Ans-XX

*IF ANY, ASK A:

A. How many have been baptized--all, some, or none of them?

All . [ASK (1)]. 7**	<u>43</u>/
Some [ASK (1) . 8**	NR MAR- 4
None 9	No Cld- 5
	No Ans- 6

**IF ANY BAPTIZED:

(Of those baptized) How many have been raised as Catholics--all, some, or none of them?

All 2	<u>44</u>/
Some 3	NR MAR- y
	No Cld- X
None 4	No Bpt- 0
	No Ans- 1

39. Do you expect to have any (more) children?

Yes . . . (ASK A) 7*	<u>45</u>/
No 8	NR MAR- 5
Don't know . . . 9	No Ans- 6

*IF YES:

A. How many? _____
               number

	46-47/
	NR MAR - y
	If No - 2
	No Ans-

40. If you had your choice, what would be the ideal number of children you would like to have in your family?

‾‾‾‾‾‾‾‾‾‾
number

48-49/
NR MAR-yy
No Ans-XX

41. In what year were you and your (husband) (wife) married?

‾‾‾‾‾‾‾‾‾‾
year

50-51/
NR MAR-yy
No Ans-XX

42. Were you married by a priest?

Yes 8
No (ASK A) 9*

52/
NR MAR- 6
No Ans- 7

*IF NO:

A. What were your reasons for not being married by a priest?

53/
NR MAR- y
Priest- X
No Ans- 0

IF ALL CHILDREN ARE PRE-SCHOOL AGE, SKIP TO Q. 48.

43. Did any of your children (Did your child) go to Catholic school(s)?

Yes . . . . . . (ASK A) 7*
No 8

54/
No Cld- 5
No Ans- 6

*IF YES:

A. Was that elementary school?
High school? College?

Elementary school . . . 2
High school 3
College 4

55/
No Cld- X
If No - 0
No Ans- 1

44. Did any of your children (Did your child) go to any public or other non-Catholic schools?

Yes . . . . : . . . (ASK A) 8*
No . . . . . (SKIP TO Q. 47) 9

56/
No Cld- 6
No Ans- 7

*IF YES:

A. Was that elementary school?
High school? College?

Elementary school [ASK (1)] 3#
High school . . . [ASK (2)] 4##
College . . . . . [ASK (3)] 5+

57/
No Cld- 0
If No - 1
No Ans- 2

#IF ELEMENTARY SCHOOL:

(1) Why did your child (children) attend non-Catholic elementary school(s)?

58/
No Cld- y
If No - X
No Elm- 0
No Ans- 1

##IF HIGH SCHOOL:

(2) Why did your child (children) attend a non-Catholic high school?

59/
No Cld- y
If No - X
No HS - 0
No Ans- 1

+IF COLLEGE:

(3) Why did your child (children) attend a non-Catholic college?

60/
No Cld- y
If No - X
No Col- 0
No Ans- 1

IF CHILD OR CHILDREN ATTENDS (OR ATTENDED) NON-CATHOLIC ELEMENTARY SCHOOL(S) ASK:

45. While in elementary school, (has your child) (have your children) received religious instruction regularly from your church?

Yes, all . 6	61/	
Yes, some . 7	No Cld- 2	
No 8	If No - 3	
DK 9	No Elm- 4	
	No Ans- 5	

IF CHILD OR CHILDREN ATTENDS (ATTENDED) NON-CATHOLIC HIGH SCHOOL(S) ASK:

46. While in high school did your child(ren) receive religious instruction regularly or (was) (were) your child(ren) a member (members) of a high school religious club?

Yes, all . 6	62/	
Yes, some . 7	No Cld- 2	
No 8	If No - 3	
DK 9	No HS - 4	
	No Ans- 5	

47. If you spent any money on Catholic school tuition for your children, on the average how much did you spend per year?

Check if none /__/

$ _____

63-66/
No Cld-yyyy
No Cth-yXXX
None -Xyyy
No Ans-XXXX

48. Did you ever speak to a child of yours about being a priest or a nun?

Yes . . 0	67/
No . . . 1	No Cld- y
	No Ans- X

ASK EVERYONE:

49. As you see it, what, if any, are the advantages of sending a child to a Catholic school?

68/
y

69/
y

50. Where do you think improvements should be made in the Catholic schools?

70/
y

71/
y

51. Here is a list of things people generally like when they see them in young children. Which two of the things on the list (do) (did) you find the nicest? (HAND RESPONDENT CARD E.)

BEGIN DECK 4

__ _____

(CIRCLE TWO)

A. When they listen to what you tell them to do 1   7/
B. When they are neat and clean 2   0
C. When they are polite and well-behaved with other people . 3
D. When they hug and kiss you 4
E. When they play nicely with other children 5
F. When they learn to do something after they have tried
   for a long time 6
G. When they play with you 7

52. I am going to read you a list of jobs. If a son of yours chose each job tell me whether you would feel <u>very pleased</u>, <u>somewhat pleased</u>, <u>somewhat disappointed</u>, or <u>very disappointed</u>. (CIRCLE CODES IN TABLE BELOW.)

		Very Pleased	Somewhat Pleased	Somewhat Dis-appointed	Very Dis-appointed	Don't Know	
A.	Business executive.	X	0	2	3	1	8/y
B.	High school teacher.	5	6	8	9	7	9/4
C.	Priest.	X	0	2	3	1	10/y
D.	Bank teller.	5	6	8	9	7	11/4
E.	Author.	X	0	2	3	1	12/y
F.	Carpenter.	5	6	8	9	7	13/4
G.	Stock broker.	X	0	2	3	1	14/y
H.	Furniture mover.	5	6	8	9	7	15/4

53. Would you prefer a job where you are <u>part of a team</u>, all working together, even if you don't get personal recognition for your work, or a job where you <u>worked alone</u> and others could see what you have done?

Part of a team 7   16/6

Work alone . . 9

Can't decide . 8

54. Which of these opinions comes closer to the way you feel? Some people feel that <u>other persons can be counted on</u> for important help in an emergency. Other people feel that these days <u>one never knows whom he can count on</u>.

Other persons can be counted on X   17/y

One never knows whom he can count on . . 1

Can't decide 0

55. Some people say that <u>anyone who looks for meaning in life is just kidding himself</u>. Other people say that you <u>don't have to look too hard</u> to find meaning in life. What do you think?

Anyone who looks for meaning is kidding himself . . . 3   18/2

Don't have to look too hard to find it 5

Can't decide 4

56. A. Some people say that for the average man things are getting worse. Other people say things are getting better. Which opinion comes closest to the way you feel? Would you say things are getting <u>better</u> or <u>worse</u>?

Better 7   19/6

Worse 9

Can't decide . . 8

B. Some people say that hard work is more important for getting ahead than having a nice personality and being well-liked. Other people say that having a nice personality and being well-liked are more important for getting ahead than hard work. Would you say <u>hard work</u> or a <u>nice person-ality</u> is more important?

Hard work X   20/y

Nice personality 1

Can't decide 0

57. Now we would like to ask about your religious practices.

		Every day	Several times a week	Every week	Several times a month	About once a month	Several times a year	About once a year	Practically never or not at all	
A.	How often do you go to Mass?	1	2	3	4	5	6	7	8	21/0
B.	About how often do you receive Holy Communion?	1	2	3	4	5	6	7	8	22/0
C.	How often do you go to confession?	1	2	3	4	5	6	7	8	23/0
D.	About how often do you stop in church to pray?	1	2	3	4	5	6	7	8	24/0
E.	How often does your spouse go to church?	1	2	3	4	5	6	7	8	25/0

58. Here is a list of things that some Catholics do. During the last two years have you managed to-- (CIRCLE ANY WHICH APPLY.)

    A. go on a retreat? 3   26/1

    B. make a day of recollection? 4

    C. read a spiritual book (or books)? 5

    D. make a mission? 6

    E. read Catholic magazines or newspapers regularly? 7

    F. listen to a Catholic radio or TV program? 8

    G. have a serious conversation with a priest about religious problems? 9

    H. None of the above 2

59. Thinking of your three closest friends, what religion does each belong to? (ASK ABOUT FIRST, SECOND, THIRD CLOSE FRIEND AND ENTER BELOW.)

	First Friend	Second Friend	Third Friend
Protestant	1	1	1
Catholic	2	2	2
Jewish	3	3	3
No religion	4	4	4
Other (SPECIFY) _____	5	5	5
Don't know religion	0	0	0
No (1st)(2nd)(3rd) friend	y	y	y
	27/X	28/X	29/X

60. Of your <u>other</u> friends, how many would you say are Catholic--more than half, about half, less than half, or none?

More than half 6	<u>30</u>/4
About half 7	
Less than half 8	
None 9	
Don't know 5	
Doesn't have any other friends . 3	

61. Of your <u>Catholic</u> friends, about how many belong to the same parish as you do--more than half, about half, less than half, or none?

More than half 1	<u>31</u>/X
About half 2	
Less than half 3	
None 4	
Don't know 0	
Don't have any Catholic friends. y	

62. As a general rule, how important do you think it is for young people to marry a member of their own religion--<u>very important</u>, <u>fairly important</u>, or <u>not important at all</u>?

Very important 7	<u>32</u>/5
Fairly important 8	
Not important at all 9	
Don't know 6	

63. If a child of yours wanted to marry someone who was not a Catholic, how do you think you would react?

<u>33</u>/y

64. How would you feel about a teen-ager of yours dating a non-Catholic? Would you oppose it strongly, oppose it but not strongly, or not oppose it at all?

Oppose strongly 7	<u>34</u>/5
Oppose but not strongly . . 8	
Not oppose at all 9	
Don't know 6	

65. How much money would you say your family contributes to the Church each year (not counting school tuition)?

Check if **none** /__/ $_____

<u>35-38</u>/
No Ans-yyyy
None -XXXX

66. Would you say that you have neighbors in your home very often, often, not too often, or not at all?

Very often . . X	39/y
Often 0	
Not too often . 1	
Not at all . . 2	

67. Of the neighbors that visit you at home, what proportion of these is Catholic?

All or almost all 5	40/4
Most 6	
Some 7	
A few 8	
None or almost none 9	
Never have neighbors . . . 3	

68. How many of your neighbors are Catholic? Would you say almost all, more than half, about half, less than half, or almost none?

Almost all 0	41/y
More than half 1	
About half 2	
Less than half 3	
Almost none 4	
Don't know X	

69. How important do you feel it is for Catholics to choose other Catholics as their really close friends--very important, fairly important, or not important?

Very important 7	42/6
Fairly important 8	
Not important 9	

70. About how often do you pray privately?

Once a day . . . . . (ASK A AND B) 0*	43/y
Several times a week (ASK A AND B) 1*	
About once a week . (ASK A AND B) 2*	
Less than once a week(ASK A AND B) 3*	
Never. . . . . . (SKIP TO Q. 71) X	

*IF EVER:

A. As far as you're concerned, which <u>two</u> of the statements on this card are the most important reasons for praying? (HAND RESPONDENT CARD F.)

(CIRCLE TWO)

A) Prayer gives me peace of mind 0	44/
B) Prayer honors God 1	NEVER-
C) Prayer makes up for past failings in some degree 2	No Ans-
D) Prayer helps me adjust to life and its problems 3	
E) Prayer offers thanks to God 4	
F) Prayer helps me get something special when I want it . . . 5	

B. For what do you usually pray?

45/
NEVER-
No Ans-

71. Have there been times in your life when you felt especially religious?

Yes . . . . . (ASK A) X* 46/y

No 0

┌─*IF YES:*

  A. When was that?

                                               47/

                                             NAP- 1

                                             NAN- 2

72. What is the name of your parish church?

                                           48/

                                   Answered- y

                                   No Ans- X

                                   D.K. - 0

                                   No Par- 1

73. Are you a member of any religious organizations?

Yes (ASK A, B, AND C) 8* 49/7

No. . (SKIP TO Q.74) 9

IF YES:

  A. What are the names of these organizations?

  B. Are you active in (NAME OF ORGANIZATION)?

  C. Have you ever been an officer of (NAME OF ORGANIZATION)?

	A. Name	B. Active	C. Officer
1.	50/ NAP-y NAN-X	Yes . 4 51/ No . 5 NAP-2 NAN-3	Yes . 8 52/ No . 9 NAP-6 NAN-7
2.	53/ NAP-y NAN-X	Yes . 4 54/ No . 5 NAP-2 NAN-3	Yes . 8 55/ No . 9 NAP-6 NAN-7
3.	56/ NAP-y NAN-X	Yes . 4 57/ No . 5 NAP-2 NAN-3	Yes . 8 58/ No . 9 NAP-6 NAN-7
4.	59/ NAP-y NAN-X	Yes . 4 60/ No . 5 NAP-2 NAN-3	Yes . 8 61/ No . 9 NAP-6 NAN-7

74. Most parishes are so big nowadays that it is very difficult for the priests to know their parishioners by name. Do you think (your priest) (any of your priests) knows (know) you by name?

Yes . X 62/y

No . 0

75. What is the name of your pastor?

_____

<u>63</u>/
Answer- 1
No Ans- 2
No Pst- 3
D.K. - 4

76. Have your parish priests or other priests ever visited your home?

Yes . (ASK A) 2* <u>64</u>/1

No 3

*IF YES:

| A.   About how often do they visit? |

About once a month or more . 6   <u>65</u>/
Several times a year . . . . 7 If No-4
Once a year . . . . 8 NAN -5
Once every few years 9

77. I am going to read to you a list of things about which many people disagree. Do you think that the Church has the right to teach what position Catholics should take on such issues?

		Yes	No	Don't Know	
A.	Government regulation of business and labor	X	1	0	<u>66</u>/y
B.	Racial integration	3	5	4	<u>67</u>/2
C.	Whether the U.S. should recognize Red China	7	9	8	<u>68</u>/6
D.	What are immoral books or movies	X	1	0	<u>69</u>/y
E.	Proper means for family limitation	3	5	4	<u>70</u>/2
F.	Federal aid to education	7	9	8	<u>71</u>/6
G.	Communist infiltration into government	X	1	0	<u>72</u>/y

BEGIN DECK 5

78. Here is another sheet with a number of statements on it. Please circle the letter which indicates how much you personally agree or disagree with each statement.
(HAND RESPONDENT PINK SHEET.)

		Agree Strongly	Agree Somewhat	Disagree Somewhat	Disagree Strongly	D. K.	
A.	Love of neighbor is more important than avoiding meat on Friday.	X	0	2	3	1	_8_/y
B.	It is always wrong to say something that might make a person question his faith, even if what one says is true.	5	6	8	9	7	_9_/4
C.	The Catholic Church teaches that large families are more Christian than small families.	X	0	2	3	1	10/y
D.	Although Christ saved the spiritual world by his death and resurrection, the material world is under the control of the devil.	5	6	8	9	7	11/4
E.	Husband and wife may have sexual intercourse for pleasure alone.	X	0	2	3	1	12/y
F.	The world is basically a dangerous place where there is much evil and sin.	5	6	8	9	7	13/4
G.	The Catholic Church teaches that a good Christian ought to think about the next life and not worry about fighting against poverty and injustice in this life.	X	0	2	3	1	14/y
H.	The Catholic Church teaches that if there is ever a majority of Catholics in the country, Catholicism must become the official religion of the United States.	5	6	8	9	7	15/4
I.	Even people who won't work should be helped if they really need it.	X	0	2	3	1	16/y
J.	Parts of the Mass ought to be said out loud and in English.	5	6	8	9	7	17/4
K.	There is basic opposition between the discoveries of modern science and the teaching of the Church.	X	0	2	3	1	18/y
L.	Most Protestants are inclined to discriminate against Catholics.	5	6	8	9	7	19/4
M.	Most priests don't expect the laity to be leaders, just followers.	X	0	2	3	1	20/y
N.	Protestants don't really take their religion seriously as compared to Catholics.	5	6	8	9	7	21/4
O.	Catholics must support laws which outlaw the sale of birth control devices.	X	0	2	3	1	22/y
P.	Only people who believe in God can be good American citizens.	5	6	8	9	7	23/4
Q.	It would make me somewhat unhappy if a daughter of mine became a nun.	X	0	2	3	1	24/y
R.	Protestant ministers should not be permitted to publicly teach things which are opposed to Catholic doctrine.	5	6	8	9	7	25/4
S.	God's purpose is clear to me in all the events of my life.	X	0	2	3	1	26/y
T.	My religion provides me with answers to all the important problems in my life.	5	6	8	9	7	27/4

79. In national politics, do you consider yourself a Democrat or Republican?

> Democrat 0   28/y
> Republican 1
> Independent (ASK A) 2*
> Other . . (ASK A) 3*
> Don't know (ASK A) X*

*IF INDEPENDENT, OTHER OR DON'T KNOW:

> A. In general, would you say you are closer to the Democratic or Republican party in national politics?
>
> > Democratic 7   29/
> > Republican 8   NAP-4
> > Neither 9   NAN-5
> > Don't know 6

80. How many organizations do you belong to besides religious ones--such as unions, professional organizations, clubs, neighborhood organizations, etc.?

> None 0   30/X
> One . . . . . (ASK A & B) 1*
> Two . . . . . (ASK A & B) 2*
> Three or four (ASK A & B) 3*
> Five or more. (ASK A & B) 5*

*UNLESS "NONE":

> A. In general, would you say you are <u>very active</u> in these organizations, <u>fairly active</u>, or <u>inactive</u>?
>
> > Very active 7   31/
> > Fairly active 8   None-5
> > Inactive 9   No Ans-6
>
> B. How many of the members of these organizations you belong to are the same religion as you are? Would you say <u>more than half</u>, <u>about half</u>, <u>less than half</u>, or <u>almost none</u>?
>
> > More than half 1   32/
> > About half 2   None-y
> > Less than half 3   No Ans-X
> > Almost none 4
> > Don't know 0

81. Do you read any <u>non</u>-religious magazines regularly?

> Yes 6   33/5
> No 7

82. How interested are you in what goes on in the world today? For instance, do you follow the international news <u>very closely</u>, <u>fairly closely</u>, or <u>not too closely</u>?

> Very closely . . . 0   34/X
> Fairly closely . . 1
> Not too closely . 2

83. What about local news--the things that happen here in your (town) (area)?
Do you follow local news <u>very closely</u>, <u>fairly closely</u>, or <u>not too closely</u>?

Very closely 4   <u>35</u>/3
Fairly closely 5
Not too closely 6

---

84. Do you ever get as worked up by something that happens in the news as you
do by something that happens in your personal life?

Yes 8   <u>36</u>/7
No 9

---

85. Here is a list of ways we might know different people. Which kind of person
on that card is the <u>closest relationship</u> you have with each of the following
groups? (HAND RESPONDENT CARD G.)

First, an Irish-American--what is the closest association you have had with
an Irish-American?

(READ LIST OF ETHNIC GROUPS BELOW,
CODING ONE RESPONSE FOR EACH.)

	Relative	Best Friend	Close Friend	Friend	Neighbor	Co-worker	Knew in School	Acquaintance	Stranger or Never Met One	
A. Irish-American.	1	2	3	4	5	6	7	8	9	<u>37</u>/0
B. Protestant.	1	2	3	4	5	6	7	8	9	<u>38</u>/0
C. Italian-American.	1	2	3	4	5	6	7	8	9	<u>39</u>/0
D. German-American.	1	2	3	4	5	6	7	8	9	<u>40</u>/0
E. Jew.	1	2	3	4	5	6	7	8	9	<u>41</u>/0
F. Scandinavian.	1	2	3	4	5	6	7	8	9	<u>42</u>/0
G. Polish-American.	1	2	3	4	5	6	7	8	9	<u>43</u>/0
H. Negro.	1	2	3	4	5	6	7	8	9	<u>44</u>/0

---

86. Here is a short quiz which touches on practices and beliefs of the Catholic
Church. You are not expected to get them all correct--some you may find
rather difficult. (HAND RESPONDENT YELLOW SHEET.)

Please circle the number in front of the answer which comes closest to
being correct, in your opinion.

A. The word we use to describe the   Transfiguration 1   <u>45</u>/0
fact that the Second Person of   Incarnation 2
the Trinity became man is--   Transubstantiation 3
   Immaculate Conception . . 4

Q. 86 continued on facing page.

86. Continued

B. Supernatural life is--   the life we receive from our parents 6 <u>46</u>/5
                              sanctifying grace in our souls . . . 7
                              our life after death 8
                              the power to work miracles 9

C. The "mystical body" is-- Christ's body in heaven . . . . . 1 <u>47</u>/0
                              Christ in Holy Communion 2
                              Christ united with His followers . . 3
                              None of the above 4

D. Uncharitable talk is   the second commandment . . . . . . 6 <u>48</u>/5
    forbidden by--   the fourth commandment 7
                              the eighth commandment 8
                              the tenth commandment 9

E. A man is judged immedi-   general judgment . . . . 1 <u>49</u>/0
    ately after he dies. This natural judgment 2
    judgment is called--   particular judgment 3
                              final judgment 4

F. The Encyclicals "Rerum   Christian marriage . . . . 6 <u>50</u>/5
    Novarum" of Leo XIII and Christian education 7
    "Quadragesimo anno" of   the condition of labor 8
    Pius XI both deal with-- Papal infallibility 9

87. Here are some questions which might be used on a radio or television quiz
     program. Some of them are fairly hard--let's see how many you can answer.

A. What ocean would one cross in going from the United States to   51/
    England?   NAN-y
    _____   Don't know . . X   R -0
                                                         W -1

B. Could you tell me who Billy Graham is?   52/2
                                                                      NAN-2
    _____   Don't know . . 3   R -4
                                                         W -5

C. What mineral or metal is important in the making of the atomic bomb? 53/
                                                                      NAN-6
    _____   Don't know . . 7   R -8
                                                         W -9

Q. 87 continued on next page.

87. Continued

    D. Will you tell me who Plato was?

                                             Don't know X

                      54/
                      NAN-y
                      R -0
                      W -1

    E. Will you tell me who Robert McNamara is?

                      Don't know 3

                      55/
                      NAN-2
                      R -4
                      W -5

    F. How about Charles Lindberg--can you tell me what he was famous for?

                      Don't know 7

                      56/
                      NAN-6
                      R -8
                      W -9

    G. Who wrote <u>War and Peace</u>?

                      Don't know X

                      57/
                      NAN-y
                      R -0
                      W -1

    H. What is the name of the Pope?

                      Don't know 3

                      58/
                      NAN-2
                      R -4
                      W -5

88. What kind of work do you do?

                      59-60/
                      NAP- yy
                      NAN- XX

             Occupation   *   Industry

*IF EMPLOYED:

    A. What proportion of the people with whom you work are Catholic--<u>more than half</u>, <u>about half</u>, <u>less than half</u>, or <u>almost none</u>?

                      More than half 6
                      About half 7
                      Less than half 8
                      None 9
                      Don't know 5

                      61/
                      NAP- 3
                      NAN- 4

IF RESPONDENT IS A MARRIED FEMALE:

89. What kind of work does your husband do?

Occupation	Industry

62-63/
NAP- yy
NAN- XX

90. (HAND RESPONDENT CARD H.) Adding up the income from all sources, what was (will be) your total family income in 1963?

A. Under $2,000 . . . . 0 64/y
B. $2,000 to $2,999 1
C. $3,000 to $3,999 2
D. $4,000 to $4,999 3
E. $5,000 to $5,999 4
F. $6,000 to $6,999 5
G. $7,000 to $7,999 6
H. $8,000 to $9,999 7
I. $10,000 to $14,999 8
J. $15,000 and over 9
   Don't know X

91. One final question. There has been much talk lately about change in the Catholic Church. Do you think there ought to be any changes?

Yes . . . . (ASK A) X* 65/y
No 0

*IF YES:

A. What kind of changes would you like to see?

66/
NAP- 1
NAN- 2

92. At some date in the future, we may want to ask for brief interviews with the parents of the people who have granted interviews on this study so far. Could I have the name and address of each of your parents, if they are still living?

Father's Name _____   Mother's Name:_____

Street Address:_____   Street Address:_____

City and State:_____   City and State:_____

Father deceased: ⎣_/   Mother deceased: ⎣_/

```
TIME
INTER-
VIEW
ENDED
 :
```

INTERVIEWER'S REMARKS

A. Length of interview:

_____ hrs. _____ minutes

B. Sex of respondent:

Male 1 67/0
Female 2

C. We want to determine whether obtaining a number of personal interviews in a household affects the second, and subsequent respondents.

We shall compare all first interviews with all subsequent ones, to see if the responses are different.

Therefore, please circle the appropriate code below.

This was the <u>first personal interview</u> obtained in the household on this study . . 5 68/4

This was the <u>second or subsequent personal interview</u> obtained in this household on this study . . 6*

*IF SECOND OR SUBSEQUENT INTERVIEW:

(1) Do you have any evidence that this respondent and the first respondent talked over the interview before this interview was conducted?

Yes . . . . . 8# 69/7
No 9

#IF YES:

a) What evidence do you have? What effect, if any, do you think this had on this respondent's answers?

70/y

D. Was anyone else present during all or part of the interview?

No 1 71/0
Yes, spouse 2
Yes, parent 3
Yes, child(ren) 4
Yes, other relative . . 5

E. Did this respondent ask any questions about the study's "approval," or about its "clearance" with the Roman Catholic hierarchy in your area (the Diocese, parish priests, etc.)?

If anything like this occurred in this case, please describe the respondent's questions, your answers, and any action the respondent took or wanted to take before acquiescing to the interview.

72/y

Date of interview: _____

_____
Interviewer's Signature

THE ADOLESCENT QUESTIONNAIRE

NORC 476 YG
11/63

NATIONAL OPINION RESEARCH CENTER
University of Chicago

(1-4)

STUDY OF YOUNG ADULT
ATTITUDES AND OPINIONS

Segment	
Case		(5-9)

Your household is one of about 3,000 in the United States in which young
people are filling out this questionnaire.

The research is designed to give important data on people's past experiences
and attitudes toward school, and opinions on current events of the day.

Feel free to answer exactly the way you feel, for no one you know will ever
see the answers. Information obtained will be reported in terms of statistics; the report will read something like this: "Fifty per cent of the young
men reported that they were members of elementary school clubs."

Almost all of the questions can be answered by circling one or more numbers
or letters beneath the questions. For example:

I am a resident of.... (Circle one.)

Canada 1

United States . . . . . (2)

England 3

NOTE: After each question there is an instruction in parentheses.

1. If it says "(Circle one)," circle only the one number [or letter]
   which best describes your answer, even though some of the other
   answers might also seem true.

2. If it says "(Circle one number [or letter] on each line),"
   please look to see that you have circled one and only one
   number [or letter] on each of the lines. For example:

	Agree	Disagree	
A. There are 12 months in the year.	(1)	2	25/X
B. The sun rises in the North.	4	(5)	Please ignore
C. In the summer, grass is green.	(7)	8	these numbers.

The numbers appearing in the right hand margin of the questionnaire are for office use only.

===

PLEASE BEGIN THE QUESTIONNAIRE WITH QUESTION 1 BELOW. THANK YOU!

===

1. What is your date of birth? _____ _____ , _____   17-18/y
                               (Month) (Day)   (Year)

2. What is your sex? (Circle one.)   Male 1   19/

                                       Female 2

3. Here are some statements. How much do you agree or disagree with each one? (Circle one number on each line.)

		Agree Strongly	Agree Somewhat	Disagree Somewhat	Disagree Strongly	
A.	Only people who believe in God can be good American citizens.	1	2	3	4	20/0
B.	The teachings of my church are old-fashioned and superstitious.	6	7	8	9	21/5
C.	A family should have as many children as possible and God will provide for them.	1	2	3	4	22/0
D.	Negroes would be satisfied if it were not for a few people who stir up trouble.	6	7	8	9	23/5
E.	A student should be free to make up his own mind on what he learns in school.	1	2	3	4	24/0
F.	Love of neighbor is more important than avoiding meat on Friday.	6	7	8	9	25/5
G.	Negroes shouldn't push themselves where they are not wanted.	1	2	3	4	26/0
H.	The teachings of my church are too negative and not positive enough.	6	7	8	9	27/5
I.	Books written by Communists should not be permitted in public libraries.	1	2	3	4	28/0
J.	My religion teaches that a good Christian ought to think about the next life and not worry about fighting against poverty and injustice in this life.	6	7	8	9	29/5
K.	Jewish businessmen are about as honest as other businessmen.	1	2	3	4	30/0
L.	Working men have the right and duty to join unions.	6	7	8	9	31/5

4. Below are some statements about religion. Some people think they are true and some think they are false. (Circle the number on each line that comes closest to your own personal opinion about each statement.)

		Certainly True	Probably True	Probably False	Certainly False	
A.	When you come right down to it, there is no definite proof that God exists.	6	7	8	9	32/5
B.	God doesn't really care how He is worshipped, so long as He is worshipped.	1	2	3	4	33/0
C.	There is a life after death.	6	7	8	9	34/5
D.	God will punish the evil person for all eternity.	1	2	3	4	35/0

5. Below is a list of things some people feel are wrong and some people feel are right things to do. (Read each statement, starting with statement A, and circle one number on each line that comes closest to your own <u>personal</u> feelings about each action.)

		Certainly right to do	Probably right to do	Neither right nor wrong	Probably wrong to do	Certainly wrong to do	Depends on why the person does it	
A.	Help another student during an exam.	1	2	3	4	5	6	36/0
B.	Heavy necking on a date.	1	2	3	4	5	6	37/0
C.	Having as little to do with Jews as possible.	1	2	3	4	5	6	38/0
D.	Handing in a school report that is not your own work.	1	2	3	4	5	6	39/0
E.	Joining a protest against a Negro who moved into an all-white neighborhood.	1	2	3	4	5	6	40/0
F.	Marrying someone with a different religion from your own.	1	2	3	4	5	6	41/0
G.	Sex relations with the person you intend to marry.	1	2	3	4	5	6	42/0

6. <u>FOR BOYS</u>: Below is a list of jobs. How would you feel if you had such a job?

<u>FOR GIRLS</u>: Below is a list of jobs. How would you feel if your future husband had such a job?

<u>ALL</u>: Circle one number on each line that best describes how you would feel--whether very pleased, somewhat pleased, somewhat disappointed, or very disappointed.

		Very Pleased	Somewhat Pleased	Somewhat Dis-appointed	Very Dis-appointed	
A.	Business executive.	0	1	2	3	43/y
B.	High school teacher.	6	7	8	9	44/4
C.	Priest.	0	1	2	3	45/y
D.	Bank teller.	6	7	8	9	46/4
E.	Author.	0	1	2	3	47/y
F.	Carpenter.	6	7	8	9	48/4
G.	Stock broker.	0	1	2	3	49/y
H.	Furniture mover.	6	7	8	9	50/4

7. Would you prefer a job where you are <u>part of a team</u>, all working together, even if you don't get personal recognition for your work, or a job where you <u>worked alone</u> and others could see what you have done? (Circle one choice.)

  Part of a team with no personal recognition . . . . 7 <u>51</u>/6

  Work alone with personal recognition 8

  Can't decide 9

8. Some people say that hard work is more important for getting ahead than having a nice personality and being well-liked. Other people say that having a nice personality and being well-liked are more important for getting ahead than hard work. Would you say <u>hard work</u> or a <u>nice personality</u> is more important? (Circle one choice.)

          Hard work . . . . X <u>52</u>/y

          Nice personality . 1

          Can't decide . . . 0

9. Are you presently in high school?

       Yes, I'm a freshman (1st year) . . . . . 1 <u>53</u>/9

       Yes, I'm a sophomore (2nd year) 2

       Yes, I'm a junior (3rd year) 3

       Yes, I'm a senior (4th year) 4

       No, I have not yet begun 5

       No, I left school without graduating . . 6

       No, I have graduated 7

       No, I have graduated and am in college . 8

IF YOU HAVE NOT YET BEEN TO HIGH SCHOOL: SKIP TO QUESTION 36 AND GO ON FROM THERE.

IF YOU ARE IN HIGH SCHOOL NOW: CONTINUE BELOW.

IF YOU HAVE BEEN TO HIGH SCHOOL: ANSWER QUESTIONS 10 THROUGH 35 AS YOU WOULD HAVE IN YOUR LAST YEAR OF HIGH SCHOOL.

10. A. <u>BOYS ONLY:</u>
  If you could be remembered here at school for one of the following, which would you want it to be? (Circle one choice.)

        An "A" student . . . . 6 <u>54</u>/R

        Star athlete 7

        Most popular 8

        A leader in clubs and activities 9

  B. <u>GIRLS ONLY:</u>
  If you could be remembered here at school for one of the following, which would you want it to be? (Circle one choice.)

        An "A" student . . . . 1 <u>55</u>/R

        Cheer leader 2

        Most popular 3

        A leader in clubs and activities 4

11. How much time on the average do you spend doing homework outside of school?
(Circle one choice.)

> None or almost none . . . . 3 <u>56</u>/2
>
> Less than one-half hour a day 4
>
> About one-half hour a day 5
>
> About one hour a day 6
>
> About one and one-half hours a day . . . 7
>
> About two hours a day 8
>
> Three or more hours a day 9

12. If you feel that you were treated unfairly in some way by a teacher, do you--
(Circle one choice.)

> feel free to talk to the teacher about it? . . . . X <u>57</u>/y
>
> feel a bit uneasy about talking to the teacher? 0
>
> feel it would be better not to talk to the teacher? . . . 1

13. What if you disagree with something the teacher said. Do you--
(Circle one choice.)

> feel free to disagree with the teacher in class? . . . . 7 <u>58</u>/6
>
> feel uneasy about disagreeing in class? 8
>
> feel it would be better not to disagree in class? 9

14. Do you ever remember disagreeing in class with what one of your high school teachers said? (Circle one choice.)

> Yes, often . . . . 1 <u>59</u>/0
>
> Yes, occasionally 2
>
> Yes, once or twice 3
>
> Never 4

15. Do your teachers treat everyone equally, or are some students treated better than others in school? (Circle one choice.)

> Some students receive much better treatment than others . . . . . 6 <u>60</u>/5
>
> Some students receive somewhat better treatment than others . . . 7
>
> Some students receive a little better treatment than others . . . 8
>
> Everyone is always treated equally 9

16. Thinking of all of the teachers you have this year, what words below best describe most of them? (Circle as many numbers as apply in each group.)

Interested in the subject . 1 <u>61</u>/R	Interested in books . . . . . . 1 <u>62</u>/R
Stern 2	Narrow-minded 2
Devout 3	Intelligent 3
Nervous 4	Patient 4
Fair 5	Unhappy 5
Hard to please 6	Knows the score 6
Self-controlled 7	Easy to talk to 7
Interested in students . . 8	Quick-tempered 8

17. Teachers sometimes like certain kinds of students. Here is a list (Circle all the numbers which describe the kinds of <u>students</u> you think your teachers like best.)

Quiet . . . . 1 <u>63</u>/R	Asks questions . . . . 1 <u>64</u>/R
Thinks for himself . . . 2	Polite 2
Obedient 3	Interested in ideas 3
Quick to memori . . . 4	Voices his own opinions . . . 4
Neatly dressed 5	Active on teams or clubs . . . 5
Likes to work on his own 6	Interested in books 6

18. Is your high school co-educational or not?   (Circle one choice.)

All male only 1   <u>65</u>/0

All female only 2

Co-educational, boys and girls attend the same classes 3

Co-educational, but boys and girls <u>rarely</u> or never attend the
same classes 4

19. **Which of the items below fit most of the <u>boys</u> in your high school?** (Circle **as many as apply.)** (If you attend an all-girls' school, skip this question.)

Friendly 0	Cheat on some exams . . . . 5 <u>66</u>/R
Girl-crazy 1	Sports-minded 6
Studious 2	Active around the school . . . 7
Out for a good time 3	Hard to get to know 8
Religious 4	Uninterested in school 9

20. **Which of the items below fit most of the <u>girls</u> in your high school?** (Circle as many as apply.) (If you attend an all-boys' school, skip this question.)

Think for themselves 0	Boy-crazy . . . . 5 <u>67</u>/R
Friendly 1	Studious 6
Hard to get to know 2	Out for a good time 7
Mad about clothes 3	Snobbish to girls outside their group 8
Active around school 4	Cheat on some exams 9

21. Suppose the circle below represented the life at your school. The center of the circle represents the center of things in school. How far out from the center of things are you? (Underline the number which you think represents where you are.)

BEGIN DECK 2

22. Which is more important to you--activities or friends associated with school, or activities and friends in the neighborhood, or somebody else not related to school?
    (Circle   Groups, activities or friends related to school 3   10/2
    one.)   Groups, activities or friends not related to school . . . 4

23. How active would you say you have been in school activities?
    (Circle one.)
                                            Very active 6   11/5
                                            Pretty active 7
                                            Not too active 8
                                            Not active at all 9

24. Thinking of the teachers you now have in class, how good do you think they are in getting ideas across and gaining the students' interest?
    (Circle one choice.)
                                            Very good X   12/y
                                            Somewhat good 0
                                            Good 1
                                            Not too good 2
                                            Not good at all 3

25. How often were you unprepared for class because you didn't study enough before it, or skipped doing your homework?
    (Circle one choice.)
                                            Very often 5   13/4
                                            Sometimes 6
                                            Once or twice 7
                                            Never 8

26. How often have you used crib notes, copied, or helped someone else out during an exam?   (Circle one choice.)
                                            On all or almost all exams. X   14/y
                                            Very often 0
                                            Often 1
                                            More than once or twice . . 2
                                            Once or twice 3
                                            Never 4

27. Which items below apply to your best friends who attend the same school as you do and are of your own sex?   (Circle as many numbers as apply in each group.)

Quiet 1 15/R	Interested in ideas 1 16/R
Out for a good time . . . 2	Date a lot 2
Active around school . . . 3	Plan to go to college 3
Religious 4	Interested in cars 4
Think for themselves . . . 5	Intellectual 5
Uninterested in school . . 6	Sports-minded 6
Studious 7	BOYS ONLY: Girl-crazy 7
Same religion as I am . . 8	GIRLS ONLY: Mad about clothes . 8

28. What is the total number of students in the student body of your high school (or the one you graduated from)?
    (Circle one choice.)
                                            Less than 200 1   17/0
                                            200 to 500 2
                                            500 to 800 3
                                            800 to 1,500 4
                                            1,500 to 3,000 5
                                            3,000 or more 6

29. Different schools use different marking systems. Circle below the one number
    that indicates your general average through high school so far.

                                100 - 90% (Superior) . . 3 *18*/2
                                90 - 86% (Excellent) . . 4
    85 - 81% (Good) 5
    80 - 76% (Fair) 6
    75 - 71% (Average) . . . 7
    70 - 65% (Passing) . . . 8
    65 or less (Unsatisfactory)9

30. Did you ever attend any other high school besides the one you presently
    attend? (Circle one choice.)

    No, this is the only high school I ever attended . . . . X *19*/y
    Yes, and I only attended public high schools 0
    Yes, and I attended church-related high schools 1
    Yes, and I attended both public and church-related high schools . 2

31. What is the name of the high school you presently attend?

                                                                      20-21/

32. Is your high school a public, religious, or private high school? (Circle
    one choice.)

                            Public high school 0 *22*/X
                            Private (Catholic) high school 1
                            Private (other religious) high school . . 2
                            Private (non-religious) high school . . . 3

IF YOU ATTEND PUBLIC HIGH SCHOOL OR PRIVATE NON-RELIGIOUS HIGH SCHOOL: CONTINUE
BELOW.

IF YOU ATTEND CATHOLIC HIGH SCHOOL OR OTHER RELIGIOUS HIGH SCHOOL: SKIP TO
QUESTION 36 AND GO ON FROM THERE.

33. Are you getting any formal religious training from your church while you are
    in high school (or were you a member of a high school religious club)?
    (Circle all the numbers which apply.)

    Yes, I attend formal religious education classes 6 *23*/R
    Yes, I am a member of a religious club in school 7
    No, I am not a member of either a religious club or class 8
    No, I am not a member of either a religious club or class and
    neither is available 9

34. What proportion of the teachers in your high school are from the same re-
    ligion as you are? (Circle one choice.)

                                  All or almost all . . . . y *24*/R
                                  Over half X
                                  About half 0
                                  Less than half 1
                                  Few or none 2

35. How well do you know the teachers at school who are from your own religious
    background? (Circle one choice.)

                                  I know some very well 4 *25*/R
                                  I know one or two very well . . 5
                                  I know them a little 6
                                  I don't know any very well . . 7
                                  I don't know any at all 8
                                  There are none 9

EVERYONE ANSWER THE FOLLOWING QUESTIONS:

36. Thinking of your last elementary school teacher, what items best describe him or her? (Circle all the choices that apply.)

Fair 1	26/R	Narrow-minded 1	27/R
Hard worker 2		Intelligent 2
Nervous 3		Patient 3
Treated me as an adult . . . 4		Unrealistic 4
Devout 5		Let me do things on my own 5
Hard to please 6		Quick-tempered 6
Self-controlled 7		Easy to talk to 7
Stern 8		Unhappy 8

37. Teachers have different ways of keeping students in order. How often, if at all, did your elementary school teacher do the following things when displeased by a student?

(Circle one number on each line.)

	Often	Some-times	Once in a while	Never	
A. Waited until the student stopped what he was doing.	1	2	3	4	28/0
B. Lost his or her temper.	6	7	8	9	29/5
C. Ridiculed or made fun of the student.	1	2	3	4	30/0
D. Put him in a special place or gave him something silly to do or wear.	6	7	8	9	31/5
E. Gave him extra work to do.	1	2	3	4	32/0
F. Kept him after school.	6	7	8	9	33/5
G. Sent for the student's parent.	1	2	3	4	34/0

38. Teachers sometimes like certain kinds of students more than others. (Circle all the items that apply to the kinds of students your last elementary school teacher liked best.)

Quiet X	35/R	Likes to work on his own . 5	36/R
Obedient 0		Polite 6
Quick to memorize 1		Thinks for himself 7
Interested in books 2		Active on teams or clubs . 8
Neatly dressed 3		Voices his own opinions . 9

39. What kind of elementary school did you attend? (Circle one choice.)

I only attended public school(s) 6 37/5
I only attended religious schools 7
I attended public and religious schools, but spent my 8th grade in public school 8
I attended public and religious schools but spent my 8th grade in a religious school 9

IF YOU ATTENDED PUBLIC ELEMENTARY SCHOOL AT ANY TIME: ANSWER QUESTION 40; IF NOT, SKIP QUESTION 40.

40. Did you regularly attend religious instruction classes?

Yes . . . . X 38/R
No, although some were available 0
No, none was available 1

41. About how many evenings a week do you spend at home? (Circle the total number.)

								39/X
0	1	2	3	4	5	6	7	

---

42. How much time do you spend <u>outside</u> of school with one or more members of the opposite sex, but not on a regular date?

None, or almost no time .	X	40/y
About an hour a day . . .	0	
About two hours a day . .	1	
About three hours a day .	2	
More than three hrs. a day	3	

---

43. Do you date?

No	3	41/3
Yes, very irregularly	4	
Yes, about once a month	5	
Yes, once every two or three weeks	6	
Yes, about once a week	7	
Yes, about twice a week or more	8	

---

44. Do you go steady or not?

Yes, I go steady	X	42/y
No, I don't go steady . .	0	

---

45. Suppose you had a problem and you knew that however you solved it, someone would be disappointed in you. Which would be hardest for you to take? (Put a <u>1</u> next to the kind of disapproval you would find hardest to take, a <u>2</u> for the next hardest, a <u>3</u> for the third hardest, and a <u>4</u> for the least difficult one to take.)

A. Parents' disapproval ___	43/0
B. Disapproval of a favorite priest or minister ___	44/0
C. A closest friend's disapproval ___	45/0
D. A favorite teacher's disapproval ___	46/0

---

46. Below is a list of items on which some parents have rules for their teen-age children, while others do not. (Circle the number after each situation that your parents have definite rules for.)

Against use of the family car	0	48/X
Time for being in at night on weekends	1	
Amount of dating	2	
Against going steady	3	
Time spent watching TV	4	
Time spent on home work	5	
Against going out with certain boys	6	
Against going out with certain girls	7	
Against dating someone of a different religion	8	
No rules for any of the above items	9	

---

47. Below is a list of items. (Circle the number next to the items which best describe what your father is like. Circle all that apply.)

Treats me as an adult . . .	4	49/R	Knows the score 1	50/R
Fair	5		Hard to please 2	
Patient	6		Self-controlled 3	
Intelligent	7		Easy to talk to 4	
Stern	8		Quick-tempered 5	
Head of the house	9		Lets me work things out myself. 6	

48. Below is a list of items. (Circle only those which are most true of you as a person. Most people choose three or four items, but you can choose more or fewer if you want to.)

Quiet 1 51/R	Ambitious 1 52/R
Out for a good time 2	Interested in ideas . . . . . 2 —
Unhappy 3	Interested in cars 3
Active around school 4	Rebellious 4
Religious 5	Plan to go to college 5
Think for myself 6	Sports-minded 6
Uninterested in school . . . 7	Intellectual 7

49. What proportion of your friends are Protestant? Catholic? Jewish? (Circle one choice on each line.)

	All	Almost All	Most	About Half	Less Than Half	Very Few	None	
Protestant.	1	2	3	4	5	6	7	53/0
Catholic.	1	2	3	4	5	6	7	54/0
Jewish.	1	2	3	4	5	6	7	55/0

50. How close do you feel toward your church or religion--very close, pretty close, not too close, or not at all close? (Circle one.)

Very close 0   56/X
Pretty close . . . 1
Not too close . . 2
Not at all close . 3

51. What is your religious preference? (Circle one.)

Protestant (Denomination) _____ 5   57/4
Catholic 6
Jewish 7
Other (What?) _____ 8
None 9

IF YOU ARE CATHOLIC: ANSWER QUESTIONS 52 AND 53.
IF YOU ARE NON CATHOLIC: SKIP TO QUESTION 54.

52. Below is a list of religious practices. (Circle one number on each line to indicate how often, if at all, you do these various things.)

	About once a year or less?	A few times a year?	About once a month?	2 or 3 times a month?	Every week?	More than once a week?	
A. Do you attend Mass...	1	2	3	4	5	6	58/
B. Do you receive Holy Communion...	1	2	3	4	5	6	59/
C. Do you go to Confession...	1	2	3	4	5	6	60/
D. Do you pray...	1	2	3	4	5	6	61/
E. Do you talk to a priest, brother or nun about things that bother you...	1	2	3	4	5	6	62/
F. Do you attend Church-(parish) sponsored meetings or activities (other than religious instruction)...	1	2	3	4	5	6	63/

53. Here is a short quiz which touches on practices and beliefs of the Catholic Church. You are not expected to get them all correct--some you may find rather difficult.
Please circle the number after the answer which comes closest to being correct, in your opinion.

A. The word we use to describe the fact that the Second Person of the Trinity became man is...

Transfiguration 1   <u>64</u>/0
Incarnation 2
Transubstantiation . . 3
Immaculate Conception . 4

B. Supernatural life is...

the life we receive from our parents . 6   <u>65</u>/5
sanctifying grace in our souls 7
our life after death 8
the power to work miracles 9

C. The "mystical body" is...

Christ's body in heaven 1   <u>66</u>/0
Christ in Holy Communion 2
Christ united with His followers . . . 3
None of the above 4

D. Uncharitable talk is forbidden by...

the second commandment 6   <u>67</u>/5
the fourth commandment 7
the eighth commandment 8
the tenth commandment 9

E. A man is judged immediately after he dies. This judg- is called...

general judgment 1   <u>68</u>/0
natural judgment 2
particular judgment 3
final judgment 4

F. The Encyclicals "Rerum Novarum" of Leo XIII and "Quadragesimo anno" of Pius XI both deal with...

Christian marriage 6   <u>69</u>/5
Christian education 7
the condition of labor 8
Papal infallibility 9

IF YOU ARE NON-CATHOLIC, PLEASE ANSWER QUESTION 54.

54. Below is a list of religious practices. (Circle the number that indicates how often you do the various things listed.)

	About once a year or less	A few times a year	About once a month	2 or 3 times a month	Every week	More than once a week	
A. Go to Church services.	1	2	3	4	5	6	<u>70</u>/0
B. How often do you pray?	1	2	3	4	5	6	<u>71</u>/0
C. How often do you say grace before meals, or morning or evening prayers?	1	2	3	4	5	6	<u>72</u>/0
D. How often do you talk to your minister or rabbi about things that are bothering you?	1	2	3	4	5	6	<u>73</u>/0
E. How often do you attend a Church sponsored group, meeting, or activity?	1	2	3	4	5	6	<u>74</u>/0

THANK YOU FOR YOUR COOPERATION!

THE PROTESTANT QUESTIONNAIRE

TIME INTER- VIEW BEGAN	:

NORC 476 PR
11/63

NATIONAL OPINION RESEARCH CENTER
University of Chicago   _____(1-4)

Segment	
Case Number		(5-9)

Mr.
Mrs.
Miss   _____   _____
    (first name)   (last name)

_____
(street address)

_____
(city and state)

Hello, I'm _____ from the National
Opinion Research Center. We're making a study
which deals mostly with the kinds of schools
people have attended, and also with other topics
of current interest. I believe you received a
letter a few weeks ago telling you I would be
stopping by.

HOUSEHOLD ENUMERATION

First, I have to ask for a little information about the members of your household.

How many people are living in this household? (BE SURE TO INCLUDE ALL CHILDREN LIVING IN THE HOUSEHOLD, PEOPLE TEMPORARILY AWAY, ROOMERS, ETC.)

_____
number

Let's go from the oldest person in the household to the youngest.

    A. What is the name of the oldest person? The next oldest person? (ENTER NAME IN COLUMN A OF THE ENUMERATION TABLE.)

    B. How old was (he) (she) at (his) (her) last birthday? (ENTER AGE IN COLUMN B BELOW.)

    C. What is (his) (her) relation to the head of the household? (ENTER RELATION IN COLUMN C BELOW.)

    D. (ENTER M FOR MALE AND F FOR FEMALE IN COLUMN D.)

    E. What is (his) (her) marital status? (ENTER IN COLUMN E BELOW.)

	A	B	C	D	E	F
	Name	Age	Relation to Household Head	Sex	Marital Status	Indicate Respondent by ✓
1						
2						
3						
4						
5						
6						
7						
8						
9						
10						

BEGIN DECK 1

---

1. Taken altogether, how would you say things are these days--would you say that you are very happy, pretty happy, or not too happy?

Very happy . . . 7 15/6

Pretty happy . . 8

Not too happy . . 9

---

2. Has anyone talked to you about his personal problems in the last few months?

Yes . . (ASK A AND B). X*16/y

No . . (SKIP TO Q. 3) 0

*IF YES:

A. Who was that?

17/
NAP- 1
NAN- 2

B. What was the problem?

18/
NAP- 1
NAN- 2

---

3. Have you spent any time in the past few months helping someone who needed help?

Yes . . (ASK A AND B). X*19/y

No . . (SKIP TO Q. 4) 0

*IF YES:

A. Did you do that by yourself, or did others join in giving this help?

By myself 3 20/

With others 4

NAP- 1
NAN- 2

B. What did you do? Could you tell me a bit about it?

21/
NAP- 1
NAN- 2

4. We are interested in how Americans judge certain actions. Here is a card with some answers on it. Which answer comes closest to telling whether you agree or disagree with each statement?

(HAND RESPONDENT CARD A.)

		Agree Strongly	Agree Somewhat	Disagree Somewhat	Disagree Strongly	Don't Know	
A.	It is all right to ask an insurance company for more money than you deserve after an auto accident if you think they might cut your claim.	X	0	2	3	1	22/y
B.	Even though you find some people unpleasant, it is wrong to try to avoid them.	5	6	8	9	7	23/4
C.	A married couple who feel they have as many children as they want are really not doing anything wrong when they use artificial means to prevent conception.	X	0	2	3	1	24/y
D.	A salesman has the right to exaggerate how good his product is when a customer is too suspicious.	5	6	8	9	7	25/4
E.	Two people who are in love do not do anything wrong when they marry, even though one of them has been divorced.	X	0	2	3	1	26/y
F.	There is an obligation to work for the end of racial segregation.	5	6	8	9	7	27/4
G.	It is all right to refuse to talk to some member of the family after a disagreement, especially if the argument was the fault of the other.	X	0	2	3	1	28/y
H.	If the government wastes tax money, people don't have to be too exact on their income tax returns.	5	6	8	9	7	29/4
I.	It would be wrong to take considerable time off while working for a large company, even though the company would not be hurt by it at all.	X	0	2	3	1	30/y
J.	It is not really wrong for an engaged couple to have some sexual relations before they are married.	5	6	8	9	7	31/4
K.	Even though a person has a hard time making ends meet, he should still try to give some of his money to help the poor.	X	0	2	3	1	32/y

Now I would like to ask about your background.

5. First of all, where were you born? (STATE OR COUNTRY)

_____ *   33-34/
                                                    yy

*IF OUTSIDE U.S.:

> A. How old were you when you came to the U.S.?   35-36/
>   NAP-yy
>   NAN-XX

6. Were you brought up <u>mostly on a farm</u>, in <u>open country but not on a farm</u>, in a <u>small town</u>, in a <u>small city</u>, or in a <u>large city or its suburbs</u>?

    Farm X   37/y
    Open country (not farm) 0
    Small town - 10,000 1
    Small city - 10,000-500,000 . . . 2
    Large city or suburb - 500,000+ . 3

7. Where were your father and mother born?

    A. First your father _____   38-39/
                          (STATE OR COUNTRY)   NAP-yy
                                                            NAN-XX
                                                            DK -99

    B. And your mother? _____   40-41/
                        (STATE OR COUNTRY)   NAP-yy
                                                           NAN-XX
                                                           DK -99

(ASK ONLY IF BOTH PARENTS WERE BORN IN THIS COUNTRY.)

8. How many of your grandparents were born in this country?

    None 0   42/
    One   1   NAP- y
                        NAN- X
    Two   2
    Three 3
    Four 4
    Don't know . . 5

9. A. What is your main national background--on your father's side? On your mother's side?

IF CURRENTLY MARRIED, ASK B:

B. What is your (husband's, wife's) main national background? First on (his) (her) father's side? On (his) (her) mother's side?

	A. Respondent's		B. Spouse's	
	Father	Mother	Father	Mother
English, Scotch, Welsh, English Canadian, Australian, New Zealand	00	00	00	00
Irish	01	01	01	01
German, Austrian, Swiss	02	02	02	02
Scandinavian	03	03	03	03
Italian	04	04	04	04
French, French Canadian, Belgian	05	05	05	05
Polish	06	06	06	06
Russian or other Eastern European	07	07	07	07
Lithuanian	08	08	08	08
Spanish, Portuguese, Latin American, including Puerto Rican	09	09	09	09
Other (SPECIFY) _____	OX	OX	OX	OX
Don't know	3y	3y	3y	3y
Not currently married	—	—	1y	1y
	43-44/ 2y	45-46/ 2y	47-48/ 2y	49-50/ 2y

10. Did you always live together with both of your __real__ parents up to the time you were 16 years old?

Yes . . . . X 51/y

No . (ASK A AND B) . 0*

*IF NO:

A. What happened?	52/ NAP- y NAN- X
B. How old were you when it happened? _____ years	53-54/ NAP- yy NAN- XX

BEGIN DECK 2

12. Here is a sheet with a number of statements about which different people have different opinions. Please circle the letter of the answer which is closest to your own feeling. (HAND RESPONDENT GREEN SHEET.)

For example, if you agree strongly, you would circle "A"; if you disagree strongly, you would circle "D." You can choose any of the four answers on the sheet.

		Agree Strongly	Agree Somewhat	Disagree Somewhat	Disagree Strongly	Don't Know	
A.	In the long-run, war with the Communists is almost certain.	X	0	2	3	1	8/y
B.	I would try to stop the planned parenthood association from having a meeting in my community.	5	6	8	9	7	9/4
C.	Usually parents are just too busy to explain the reasons behind the orders they give their children.	X	0	2	3	1	10/y
D.	The Federal government should give religious schools money to help pay teachers' salaries and build new buildings.	5	6	8	9	7	11/4
E.	Negroes shouldn't push themselves where they are not wanted.	X	0	2	3	1	12/y
F.	A student should be free to make up his own mind on what he learns in school.	5	6	8	9	7	13/4
G.	Laws should change with the times.	X	0	2	3	1	14/y
H.	White people have a right to live in an all-white neighborhood if they want to, and Negroes should respect that right.	5	6	8	9	7	15/4
I.	The United States should do more to help the poorer nations by building hospitals, schools, and homes in those places.	X	0	2	3	1	16/y
J.	Each country should be willing to give up some of its power so that the United Nations could do a better job.	5	6	8	9	7	17/4
K.	A family should have as many children as possible and God will provide for them.	X	0	2	3	1	18/y
L.	I would strongly disapprove if a Negro family moved next door to me.	5	6	8	9	7	19/4
M.	Working men have the right and duty to join unions.	X	0	2	3	1	20/y
N.	The government is responsible for preventing wide-spread unemployment.	5	6	8	9	7	21/4
O.	The Federal government ought to provide aid for the local public schools.	X	0	2	3	1	22/y
P.	Jews have too much power in the United States.	5	6	8	9	7	23/4
Q.	When parents are wrong, they should always be willing to admit it to their children.	X	0	2	3	1	24/y

Q. 12 continued on facing page.

11. We are also interested in what Americans think about religious matters. I am going to read you a number of statements. Please tell me the statement that comes closest to your own personal opinion about each of the statements.

(HAND RESPONDENT CARD B.)	Certainly True	Probably True	I am uncertain whether this is true or false	Probably False	Certainly False	
A. There is no definite proof that God exists.	X	0	1	2	3	<u>55</u>/y
B. God doesn't really care how He is worshipped, so long as He is worshipped.	5	6	7	8	9	<u>56</u>/4
C. God will punish the evil for all eternity.	X	0	1	2	3	<u>57</u>/y
D. Science proves that Christ's Resurrection was impossible.	5	6	7	8	9	<u>58</u>/4
E. Jesus directly handed over the leadership of His Church to Peter and the Popes.	X	0	1	2	3	<u>59</u>/y
F. A good man can earn heaven by his own efforts alone.	5	6	7	8	9	<u>60</u>/4

12. Continued

		Agree Strongly	Agree Somewhat	Disagree Somewhat	Disagree Strongly	Don't Know	
R.	It is as important for a child to think for himself as to be obedient to his parents.	5	6	8	9	7	25/4
S.	Rules should never be relaxed, because children will take advantage of it.	X	0	2	3	1	26/y
T.	Negroes would be satisfied, if it were not for a few people who stir up trouble.	5	6	8	9	7	27/4
U.	Jewish businessmen are about as honest as other businessmen.	X	0	2	3	1	28/y
V.	People who don't believe in God have as much right to freedom of speech as anyone else.	5	6	8	9	7	29/4
W.	Complete abstention from liquor is the best thing.	X	0	2	3	1	30/y
X.	Books written by Communists should not be permitted in public libraries.	5	6	8	9	7	31/4
Y.	The Catholic Church won't let its members think for themselves.	X	0	2	3	1	32/y
Z.	Catholics are getting too much power in America.	5	6	8	9	7	33/4

13. What was the highest grade in school your father completed?

No schooling 3   34/1
6th grade or less 4
7th or 8th grade 5
Some high school 6
High school graduate . . . 7
Some college 8
College graduate or more . 9
Don't know 2

14. What was the highest grade in school your mother completed?

No schooling 3   38/1
6th grade or less 4
7th or 8th grade 5
Some high school 6
High school graduate . . . 7
Some college 8
College graduate or more . 9
Don't know 2

15. What was your father's (or stepfather's) main occupation during the time you were growing up?

        Occupation: _____

        Industry: _____

42-43/
NAP-yy
NAN-XX

16. On the whole, how happy would you say your childhood was--<u>extremely happy</u>, <u>happier than average</u>, <u>average</u>, or <u>not too happy</u>?

        Extremely happy . . . . . 5 <u>44</u>/4

        Happier than average . . 6

        Average 7

        Not too happy 8

        Other (SPECIFY) _____

        _____ 9

17. Everything considered, how happy would you say your parents' marriage was while you were growing up? Would you say <u>extremely happy</u>, <u>happier than average</u>, <u>average</u>, or <u>not too happy</u>?

        Extremely happy . . . . . 0 <u>45</u>/

        Happier than average . . 1 NAP- y

        Average . . . . 2 NAN- X

        Not too happy 3

        Other (SPECIFY) _____

        _____ 4

18. A. When you were growing up, what was your father's (stepfather's) religious preference? (CIRCLE CODE UNDER <u>A</u> BELOW.)

    B. When you were growing up, what was your mother's (stepmother's) religious preference? (CIRCLE CODE UNDER <u>B</u> BELOW.)

A. Father's (stepfather's) religious preference	B. Mother's (stepmother's) religious preference
Protestant . . . . . 0 <u>46</u>/	Protestant . . . . . . 0 <u>47</u>/
Catholic . . . . . . 1 NAP- y	Catholic . . . . 1 NAP- y
Jewish . . . . 2 NAN- X	Jewish . . . . 2 NAN- X
Other (SPECIFY) ____	Other (SPECIFY) ____
_____ 3	_____ 3
None 4	None 4

19. A. What is your religious preference?

          Protestant . . . . (ASK B AND C) 5*+
          Catholic . . (ASK C, THEN DISCONTINUE INTERVIEW) 6+
          Jewish . . . (ASK C, THEN DISCONTINUE INTERVIEW) 7+
          Other . . . . (ASK C, THEN DISCONTINUE INTERVIEW) 8+
          None . . . . (DISCONTINUE INTERVIEW) 9

*IF PROTESTANT:
  B. What denomination?

          _____ 48/y

+IF ANY RELIGION:
  C. Were you raised a (Protestant) (Catholic) (Jew)?

                    Yes 2   49/
                                                      NAP- 0
                    No . . . . [ASK (1)] 3# NAN- 1

      #IF "NO" TO C:
      (1) How old were you when you became a (Protestant)
           (Catholic) (Jew)?
                        _____   50-51/
                          age |____|____| NAP-yy
                                                      NAN-XX

20. A. How religious would you say your father was while you were growing up--
         very, somewhat, not too, or not religious at all?

     B. How religious was your mother?

	A. Father	B. Mother
Very religious	6	1
Somewhat religious	7	2
Not too religious	8	3
Not at all religious	9	4
Don't know	5	0
No (father) (mother) present	3	y
	52/4	53/X

21. When you were growing up--
    (HAND RESPONDENT CARD C.)

    ASK A UNLESS NO FATHER
    PRESENT:

	More Than Weekly	Weekly	1-3 Times a month	Couple Times a Year	Almost Never	Don't Know	
A. About how often did your father attend church?	5	6	7	8	9	4	54/ NAP- 2 NAN- 3
ASK B UNLESS NO MOTHER PRESENT:							
B. About how often did your mother attend church?	5	6	7	8	9	4	56/ NAP- 2 NAN- 3
C. About how often did your parents send you to Sunday School?	5	6	7	8	9	4	57/ NAP- 2 NAN- 3

22. A. How religious would you say you are at the present time?

IF CURRENTLY MARRIED:
B. How religious would you say your (wife) (husband) is at the present time?

	A. Respondent	B. Spouse
Very religious	X	6
Somewhat religious . .	0	7
Not too religious . .	1	8
Not at all religious .	2	9
Not currently married	-	4
	58/y	59/5

IF CURRENTLY MARRIED:
23. What is your (husband's) (wife's) religious preference?

Protestant 1   60/X
Catholic 2
Jewish 3
Other (SPECIFY) _____
_____ 4
None 0
Not currently married . . y

24. A. How many brothers do you have? (Includes any no longer living.)

_____   61-62/
Number   NAN-yy

B. How many sisters do you have? (Includes any no longer living.)

_____   63-64/
Number   NAN-yy

IF NO BROTHERS OR SISTERS, SKIP TO Q. 26.

25. Have any of your brothers or sisters married a Catholic?

Yes 2   65/1
No 3

BEGIN DECK 3

_____

26. Think of the neighborhood in which you grew up.
How many of your neighbors were Protestants--more
than half, about half, less than half, or none?

More than half 1	_8_/0
About half 2	
Less than half . . . 3	
None 4	

27. A. How far did you go in school?

ASK IF CURRENTLY MARRIED:

B. How far did your spouse go in school?

	A. Self	B. Spouse
No schooling	1	1
6th grade or less	2	2
7th or 8th grade	3	3
Some high school	4	4
High school graduate	5	5
Some college	6	6
College graduate or more	7	7
Don't know	8	8
Not currently married	-	9
	22/0	23/0

IF RESPONDENT IS SINGLE (NEVER MARRIED), SKIP TO Q. 32.

28. How many children have you and your (husband)
(wife) had?

_____
number

41-42/
NR MAR-yy
No Ans-XX

29. Do you expect to have any (more) children?

Yes . . . (ASK A) 7*	45/
No 8	NR MAR- 5
Don't know . . . 9	No Ans- 6

*IF YES:

A. How many?

_____
number

46-47/
NR MAR-yy
If No -XX
No Ans-99

30. If you had your choice, what would be the ideal number of children
you would like to have in your family?

                                  48-49/
                                  NR MAR-yy

_____
    number   No Ans-XX

31. In what year were you and your (husband) (wife) married?

                                  50-51/
                                  NR MAR-yy

_____
    year   No Ans-XX

ASK EVERYONE:
32. Parochial schools are those that are supported by religious organizations
or churches. <u>What advantages</u>, if any, do you see in having parochial
schools in the United States?

                                     68/
                                     y

                                     69/
                                     y

33. What <u>disadvantages,</u> if any, do you see in having parochial schools
in this country?

                                     70/
                                     y

                                     71/
                                     y

IF RESPONDENT IS SINGLE, OR HAS NO CHILDREN, SKIP TO Q. 35.

34. Here is a list of things people generally like when they   BEGIN DECK 4
see them in young children. Which two of the things on
the list (do) (did) you find the nicest? (HAND   _____
RESPONDENT CARD E.)   (CIRCLE TWO)

   A. When they listen to what you tell them to do 1 7/
   B. When they are neat and clean 2 0
   C. When they are polite and well-behaved with other people 3
   D. When they hug and kiss you 4
   E. When they play nicely with other children 5
   F. When they learn to do something after they have tried
      for a long time 6
   G. When they play with you 7

35. I am going to read you a list of jobs. If a son of yours chose each job, tell me whether you would feel <u>very pleased</u>, <u>somewhat pleased</u>, <u>somewhat disappointed</u>, or <u>very disappointed</u>. (CIRCLE CODES IN TABLE BELOW.)

		Very Pleased	Somewhat Pleased	Somewhat Dis-appointed	Very Dis-appointed	Don't Know	
A.	Business executive	X	0	2	3	1	<u>8</u>/y
B.	High school teacher	5	6	8	9	7	<u>9</u>/4
C.	Clergyman	X	0	2	3	1	<u>10</u>/y
D.	Bank teller	5	6	8	9	7	<u>11</u>/4
E.	Author	X	0	2	3	1	<u>12</u>/y
F.	Carpenter	5	6	8	9	7	<u>13</u>/4
G.	Stock broker	X	0	2	3	1	<u>14</u>/y
H.	Furniture mover	5	6	8	9	7	<u>15</u>/4

36. Would you prefer a job where you are <u>part of a team</u>, all working together, even if you don't get personal recognition for your work, or a job where you <u>worked alone</u> and others could see what you have done?

Part of a team. . 7   <u>16</u>/6

Work alone . . . 9

Can't decide . . 8

37. Which of these opinions comes closer to the way you feel? Some people feel that <u>other persons can be counted on</u> for important help in an emergency. Other people feel that these days <u>one never knows whom he can count on</u>.

Other persons can be counted on X   <u>17</u>/y

One never knows whom he can count on . . 1

Can't decide 0

38. Some people say that <u>anyone who looks for meaning in life is just kidding himself</u>. Other people say that <u>you don't have to look too hard</u> to find meaning in life. What do you think?

Anyone who looks for meaning is kidding himself . . . 3   <u>18</u>/2

Don't have to look too hard to find it 5

Can't decide 4

39. A. Some people say that for the average man things are getting worse. Other people say things are getting better. Which opinion comes closest to the way you feel? Would you say things are getting <u>better</u> or <u>worse</u>?

Better 7   <u>19</u>/6

Worse 9

Can't decide . . . 8

B. Some people say that hard work is more important for getting ahead than having a nice personality and being well-liked. Other people say that having a nice personality and being well-liked are more important for getting ahead than hard work. Would you say <u>hard work</u> or a <u>nice personality</u> is more important?

Hard work X   <u>20</u>/y

Nice personality . . . 1

Can't decide 0

40. Now we would like to ask about your religious practices.

    (CIRCLE PROPER CODES BELOW.)

	Every day	Several times a week	Every week	Several times a month	About once a month	Several times a year	About once a year	Practically never or not at all	
A. How often do you go to church?	1	2	3	4	5	6	7	8	21/0
IF CURRENTLY MARRIED:									
B. How often does your spouse go to church?	1	2	3	4	5	6	7	8	25/0

41. Thinking of your three closest friends, what religion does each belong to? (ASK ABOUT FIRST, SECOND, THIRD CLOSE FRIEND AND ENTER BELOW.)

	First Friend	Second Friend	Third Friend
Protestant	1	1	1
Catholic	2	2	2
Jewish	3	3	3
No religion	4	4	4
Other (SPECIFY) _____	5	5	5
Don't know religion	0	0	0
No (1st) (2nd) (3rd) friend	y	y	y
	27/X	28/X	29/X

42. Of your <u>other</u> friends, how many would you say are Catholic--<u>more than half</u>, <u>about half</u>, <u>less than half</u>, or <u>none</u>?

    More than half 6   30/4
    About half 7
    Less than half 8
    None 9
    Don't know 5
    Doesn't have any other friends . 3

43. As a general rule, how important do you think it is for young people to marry a member of their own religion--<u>very</u> important, <u>fairly</u> important, or <u>not</u> important at all?

Very important	. . . .	7	<u>32</u>/5
Fairly important	. . . .	8	
Not important at all	. . . . .	9	
Don't know	. . . .	6	

44. How would you feel about a teen-ager of yours dating a Catholic? Would you <u>oppose it strongly,</u> <u>oppose it but not strongly,</u> or <u>not oppose it at all</u>?

Oppose strongly	. . . .	7	<u>34</u>/5
Oppose but not strongly	. . . .	8	
Not oppose at all	. . . .	9	
Don't know	. . . .	6	

45. About how much money would you say your family contributes to the church each year?

Check if none [ ] $ _____
(Amount)

[ ][ ][ ][ ]   35-38/
No Ans-yyyy
None -XXXX

46. Would you say that you have neighbors in your home very often, often, not too often, or not at all?

Very often	. . . .	X	<u>39</u>/y
Often	. . . .	0	
Not too often	. . . . . .	1	
Not at all	. . . .	2	

47. How many of your neighbors are Protestant? Would you say <u>almost all,</u> <u>more than half,</u> <u>about half,</u> <u>less than half,</u> or <u>almost none</u>?

Almost all	. . . .	0	<u>41</u>/y
More than half	. . . . .	1	
About half	. . . .	2	
Less than half	. . . . .	3	
Almost none	. . . .	4	
Don't know	. . . .	X	

48. How important do you feel it is for Protestants to choose other Protestants as their really close friends--very important, fairly important, or not important?

Very important	. . . . .	7	<u>42</u>/6
Fairly important	. . . .	8	
Not important	. . . . . .	9	

49. About how often do you pray privately?

Once a day	(ASK A AND B)	0* <u>43</u>/y
Several times a week . .	(ASK A AND B)	1*
About once a week . . .	(ASK A AND B)	2*
Less than once a week .	(ASK A AND B)	3*
Never	(SKIP TO Q. 50)	X

*IF EVER:

A. As far as you're concerned, which <u>two</u> of the statements on this card are the most important reasons for praying? (HAND RESPONDENT CARD F.)

(CIRCLE TWO)

A) Prayer gives me peace of mind 0   <u>44</u>/
B) Prayer honors God . . . . 1 NEVER- y
C) Prayer makes up for past failings in some degree . 2 No Ans-X
D) Prayer helps me adjust to life and its problems . 3
E) Prayer offers thanks to God 4
F) Prayer helps me get something special when I want it 5

B. For what do you usually pray?   <u>45</u>/
                                        NEVER- y
                                          No Ans-X

50. Have there been times in your life when you felt especially religious?

Yes . . . (ASK A) X* <u>46</u>/y
No 0

*IF YES:

A. When was that?   <u>47</u>/
                                          NAP- 1
                                          NAN- 2

51. Are you a member of any religious organizations?

Yes . (ASK A, B, AND C) 8* <u>49</u>/7
No . (SKIP TO Q. 52) 9

*IF YES:

A. What are the names of these organizations?

B. Are you active in (NAME OF ORGANIZATION)?

C. Have you ever been an officer of (NAME OF ORGANIZATION)?

	A. Name	B. Active	C. Officer

1.	<u>50</u>/
	NAP-y
	NAN-X
		Yes . 4 <u>51</u>/
		        NAP-2
		No . 5 NAN-3
			Yes . 8 <u>52</u>/
			        NAP-6
			No . 9 NAN-7

2.	<u>53</u>/
	NAP-y
	NAN-X
		Yes . 4 <u>54</u>/
		        NAP-2
		No . 5 NAN-3
			Yes . 8 <u>55</u>/
			        NAP-6
			No . 9 NAN-7

3.	<u>56</u>/
	NAP-y
	NAN-X
		Yes . 4 <u>57</u>/
		        NAP-2
		No . 5 NAN-3
			Yes . 8 <u>58</u>/
			        NAP-6
			No . 9 NAN-7

4.	<u>59</u>/
	NAP-y
	NAN-X
		Yes . 4 <u>60</u>/
		        NAP-2
		No . 5 NAN-3
			Yes . 8 <u>61</u>/
			        NAP-6
			No . 9 NAN-7

52. I am going to read to you a list of things about which many people disagree. Do you think churches have the right to teach what position their members should take on such issues?

		Yes	No	Don't Know	
A.	Government regulation of business and labor	X	1	0	66/y
B.	Racial integration	3	5	4	67/2
C.	Whether the U.S. should recognize Red China	7	9	8	68/6
D.	What are immoral books or movies	X	1	0	69/v
E.	Proper means for family limitation	3	5	4	70/
F.	Federal aid to education	7	9	8	71/ ,
G.	Communist infiltration into government	X	1	0	

53. Here is another sheet with a number of statements on it. Please circle the letter which indicates how much you personally agree or disagree with each statement.

(HAND RESPONDENT PINK SHEET.)

BEGIN DECK 5

_____

		Agree Strongly	Agree Somewhat	Disagree Somewhat	Disagree Strongly	D.K.	
A.	It is always wrong to say something that might make a person question his faith, even if what one says is true.	5	6	8	9	7	9/4
B.	Although Christ saved the spiritual world by his death and resurrection, the material world is under the control of the devil.	5	6	8	9	7	11/4
C.	Husband and wife may have sexual intercourse for pleasure alone.	X	0	2	3	1	12/y
D.	The world is basically a dangerous place where there is much evil and sin.	5	6	8	9	7	13/4
E.	The Church teaches that a good Christian ought to think about the next life and not worry about fighting against poverty and injustice in this life.	X	0	2	3	1	14/y
F.	Even people who won't work should be helped if they really need it.	X	0	2	3	1	16/y
G.	There is basic opposition between the discoveries of modern science and the teaching of the Church.	X	0	2	3	1	18/y
H.	Only people who believe in God can be good American citizens.	5	6	8	9	7	23/4
I.	God's purpose is clear to me in all the events of my life.	X	0	2	3	1	26/y
J.	My religion provides me with answers to all the important problems in my life.	5	6	8	9	7	27/4

54. In national politics, do you consider yourself a Democrat or Republican?

Democrat	0	<u>28</u>/y
Republican	1	
Independent (ASK A)	2*	
Other. . . (ASK A)	3*	
Don't know (ASK A)	4*	

*IF INDEPENDENT, OTHER OR DON'T KNOW:

   A. In general, would you say you are closer to the Democratic or Republican party in national politics?

Democratic	7	<u>29</u>/
Republican	8	NAP-4
Neither	9	NAN-5
Don't know	6	

55. How many organizations do you belong to besides religious ones--such as unions, professional organizations, clubs, neighborhood organizations, etc.?

None	0	<u>30</u>/X
One . . . . . (ASK A AND B)	1*	
Two . . . . . (ASK A AND B)	2*	
Three or four (ASK A AND B)	3*	
Five or more (ASK A AND B)	5*	

*UNLESS "NONE":

   A. In general, would you say you are <u>very active</u> in these organizations, <u>fairly active</u>, or <u>inactive</u>?

Very active	7	<u>31</u>/
Fairly active	8	None - 5
Inactive	9	No Ans-6

   B. How many of the members of these organizations you belong to are the same religion as you are? Would you say <u>more than half</u>, <u>about half</u>, <u>less than half</u>, or <u>almost none</u>?

More than half	1	<u>32</u>/
About half	2	None - **y**
Less than half	3	No Ans-X
Almost none	4	
Don't know	0	

56. Do you read any <u>non</u>-religious magazines regularly?

Yes . . .	6	<u>33</u>/5
No	7	

57. How interested are you in what goes on in the world today? For instance, do you follow the international news <u>very closely</u>, <u>fairly closely</u>, or <u>not too closely</u>?

Very closely	0	<u>34</u>/X
Fairly closely	1	
Not too closely	2	

58. What about local news--the things that happen here in your (town) (area)?
Do you follow local news <u>very closely</u>, <u>fairly closely</u>, or <u>not too closely</u>?

Very closely	4	<u>35</u>/3
Fairly closely . . .	5	
Not too closely . .	6	

59. Do you ever get as worked up by something that happens in the news as you
do by something that happens in your personal life?

Yes	8	<u>36</u>/7
No	9	

60. Here is a list of ways we might know different people. Which kind of
person on that card is the <u>closest relationship</u> you have with each of
the following groups? (HAND RESPONDENT CARD G.)

First, an Irish-American--what is the closest association you have had
with an Irish-American?

(READ LIST OF ETHNIC GROUPS
BELOW, CODING ONE RESPONSE
FOR EACH.)

		Relative	Best Friend	Close Friend	Friend	Neighbor	Co-worker	Knew in School	Acquaintance	Stranger or Never Met One	
A.	Irish-American	1	2	3	4	5	6	7	8	9	<u>37</u>/0
B.	Catholic	1	2	3	4	5	6	7	8	9	<u>38</u>/0
C.	Italian-American	1	2	3	4	5	6	7	8	9	<u>39</u>/0
D.	German-American	1	2	3	4	5	6	7	8	9	<u>40</u>/0
E.	Jew	1	2	3	4	5	6	7	8	9	<u>41</u>/0
F.	Scandinavian	1	2	3	4	5	6	7	8	9	<u>42</u>/0
G.	Polish-American	1	2	3	4	5	6	7	8	9	<u>43</u>/0
H.	Negro	1	2	3	4	5	6	7	8	9	<u>44</u>/0

61. Here are some questions which might be used on a radio or television quiz
program. Some of them are fairly hard--let's see how many you can answer.

A. What ocean would one cross in going from the United States
to England?

		<u>51</u>/
		NAN-y
Don't know . . X		R -0
		W -1

B. Could you tell me who Billy Graham is?

		<u>52</u>/2
		NAN-2
Don't know . . 3		R -4
		W -5

Q. 61 continued on next page.

61. Continued

   C. What mineral or metal is important in the making of the atomic bomb?

      _____   Don't know . . 7

        53/
        NAN-6
        R -8
        W -9

   D. Will you tell me who Plato was?

      _____   Don't know . . X

        54/
        NAN-y
        R -0
        W -1

   E. Will you tell me who Robert McNamara is?

      _____   Don't know . . 3

        55/
        NAN-2
        R -4
        W -5

   F. How about Charles Lindberg--can you tell me what he was famous for?

      _____   Don't know . . 7

        56/
        NAN-6
        R -8
        W -9

   G. Who wrote <u>War and Peace</u>?

      _____   Don't know . . X

        57/
        NAN-y
        R -0
        W -1

   H. What is the name of the Pope?

      _____   Don't know . . 3

        58/
        NAN-2
        R -4
        W -5

62. What kind of work do you do?

        59-60/
        NAP-yy
        NAN-XX

_____   *   _____
    Occupation   Industry

*IF EMPLOYED:

   A. What proportion of the people with whom you work are Protestant-- <u>more than half</u>, <u>about half</u>, <u>less than half</u>, or <u>almost none</u>?

      More than half 6
      About half 7
      Less than half 8
      None 9
      Don't know 5

        61/
        NAP- 3
        NAN- 4

IF RESPONDENT IS A MARRIED FEMALE:

63. What kind of work does your husband do?

        62-63/
        NAP-yy
        NAN-XX

_____   _____
    Occupation   Industry

64. (HAND RESPONDENT CARD H.) Adding up the income from all sources, what was (will be) your total family income in 1963?

A.	Under $2,000 0	<u>64</u>/y
B.	$2,000 to $2,999 1	
C.	$3,000 to $3,999 2	
D.	$4,000 to $4,999 3	
E.	$5,000 to $5,999 4	
F.	$6,000 to $6,999 5	
G.	$7,000 to $7,999 6	
H.	$8,000 to $9,999 7	
I.	$10,000 to $14,999 . . . 8	
J.	$15,000 and over 9	
	Don't know X	

65. One final question. There has been much talk lately about change in the Catholic Church. Do you think there ought to be any changes?

Yes . . . . (ASK A) X* 65/y

No 0

*IF YES:

A. What kind of changes would you like to see?

66/
NAP- 1
NAN- 2

```
TIME
INTER-
VIEW
ENDED

:
```

INTERVIEWER'S REMARKS

A. Length of interview:

_____ hrs. _____ minutes

B. Sex of respondent:

Male 1   67/0

Female 2

C. We want to determine whether obtaining a number of personal interviews in a household affects the second, and subsequent respondents.

We shall compare all first interviews with all subsequent ones, to see if the responses are different.

Therefore, please circle the appropriate code below.

This was the <u>first personal interview</u> obtained in the household on this study . .5   68/4

This was the <u>second or subsequent</u> personal interview obtained in this household on this study . .6

*IF SECOND OR SUBSEQUENT INTERVIEW:

(1) Do you have any evidence that this respondent and the first respondent talked over the interview before this interview was conducted?

Yes . . . 8#   69/7

No 9

#IF YES:

a) What evidence do you have? What effect, if any, do you think this had on this respondent's answers?

70/y

D. Was anyone else present during all or part of the interview?

No 1   71/0

Yes, spouse 2

Yes, parent 3

Yes, child(ren) 4

Yes, other relative . . 5

Date of interview: _____

_____

Interviewer's Signature

References

BRESSLER, M., and WESTOFF, C. F. Catholic education, economic values, and achievement. *Amer. J. Sociol.*, 1963, **49** (November), 225–33.

BROTHERS, J. *Church and school*. Liverpool: University of Liverpool Press, 1964.

CROSS, R. D. *The emergence of liberal Catholicism in America*. Cambridge, Mass.: Harvard University Press, 1958.

———. Origins of Catholic parochial schools in America. *Amer. Benedictine Rev.*, 1965, **16** (No. 2; June), 194.

DAVIS, J. A. A net partial and a multiple coefficient for Goodman and Kruskal's gamma. Unpublished MS, NORC, 1964.

DUNCAN, O. D. Chap. 6: A socioeconomic index for all occupations; Chap. 7: Properties and characteristics of the socioeconomic index. In A. J. REISS, JR., *Occupations and social status*. New York: Free Press of Glencoe, 1961. Pp. 109–61.

FICHTER, J. *Parochial school*. Notre Dame, Ind.: University of Notre Dame Press, 1958.

FREEDMAN, R., *et al. Family planning, sterility and population growth*. New York: McGraw-Hill, 1959.

GANS, H. *The urban villagers*. New York: Free Press of Glencoe, 1963.

GLAZER, N., and MOYNIHAN. D. P. *Beyond the melting pot: The ethnic groups of New York City*. Cambridge, Mass.: Harvard-M.I.T., 1963.

GOODMAN, L. A., and KRUSKAL, W. H. Measures of association for cross classifications. *J. Amer. statist. Soc.*, 1954, **49,** 732–64.

GREELEY, A. M. *Religion and career*. New York: Sheed and Ward, 1963.

———. Mixed marriages in the United States. Unpublished MS, NORC, 1964.

JOHNSTONE, J. W. C., and RIVERA, R. J. *Volunteers for learning: A study of the educational pursuits of American adults*. Chicago: Aldine, 1965.

KEYFITZ, N. Sampling probabilities proportional to size. *J. Amer. statist. Ass.*, 1951, **46** (March), 105–9.

LENSKI, G. *The religious factor*. Garden City, N.Y.: Doubleday, 1961.

MCCLELLAND, D. C. *The achieving society*. New York: Van Nostrand, 1961.

MACK, R. W., MURPHY, R. J., and YELLIN, S. The Protestant ethic, level of aspiration and social mobility. *Amer. sociol. Rev.*, 1956, **21** (June), 295–300.

MAYER, A. J., and SHARP, H. Religious preference and worldly success. *Amer. sociol. Rev.*, 1962, **27** (April), 218–27.

359

O'Dea, T. F. *American Catholic dilemma.* New York: Sheed and Ward, 1958.

Rosen, B. C. Race, ethnicity, and the achievement syndrome. *Amer. sociol. Rev.,* 1959, **24** (February), 47–60.

Rosenberg, M. The dissonant religious context and emotional disturbance. In L. Schneider (Ed.), *Religion, culture, and society.* New York: Wiley, 1964. Pp. 549–59.

Rossi, P. H., and Rossi, A. S. Some effects of parochial school education in America. *Daedalus,* 1961, **90** (No. 2; Spring), 300–328.

Sudman, S., Greeley, A. M., and Pinto, L. J. The effectiveness of self-administered questionnaires. *J. Marketing Res.,* 1965, **2** (August), 293–97.

Veroff, J., Feld, S., and Gurin, G. Achievement motivation and religious background. *Amer. sociol. Rev.,* 1962, **27** (April), 205–17.

Westoff, C. F., Potter, R. G., Sagi, P., and Mishler, E. *Family growth in metropolitan America.* Princeton, N. J.: Princeton University Press, 1961.

Westoff, C. F., *et al. The third child: A study in the prediction of fertility.* Princeton, N.J.: Princeton University Press, 1963.

Index

NOTE: numerals in *italics* are table numbers.